GILBERT AND SULLIVAN
AT LAW

GILBERT AND SULLIVAN AT LAW

Andrew Goodman

RUTHERFORD • MADISON • TEANECK
Fairleigh Dickinson University Press
LONDON: Associated University Presses

Associated University Presses, Inc.
4 Cornwall Drive
East Brunswick, NJ 08816

Associated University Presses Ltd
27 Chancery Lane
London WC2A 1NF, England

Associated University Presses
Toronto M5E 1A7, Canada

198560

Library of Congress Cataloging in Publication Data

Goodman, Andrew, LL.B.
  Gilbert and Sullivan at law.

  Bibliography: p.
  Includes index.
  1. Sullivan, Arthur, Sir, 1842–1900.   2. Gilbert,
W. S. (William Schwenck), 1836–1911.   3. Opera—England
—London—History and criticism.   I. Title.
M410.S95G73   1983   782.81′092′2   82-12175
ISBN 0-8386-3179-7

Printed in the United States of America

TO MY PARENTS

Contents

Foreword by Lord Elwyn-Jones, C.H., P.C.

This book is a fascinating account of how the law affected the lives and work of Gilbert and Sullivan and D'Oyly Carte. It has clearly involved long and devoted research into source materials both here and in the United States. The outcome will I believe delight all lovers of the theatre, describing as it does the eventful progress from a modest beginning in 1875 in the performance of *Trial by Jury* in the little Royalty (Soho) Theatre in Dean Street, to the brilliant series of operas which emanated from 'the greatest partnership in the history of musical entertainment' as the author has rightly described it. Gilbert dominated the world of the theatre for thirty years and, as the book so entertainingly shows, he asserted his authority more and more over his companions, their stars, and his managers. He had stormy relations with many of them. Yet 'while he was famous as a martinet in theatrical circles,' according to the author's researches, 'his chorus girls came to regard him very much as a father figure.'

Lawyers in particular will find this book absorbing. Gilbert's career began with an unsuccessful five years at the Bar. He tried his hand, as did Boswell, on the Northern Circuit. One of the many surprising disclosures in the book is that Gilbert's original intention for the story of Iolanthe was that the fairies should fall in love en masse with the barristers of the Northern Circuit. The fact that satire of legal beings, offices and procedures permeates the Savoy series is delightfully illustrated in this book. What is not so well known is the extent to which Gilbert was one of the most prolific litigants of his time. Unlike most lawyers, when Gilbert was aggrieved he turned to the law as a first, instead of a last resort. In his legal encounters, some of the greatest advocates of the day were engaged, either for Gilbert or against him.

9

His legal escapades involved twenty silks and came before fifteen judges. His last major case was a libel action he brought against 'The Era.' Lawson Walton, Q.C., was his Leader. His Junior was the rising star Marshall Hall. For the Defendants was Edward Carson, Q.C., then at the height of his career. Three years earlier he had cross-examined another author, Oscar Wilde. The entertaining extracts in the book from the exchanges between Gilbert and Carson show that Carson had less success with Gilbert.

The author understandably finds Gilbert's attitude to his former legal colleagues difficult to assess, as is the question how harmless his satire was, or was intended to be. Within the series of the Savoy Operas nearly every rank in the legal profession is included. For Gilbert's favourite characters, and in particular the Lord Chancellor in Iolanthe, his partner Sullivan created some of the most famous arias concerned with the law. I confess that one of the pleasantest experiences I had when I was Lord Chancellor was to sing one of the arias in a duet with John Reed, the superb interpreter of the role of the Lord Chancellor, in a Concert of the Bar Musical Society in Middle Temple Hall. This followed a splendid performance by him and the D'Oyly Carte Company of 'Trial by Jury'. Apparently Sullivan took Lord Chief Justice Cockburn to see 'Trial by Jury', in the performance in which Sullivan's elder brother, Fred, caused a sensation by being made up to look like Cockburn. The Lord Chief Justice was not amused. He thought it was 'calculated to bring the Bench into contempt.' This was not the reaction of the many members of the Judiciary who enjoyed it immensely in the Middle Temple in 1978.

While this book will have particular interest for all lawyers it will I believe give great pleasure to the countless lovers of the Savoy Operas across the world.

Preface

This little book is about an aspect of the background to the works of
Gilbert and Sullivan that has often been either glossed over or inaccu-
rately sensationalised. Many of the narrative events *are* sensational,
however, and it has been extremely rewarding to investigate them in
detail. Naturally it is impossible to say that such a wide subject has been
completely exhausted; however I have tried to show by three different
themes how 'the law' as such affected the lives of the two, or better,
three, Savoyards. These are: a narration of events, a personal analysis of
the vast number of legal references in the operas, and finally a special
look at copyright. Members of the Arthur Sullivan Society may well
complain that there is too much about Gilbert, as indeed the weight of
interest is heavily placed on the librettist in this partnership that was to
become and remain a national institution; they will have to wait, I'm
afraid, for the drama series! It was not intended that W. S. Gilbert be
shown as living his life in-and-out of court; nor that he was the greatest
legal brain since the date of Legal Memory. If, however, that is the
impression conveyed, it is 'merely corroborative detail intended to give
an artistic verisimilitude to an otherwise bald and unconvincing
narrative'.

My immeasurable thanks must go to a number of people; and if I have
inadvertently left any out I am sure that my publishers will produce an
addendum slip for the next edition. First, I am deeply grateful for the
splendid contribution of a Foreword by the Right Honourable the Lord
Elwyn-Jones, C.H., Lord High Chancellor of England, 1974-1979.
Second, my good friend Jesse Shereff of the New York Gilbert and
Sullivan Society whose gracious American hospitality is typically over-
whelming; Reginald Allen, Curator of the Pierpont Morgan Library in

11

New York, who kindly granted me ten minutes of his time, which turned into three hours; Harry Benford, best friend of the University of Michigan Gilbert and Sullivan Society, and Terence Barley, the London Society's librarian; Albert Truelove and the D'Oyly Carte Trust, without whose help no-one could produce a decent book on Gilbert and Sullivan; my various learned correspondents: Dr Gavin MacFarlane; A. J. Hirst, of the Performing Right Society, London; and Victor Bonham-Carter, of the Society of Authors, with whom I swapped references and ideas over coffee and the manuscript of his recent book; the most charming and helpful staff of the libraries of the Inner Temple, London; Seton Hall School of Law, Newark, New Jersey, U.S.A.; Villanova University School of Law, Pennsylvania, U.S.A.; and the Reader Services of the University of Southampton and the London Theatre Museum.

Good typists, as it is said, are worth more than pearls, and I have been fortunate indeed with Kathy Turner. My photographer, Jeremy Zeid, and my artists, Marianne and Steve Fountain, have worked wonders. Finally thanks to the many, many friends who have kept me at my task and wished me well, including a most pretty proof-reader, Anita Sams; my long-suffering pupil-master, Roger Bartlett; and Anthony Heaton-Armstrong, who has offered encouragement, proclaimed the genius of the work, and very kindly allowed me to use the edge of his desk.

ANDREW GOODMAN

Part I

'A Judicial Humourist'

Chapter 1

'A new and original plan': Practice at the Bar

Most, if not all, authorities agree that W. S. Gilbert was a total failure as a lawyer: one claims that he was not a bad lawyer, merely spectacularly unsuccessful.[1] This general view would in itself be a good enough reason to explain why in many a half-page biography his legal attainments are not thought sufficient to merit a whole line; more often they are not mentioned at all. However this opinion also seems to indicate that, even though he was unsuccessful and unlucky in private practice at the Bar, such writers, and even contemporary biographers, have little or no conception of the curious practices of the English Bar, or its condition then and now. They have even less documentary evidence relating to his short-lived career there. Biographers until now have been content to accept various anecdotes concerning Gilbert's fumblings in court, Frenchmen rushing up and kissing him for winning, women pickpockets hurling abuse (and physical objects) at him for losing, as gospel truth. It is true that little alternative was offered them; similarly most widely quoted and accepted has been the report of an interview with Gilbert himself, reminiscing about his early years, which can be shown to have also been coloured for good measure:

When in 1864, he was called to the Bar, he was, for the only time in his uneventful legal career plentifully supplied with funds. A windfall of several hundred pounds he divided into quarters. With

15

the first, he paid his student fees at the Inner Temple; with the second he procured entrance as a pupil at the chambers of Judge Watkin Wilkins; the third paid his call to the Bar; the last set him up in Clement's Inn ...

This money was the legacy of an 'elderly maiden aunt' (a phrase later to become closely associated with the dramatist), who died towards the close of 1876. This information, first given by Gilbert to the reporter of *Scribner's Monthly* in 1879[2], has been used directly or indirectly by almost every writer since[3]. It has always been assumed that the events of the four quarters of £100 all followed Gilbert's attempts first to break into the Crimean War, which ended before he could obtain a regular army commission, and secondly to break out of the civil service, in which he very nearly came to be entombed. This is plainly not so, and had any previous biographers understood the practice of undergoing a call to the Bar they would have immediately realised why:

The records of the Inner Temple are clear and concise, embraced in the Law List of the day, Foster's *Men-At-The-Bar:*

Gilbert, William Schwenck, B.A. London Univ. 1867 and a member of Convocation, dramatic author, clerk in privy council 1857-1862, late Capt. Royal Aberdeenshire Highlanders militia (1868), author of the Bab Ballads, etc., a student of the Inner Temple 11 Oct., 1855 (then aged 19), called to the bar 17 Nov., 1863 (only son of William Gilbert, Esq., of London); born 18 Nov., 1836; married 6 Aug., 1867, Lucy A, youngest dau. of late Capt. T.M. Turner, Bombay Engineers. 24, The Boltons, SW.'[4]

Gilbert had determined to go to the Bar, and had entered himself as a student of Inner Temple several months before the Crimean War ended; over a year-and-a-half before he took a position in the Education Department of the Privy Council Office, in order to earn enough to live on whilst studying for his B.A. degree in law at King's College London. He had also entered the Inner Temple a considerable time before he received the legacy which biographers portray as the key to his going into law. Another interesting point of difference is that where writers agree that he was first commissioned in the 5th West Yorks militia, the earliest biographer, Edith Browne (and hence those relying on her source), states that Gilbert took his captaincy in the 3rd Battalion Gordon Highlanders,[5] whilst the Inner Temple records show him to have been in the Aberdeenshire militia. His call to the Bar did not occur until a full eight years after he had first joined his Inn. This, however, was not unusual as the system of legal training and education then was a long process; even today Gilbert would have needed to take dinner in the Hall of his Inn on a sufficient number of occasions to 'keep' the required number of 'dining terms' to enable him to be called.

At the end of the 1840s the University of London was the only academic establishment in the whole country which gave any effective education in law. Oxford did not introduce a law degree into its curriculum until 1853 and Cambridge not until 1855. Even the Inns of Court did not have an independent legal education institution until pressed by the Page-Wood Commission which led to the foundation of the Council of Legal Education in 1852, supervised by the combined Benchers of the four Inns of Court. Thus Gilbert at King's would have had to undergo evening classes and qualify in two subjects which he could chose from Constitutional Law and Legal History, Roman Law and Jurisprudence, Common Law, Equity, or Real Property. To qualify he had either to pass an examination or attend a certain number of evening lectures for a year.

Unfortunately little evidence of his practice after his call exists. He did indeed take pupillage with Sir Charles James Watkin-Wilkins, and after his call resided first at Pump Court, probably number 4 (though this cannot be verified), and later at Clement's Inn, which no longer exists. His first appearance was reputedly in a prosecution for the Crown at the Liverpool Sessions; however this cannot be correct as he did not join the Northern Circuit until three years after his call[6]. Before then he attended at the Westminster courts of Exchequer and Common Pleas, which both sat in St Stephen's (Westminster) Hall, as well as the Old Bailey and Clerkenwell Sessions.

Clearly, but surprisingly, his problems stemmed from a lack of ability to express himself properly on his feet, which irritated judges, bored juries, and did not help his clients' cases either. The adventures that are attributed to him are really very funny, yet looking with hindsight they must have seemed tragic to him at the time; fortunately he had the talent to turn forensic weakness into narrative strength.

In *Cornhill* magazine of December 1863, Gilbert recounted the adventures of his first brief, although, very modestly for him, anonymously:

My Maiden Brief

Late on a certain May morning, as I was sitting at a modest breakfast in my 'residence chambers', Pump Court, Temple, my attention was claimed by a single knock at an outer door, common to the chambers of Felix Polter, and of myself, Horace Penditton [*auth: alias W.S.G.*], both barristers-at-law of the Inner Temple.

The outer door was not the only article common to Polter and myself. We also shared what Polter [who wrote farces] was pleased to term a 'proper' clerk, who did nothing at all, and a 'practicable' laundress, who did everything. There existed also a communion of interest in teacups, razors, gridirons, candlesticks etc.; for although neither of us was particularly well supplied with the necessities of domestic life, each happened to possess the very articles in which the other was deficient. So we got on uncommonly well together, each regarding his friend in the light of an indispensable other self. We had both embraced the 'higher walk' of the legal profession, and were patiently waiting for the legal profession to embrace us.

The single knock raised some well-founded apprehensions in both our minds.

"Walker!" said I to the property clerk.

"Sir!"

"If that knock is for me, I'm out, you know."

"Of course, sir!"

"And Walker," cried Polter.

"Sir!"

"If it's for me, I'm not at home!"

Polter always rejoiced if he could make the conversation partake of a Maddisonian Mortonic character.

Mr. Walker opened the door. "Mr. Penditton's a-breakfasting with the Master of the Rolls, if it's him you want; and if it isn't Mr. Polter's with the Attorney-General."

"You don't say so!" remarked the visitor; "then perhaps you'll give this to Mr. Penditton, as soon as the Master can make up his mind to part with him."

And, so saying, he handed to Walker a lovely parcel of brief-paper, tied up neatly with a piece of red tape, and minuted -

"Central Criminal Court, May Sessions, 1860 - The Queen on the prosecution of Ann Back v Elizabeth Briggs. Brief for the prisoner. Mr. Penditton, one guinea - Poddle and Shaddery, Hans Place."

So it had come at last! Only an Old Bailey brief it is true; but still a brief. We scarcely knew what to make of it. Polter looked at me, and I looked at Polter, and then we both looked at the brief.

It turned out to be a charge against Elizabeth Briggs, widow, of picking pockets in an omnibus. It appeared from my 'instructions' that my client was an elderly lady, and religious. On the 2nd April then last she entered an Islington omnibus, with the view of attending a tea and prayer meeting in Bell Court, Islington. A woman in the omnibus missed her purse, and accused Mrs. Briggs, who sat on her right, of having stolen it. The poor soul, speechless with horror at the charge, was dragged out of the omnibus, and as the purse was found in a pocket on the left-hand side of her dress, she was given into custody. As it was stated by the police that she had been 'in trouble' before, the infatuated magistrate who examined her committed her for trial.

"There, my boy, your fortune's made!" said Polter.

"But I don't see the use of my taking it," said I; "there's nothing to be said for her."

"Not take it? Won't you though? I'll see about that. You shall take it, and you shall get her off, too! Highly respectable old lady - attentive member of well-known congregation–parson to speak to her character, no doubt. As honest as you are!"

"But the purse was found upon her!"

"Well, sir, and what of that? Poor woman left-handed, and pocket in left of dress. Robbed woman right handed, and pocket in right of dress. Poor woman sat on right of robbed woman. Robbed woman, replacing her purse, slipped it accidentally into poor woman's pocket. Ample folds of dress you know–crinolines overlapping, and all that. Splended defence for you!"

"Well, but she's an old hand, it seems. The police knew her."

"Police always do. 'Always knew everybody' - police maxim. Swear anything, they will."

Polter really seemed so sanguine about it that I began to look at the case hopefully, and to think that something might be done with it. He talked to me to such effect that he not only convinced me that there was a good deal to be said in Mrs. Briggs' favour, but I actually began to look upon her as the innocent victim of circumstantial evidence, and determined that no effort should be wanting on my part to procure her release from a degrading but unmerited confinement.

Of the firm of Poddle and Shaddery I knew nothing whatever, and how they came to entrust Mrs. Briggs' case to me I can form no conception. As we (for Polter took so deep a personal interest in the success of Mrs. Briggs' case that he completely identified himself, in my mind, with her fallen fortunes) resolved to go to work in a thoroughly businesslike manner, we determined to commence operations by searching for the firm of Poddle and Shaddery in the Law List. To our dismay the Law List of that year had no record of Poddle, neither did Shaddery find a place in its pages. This was serious, and Polter did not improve matters by suddenly recollecting that he had once heard an old Q.C. say that, as a rule, the farther west of Temple Bar, the shadier the attorney; so that assuming Polter's friend to have come to a correct conclusion on this point, a firm dating officially from Hans Place, and whose name did not appear in Mr. Dalbiac's Law List, was a legitimate object of suspicion. But, Polter, who took a hopeful view of anything which he thought might lead to a good farce 'situation', and who probably imagined that my first appearance on any stage as counsel for the defence was likely to be rich in suggestions, remarked that they might possibly have been certificated since the publication of the last law list; and as for the dictum about Temple Bar, why, the case of Poddle and Shaddery might be one of those very exceptions whose existence is necessary to the proof of every general rule. So Polter and I determined to treat the firm in a spirit of charity, and accept their brief.

As the May sessions of Oyer and Terminer did not commence until the 8th, I had four days in which to study my brief and prepare my defence. Besides, there was a murder case, and a desperate burglary or two, which would probably be taken first, so that it was unlikely that the case of the poor soul whose cause I espoused would be tried before the 12th. So I had plenty of time to master what Polter and I agreed was one of the most painful cases of circumstantial evidence ever submitted to a British jury; and I believe that, by the first day of the May sessions, I was intimately acquainted with the details of every case of pocket-picking reported in Cox's Criminal Cases and Buckler's Short-hand Reports.

On the night of the 11th I asked Bodger of Brazenose, Norton of Gray's Inn, Cadbury of the Lancers, and three or four other men, college chums principally, to drop in at Pump Court, and hear a rehearsal of my speech for the defence, in the forthcoming cause

celebre of the Queen on the prosecution of Ann Back v Elizabeth
Briggs. At nine o'clock they began to appear, and by ten they were
all assembled. Pipes and strong waters were produced, and Norton
of Gray's was forthwith raised to the Bench by the style and dignity
of Sir Joseph Norton, one of the barons of her Majesty's Court of
Exchequer; Cadbury, Bodger and another represented the jury;
Wilkinson of Lincoln's Inn was counsel for the prosecution, Polter
was clerk of arraigns, and Walker, my clerk, was the prosecutrix.

Everything went satisfactorily: Wilkinson broke down in his
speech for the prosecution; his witness prevaricated and contra-
dicted himself in a preposterous manner; and my speech for the
defence was voted to be one of the most masterly specimens of
forensic ingenuity that had ever come before the notice of the court;
and the consequence was, that the prisoner (inadequately represented by a statuette of the Greek Slave) was discharged and
Norton (who would have looked more like a Baron of the Exchequer
if he had looked less like a tipsy churchwarden) remarked that she
left the court without a stain upon her character.

The court then adjourned for refreshment, and the conversation
took a general turn, after canvassing the respective merits of "May it
please your ludship," and "May it please you, my lud", as an
introduction to counsel's speech–a discussion which terminated in
favour of the latter form, as being a trifle more independent in its
character. I remember proposing that the health of Elizabeth Briggs
should be drunk in a solemn and respectful bumper; and, as the
evening wore on, I am afraid I became exceedingly indignant with
Cadbury, because he had taken the liberty of holding up to public
ridicule an imaginary (and highly undignified) 'Carte de visite' of
my unfortunate client.

The 12th May, big with the fate of Penditton and of Briggs,
dawned in the usual manner. At ten o'clock Polter and I drove up in
wigs and gowns to the Old Bailey; as well because we kept those
imposing garments at our chambers, not having any use for them
elsewhere, as to impress passers-by, and the loungers below the
court, with a conviction that we were not merely Old Bailey
counsel, but had come down from our usual sphere of action at
Westminster, to conduct a case of more than ordinary complication.
Impressed with a sense of the propriety of presenting an accurate
professional appearance, I had taken remarkable pains with my
toilette. I had the previous morning shaved off a flourishing

moustache, and sent Walker out for half-a-dozen serious collars, as substitutes for the unprofessional "lay-downs" I usually wore. I was dressed in a correct evening suit, and wore a pair of thin gold-spectacles, and Polter remarked, that I looked like the sucking bencher to the life. Polter, whose interest in the accuracy of my 'get-up' was almost fatherly, had totally neglected his own; and he made his appearance in the raggedest of beards and moustaches under his wig, and the sloppiest of cheap drab lounging-coats under his gown.

I modestly took my place in the back row of the seats alloted to the bar; Polter took his in the very front, in order to have an opportunity, at the close of the case, of telling the leading counsel, in the hearing of the attorneys, of the name and address of the young and rising barrister who had just electrified the court. In various parts of the building I detected Cadbury, Wilkinson, and others who had represented judge, jury and counsel on the previous evening. They had been instructed by Polter (who had had some experience in 'packing' a house) to distribute themselves about the court, and, at the termination of the speech for the defence, to give vent to their feelings in that applause which is always so quickly suppressed by the officers of a court of justice. I was rather annoyed at this, as I did not consider it altogether legitimate; and my annoyance was immensely increased when I found that my three elderly maiden aunts, to whom I had been foolish enough to confide the fact of my having to appear on the 12th were seated in that portion of the court allotted to friends of the bench and bar, and busied themselves by telling everybody within whisper-shot, that I was to defend Elizabeth Briggs, and that this was my first brief. It was some little consolation, however, to find that the unceremonious manner in which the facts of the cases that preceded mine were explained and commented upon by the judge, jury, and counsel, caused these ladies great uneasiness, and indeed compelled them, on one or two occasions, to beat an unceremonious retreat.

At length the clerk of arraigns called the case of Briggs, and with my heart in my mouth, I began to try to recollect the opening words of my speech for the defence, but I was interrupted in that hopeless task by the appearance of Elizabeth in the dock.

She was a pale, elderly widow, rather buxom, and remarkably neatly dressed, in slightly rusty mourning. Her hair was arranged in two sausage curls, one on each side of her head, and looped in two festoons over the forehead. She appeared to feel her position acutely, and although she did not weep, her red eyes showed evident traces of recent tears. She grasped the edge of the dock and rocked backwards and forwards, accompanying the motion with a low moaning sound, that was extremely touching. Polter looked back at me with an expression which plainly said, "If ever an innocent woman appeared in that dock, that woman is Elizabeth Briggs!"

The clerk of arraigns now proceeded to charge the jury. "Gentleman of the jury, the prisoner at the bar, Elizabeth Briggs, is indicted for that she did, on the 2nd April last, steal from the person of Ann Back a purse containing ten shillings and fourpence, the moneys of the said Ann Back. There is another count to the indictment, charging her with having received the same, knowing it to have been stolen. To both of these counts the prisoner has pleaded 'Not guilty' and it is your charge to try whether she is guilty or not guilty." Then to the bar, "Who appears in this case?"

Nobody replying in behalf of the Crown, I rose and remarked that I appeared for the defence.

A counsel here said that he believed the brief for the prosecution was entrusted to Mr. Porter but that that gentleman was engaged at the Middlesex Sessions, in a case which was likely to occupy several hours, and that he (Mr. Porter) did not expect that Briggs' case would come on that day.

A consultation then took place between the judge and the clerk of arraigns. At its termination, the latter functionary said, "Who is the junior counsel present?"

To my horror, up jumped Polter, and said, "I think it's very likely that I am the junior counsel in court. My name is Polter, and I was only called last term!".

A titter ran through the crowd, but Polter, whose least fault was bashfulness, only smiled benignly at those around him.

Another whispering between judge and clerk. At its conclusion the clerk handed a bundle of papers to Polter saying at the same time,

"Mr. Polter, his lordship wishes you to conduct the prosecution."

"Certainly," said Polter; and he opened the papers, glanced at them, and rose to address the court.

He began by requesting that the jury would take into consideration the fact that he had only that moment been placed in possession of the brief for the prosecution of the prisoner at the bar, who appeared, from what he could gather from a glance at his instructions, to have been guilty of as heartless a robbery as ever disgraced humanity. He would endeavour to do his duty, but he feared that, at so short a notice, he should scarcely be able to do justice to the brief with which he had been most unexpectedly entrusted. He then went on to state the case in a masterly manner, appearing to gather the facts, with which, of course, he was perfectly intimate, from the papers in his hand. He commented on the growing frequency of omnibus robberies, and then went on to say:-

"Gentlemen, I am at no loss to anticipate the defence on which my learned friend will base his hope of inducing you to acquit this wretched woman. I don't know whether it has ever been your misfortune to try criminal cases before, but if it has, you will be able to anticipate his defence as certainly as I can. He will probably tell you, because the purse was found in the left-hand pocket of that miserable woman's dress, that she is left-handed, and on that account wears her pocket on the left side, and he will then, if I am not very much mistaken, ask the prosecutrix if she is not right-handed, and, lastly, he will ask you to believe that the prosecutrix, sitting on the prisoner's left, slipped the purse accidentally into the prisoner's pocket. But, gentlemen, I need not remind you that the facts of these omnibus robberies are always identical. The prisoner always is left-handed, the prosecutrix always is right-handed, and the prosecutrix always does slip her purse accidentally into the prisoner's pocket, instead of her own. My lord will tell you that this is so, and you will know how much faith to place upon such a defence, should my friend think proper to set it up." He ended by entreating the jury to give the case their attentive consideration, and stated that he relied confidently on an immediate verdict of 'Guilty'. He then sat down, saying to the usher, "Call, Ann Back."

Ann Back, who was in court, shuffled up into the witness-box and was duly sworn. Polter then drew out her evidence, bit by bit, helping her with leading questions of the most flagrant description. I knew that I ought not to allow this, but I was too horrified at the turn matters had taken to interfere. At the conclusion of the examination in chief Polter sat down triumphantly, and I rose to cross-examine.

"You are right-handed, Mrs. Back?" (Laughter)

"Oh, yes, sir!"

"Very good. I've nothing else to ask you."

So Mrs. Back stood down and the omnibus conductor took her place. His evidence was not material, and I declined to cross-examine. The policeman who had charge of the case followed the conductor, and his evidence was to the effect that the purse was found in her pocket.

I felt that this witness ought to be cross-examined, but not having anything ready, I allowed him to stand down. A question, I am sorry to say, then occurred to me, and requested his lordship to allow the witness to be recalled.

"You say you found the purse in her pocket, my man?"

"Yes, sir."

"Did you find anything else?"

"Yes, sir."

"What?"

"Two other purses, a watch with the bow broken, three hand-kerchiefs, two silver pencil-cases, and a hymn-book."

(Roars of laughter.)

"You may stand down."

"That is the case, my lord," said Polter.

It was now my turn to address the court. What could I say? I believe I observed, that, undeterred by my learned friend's opening speech, I did intend to set up the defence he had antici-pated. I set it up, but I don't think it did much good. The jury, who were perfectly well aware that this was Polter's first case, had no idea but that I was an old hand at it; and no doubt thought me an uncommonly clumsy one. They had made every allowance for Polter, who needed nothing of the kind, and they made none at all for me, who needed all they had at their disposal. I soon relin-quished my original line of defence, and endeavoured to influence the jury by vehement assertions of my personal conviction of the prisoner's innocence. I warmed with my subject, for Polter had not anticipated me here, and I believe I grew really eloquent. I think I staked my professional reputation on her innocence, and I sat down expressing my confidence in a verdict that would restore the unfortunate lady to a circle of private friends, several of whom were waiting in the court below to testify to her excellent character.

"Call witnesses to Mrs. Briggs' character," said I.

"Witnesses to the character of Briggs!" shouted the crier.

The cry was repeated three or four times outside the court; but there was no response.

"No witnesses to Briggs' character here, my lord!" said the crier.

Of course I knew this very well; but it sounded respectable to expect them.

"Dear, dear," said I, "this is really most unfortunate. They must have mistaken the day."

"Shouldn't wonder," observed Polter, rather drily.

I was not altogether sorry I had no witnesses to adduce, as I am afraid that they would scarcely have borne the test of Polter's cross-examination; Besides, if I had examined witnesses for the defence, Polter would have been entitled to a reply, of which privilege he would, I was sure, avail himself.

Mr. Baron Bounderby proceeded to sum up, grossly against the prisoner, as I then thought, but, as I have since had reason to believe, most impartially. He went carefully over the evidence, and told the jury that if they believed the witnesses for the prosecution, they should find the prisoner guilty, and if they did not, - why, they should acquit her. The jury were then directed by the crier to "consider their verdict", which they couldn't possibly have done, for they immediately returned a verdict of "Guilty". The prisoner not having anything to say in arrest of judgement, the learned judge proceeded to pronounce sentence - inquiring first of all, whether anything was known about her?

A policeman stepped forward, and stated that she had twice been convicted at this court of felony, and once at the Middlesex Sessions.

Mr. Baron Bounderby, addressing the prisoner, told her that she had been most properly convicted, on the clearest possible evidence; that she was an accomplished thief, and, a most dangerous one; and that the sentence of the court was that she should be imprisoned and kept to hard labour for the space of eighteen calendar months.

No sooner had the learned judge pronounced this sentence than the poor soul stooped down, and taking off a heavy boot, flung it at my head, as a reward for my eloquence on her behalf; accompanying the assault with a torrent of invective against my abilities as a counsel, and my line of defence. The language in which her oration was couched was perfectly shocking. The boot missed me, but hit a reporter on the head, and to this fact I am disposed to attribute the unfavourable light in which my speech for the defence was placed in two or three of the leading daily papers next morning. I hurried out of court as quickly as I could, and, hailing a Hansom, I dashed back to chambers, pitched my wig at a bust of Lord Brougham, bowled over Mrs. Briggs' prototype with my gown, packed up, and started that evening for the West coast of Cornwall. Polter, on the other hand, remained in town, and got plenty of business in that and the ensuing session, and afterwards on circuit. He is now a flourishing Old Bailey counsel, while I am as briefless as ever.

Hesketh Pearson, in his biography of Gilbert and Sullivan, quotes from the dialogue of this short story and assures its being an authentic account. The court procedure and background picture of life in chambers at the time is very accurate, although it is almost impossible to verify much of the anecdote; several authorities either confirm as actually happening a client throwing her boot at Gilbert in open court, or use this magazine article as if it were a law report. Broadly speaking it typifies the way in which most writers intent on producing biographies of this phenomenal pair of entertainers seek to romanticise their early years: and the less concrete the evidence upon which the writings need to be based, the more romantic the various anecdotes and epigrams or witticisms of the duo become.

Under the sponsorship of Sir John Holker and others, chiefly friends of his father, Gilbert was elected to the Northern Circuit on 15th March, 1866, where for a short time he practised at the Manchester and Liverpool Assizes, the Liverpool Sessions and the Passage Court. He developed the very curious habit of inviting theatrical friends who happened to be touring in repertory companies in the vicinity, to watch him conduct the most amazingly disastrous cases. The estimates vary, but Gilbert himself [8] suggests that he only earned £75 in two years, and in consequence he beat a retreat to 1, Verulam Buildings, South Square, Gray's Inn, to take up a new career as a dramatic critic and magazine journalist.

The importance of his training for, and about five years at, the Bar, is reflected in nearly all of his dramatic works. His disappointment in being forced by economic drought to give up the profession led to scathing satires on it, closely following the Dickensian tradition. These can be seen not only in his famous collaboration with Arthur Sullivan, but in his many other works, now less well-known, which made him the nation's leading and most respected dramatist at the time of his death in

1911. There is a clear indication that he kept up-to-date in all matters of legal topicality and changes in procedure; it is unfortunate that no more is known of his time in practice. His potential as a lawyer, though, was to be seen many, many times in later life, and in the works by which his name has been immortally linked with the greatest English composer of the period, Sir Arthur Sullivan.

Chapter 2

'Professional licence': 'Bab' and the early years

Then, as now, the early years at the Bar were no way for a man to make a good living; between 1861 and 1871 Gilbert increasingly turned his attention to his writing, which kept him in relatively gainful employment in comparison to the long periods of waiting in chambers for the scant briefs to arrive. It was in magazine journalism that the budding author first found his feet, although he discovered that his education had given him a good enough grounding in French and Italian to be able to translate for British theatre the more popular operas of the day. There also appeared the gradually more ambitious sketches and burlesques for which he later became well known. Under his own name, and the pseudonym F. Latour Tomline, he wrote for a variety of magazines including *Punch, Cornhill, Temple Bar, London Society,* and *Tinsley's;* he was also the London correspondent to *Invalide Russe* and the dramatic critic for Vizetelli's *Illustrated Times.* Gilbert thus began his career as an author, much in the same way as others like Dickens, Fielding and Shaw, all of whom made use of their era's popular press.

The young barrister clearly made use of his day-to-day background wherever he could; this can readily be seen in short stories, his burlesques and translations such as *The Burglar's Story, or Committed for Trial.*[1] An early play of his, *Actors, Authors and Audiences,* showed the author of an unsuccessful play being put on trial before a jury composed of members of the audience; this theme, which occurred again in his later writing, was an early broadside at his many critics.

Real success, however, came with his association with, and contributions to, *Fun* magazine, which became a regular feature from June 1867. This association was responsible for most of his fame and the creation of most of his satire on legal themes, before his meeting with Sullivan. It led to the publication weekly of his satirical verse which he signed with the pen-name 'Bab'. These verses were later published in collected form as *The Bab Ballads*[2]; and from which were inevitably taken the ideas, and also a considerable amount of verse, for the lyrics of the Savoy Operas. *Fun* itself was an important rival to *Punch*, and its style can best be compared with *Private Eye* or *National Lampoon* today. The editor, Tom Hood, collected about him a group of young satirists, cartoonists and political commentators, much on the lines of *Punch*. Gilbert, when a member of the *Fun* board, attempted to copy the famous *Punch* weekly editorial lunches, by having Hood and the Fun editors at weekly gatherings on a Wednesday at his chambers in Gray's Inn.

The legal content in two of the *Bab Ballads* is well-known, those being *Baines Carew, Gentleman:*

> '*Of all the good attorneys who*
> *Have placed their names upon the roll,*
> *But few could equal* BAINES CAREW,
> *For tender-heartedness and soul.*
>
> *Whene'er he heard a tale of woe*
> *From client A or client B,*
> *His grief would overcome him so,*
> *He'd scarce have strength to take his fee.*
>
> *It laid him up for many days,*
> *When duty led him to distrain;*
> *And serving writs, although it pays,*
> *Gave him excruciating pain.*
>
> *He made out costs distrained for rent*
> *Foreclosed and sued with moistened eye -*
> *No bill of costs could represent*
> *The value of such sympathy.*

No charges can approximate
The worth of sympathy with woe; -
Although I think I ought to state
He did his best to make them so.

and the story of Damon v Pythias:

Two better friends you wouldn't pass
Throughout a summer's day
Than DAMON and his PYTHIAS, -
Two merchant princes they.

At school together they contrived
All sorts of boyish larks;
And, later on, together thrived
As merry merchants' clerks.

And then, when many years had flown,
They rose together till
They bought a business of their own -
And they conduct it still.

They loved each other all their lives,
Dissent they never knew
And, stranger still, their very wives
Were rather friendly too.

Perhaps you think, to serve my ends,
These statements I refute,
When I admit that these dear friends
Were parties to a suit?

But 'twas a friendly action, for
Good PYTHIAS, as you see,
Fought merely as executor,
And DAMON as trustee.

They laughed to think, as through the throng
Of suitors sad they passed,
That they, who'd lived and loved so long,
Should go to law at last.

The junior briefs they kindly let
  Two sucking counsel hold;
These learned persons never yet
  Had fingered suitors' gold.

But though the happy suitors two
  Were friendly as could be,
Not so the junior counsel who
  Were earning maiden fee.

They too, till then, were friends. At school
  They'd done each other's sums,
And under Oxford's gentle rule
  Had been the closest chums.

But now they met with scowl and grin
  In every public place,
And often snapped their fingers in
  Each other's learned face.

It almost ended in a fight
  When they on path or stair
Met face to face. They made it quite
  A personal affair.

And when at length the case was called
  (it came on rather late),
Spectators really were appalled
  To see their deadly hate.

One junior rose - with eyeballs tense,
  And swollen frontal veins:
To all his powers of eloquence
  He gave the fullest reins.

His argument was novel - for
  A verdict he relied
On blackening the junior
  Upon the other side.

"Oh," said the Judge, in robe and fur,
  "The matter is dispute
To arbitration pray refer -
  This is a friendly suit."

And PYTHIAS, *in merry mood,*
Digged DAMON *in the side;*
And DAMON, *tickled with the feud,*
With other digs replied.

But oh! those deadly counsel twain,
Who were such friends before,
Were never reconciled again -
Quarrelled more and more.

Many have commented how Gilbert's sharp legal wit made his presence felt. He came very close to libel on really too many occasions, and created an air of fear and to an extent dislike, certainly misunderstanding, about him that was to last for the rest of his life. To those that did not know him well, this later gave the impression that he was a theatrical martinet:

On the board of *Fun* less stringent laws of libel made all things possible to the naturally audacious. Gilbert attacked 'legal delinquents' by name - 'for our own part we give the rowdy portion of the Bar warning - whenever a case of this kind [defending mill-owners prosecuted for inhuman working conditions] occurs, we shall present the public with a full-length portrait of the offending barrister.[3]

A curiously autobiographical *Bab Ballad* was presented at about this time, *To My Bride (Whoever She May Be)*, which contained one of Gilbert's many pictures of himself, and which briefly sums up the way his own career at the Bar was going:

'You'll marry soon - within a year or twain -
    A batchelor of circa two-and-thirty,
Tall, gentlemanly, but extremely plain,
    And, when you're intimate, you call him "BERTIE".
Neat-dresses well; his temper has been classified
    as hasty; but he's very quickly pacified.

You'll find him working mildly at the Bar,
    After a touch at two or three professions,
From easy affluence extremely far,
    A brief or two on Circuit - "soup" at Sessions;
A pound or two from whist and backing horses,
    And say, three hundred from his own resources.

In *My Dream*, Gilbert introduces for the first time his idea of what was to become especially associated with his works and the logic of his plots in particular: in *Topsy-Turveydom*.

> *Our* magistrates, in duty bound
> Commit all robbers who are found;
> But there the beaks (so people said)
> Commit all robberies instead.
>
> *Our* judges, pure and wise in tone,
> Know crime from theory alone,
> And glean the motives of a thief
> From books and popular belief.
>
> But there, a judge who wants to prime
> His mind with true ideas of crime,
> Derives them from the common sense
> Of practical experience.

In *The Haughty Actor*, a more detailed look at legal procedure is given by the author and it illustrates clearly the fact that it was written before the changes in the legal system brought about by the Judicature Acts 1873 and 1875. The legal theme is delicately woven into a story of a haughty actor who thinks himself too much of a star to accept a lesser role: he dreams, however, that he has been involved in a swordfight and wounded in the hand. When he goes to surgeon Cobb he is refused treatment because Cobb will only do amputations, not petty surgery. Through that refusal the wound festers and the actor asks Counsel to bring an action in negligence against the surgeon. Gilbert continues the story

> Oh, bring my action, if you please,
>   The case I pray you urge on,
> And win me thumping damages
>   From COBB, that haughty surgeon.
> He culpably neglected me
> Although I proffered him his fee,
> So pray come down, in wig and gown,
>   On COBB, that haughty surgeon!

That Counsel, learned in the laws,
    With passion almost trembled,
He just had gained a mighty cause,
    Before the Peers assembled!
Said he, "How dare you have the face
To come with Common Jury case
To one who wings rhetoric flings
    Before the Peers assembled?"

Dispirited became our friend -
    Depressed his moral pecker -
"But stay! a thought! I'll gain my end,
    And save my poor exchequer.
I won't be placed upon the shelf,
I'll take it into Court myself,
And legal lore display before,
    The Court of the Exchequer."

He found a Baron - one of those
    Who with our laws supply us -
In wig and silken gown and hose,
    As if at Nisi Prius.
But he'd just given, off the reel,
A famous judgement on Appeal:
It scarce became his heightened fame
    To sit at Nisi Prius.

Our friend began, with easy wit,
    That half concealed his terror:
"Pooh!" said the Judge, "I only sit
    In Banco or in Error.
Can you suppose, my man, that I'd
O'er Nisi Prius Courts preside
Or condescend my time to spend
    On anything but Error?"

The outcome was that the actor awoke and accepted the lesser part. The actual 'ballad' shows how familiar Gilbert was with his legal terminology. More than that, it demonstrates a good example of the way in which the dramatist-to-be would place human traits and weaknesses against the background of the law as an institution. By the time his stage works are arrived at, this has become a principal philosophy in his craft, pitting balloon-like caricatures against the fantasy of institutions bulging with the vanity of self-importance. The Gilbert-to-come is only a little way off from the creator of the *Bab Ballads*.

Chapter 3

'Don't tell us what she told you': Theatrical causes

Gilbert never left the law in spirit, if he left the Bar in practice. He must have been one of the most prolific litigants of his social era and one of the rare breed that, when aggrieved, turns to law first rather than as a last resort. In later life his wrath and legal threats were felt not only by his neighbours, but also his milkman, coalman and postman. Yet for all that he was as kind as he was peppery, and whilst he was famous as a martinet in theatrical circles, his chorus girls came to regard him as very much a father figure. When he did take people, often employees or agents but even friends, to law, his injuries were often either imaginary, exaggerated or possible to solve in a friendly manner. However in this way he established a safeguard for his rights and those of others that he was trying to set up or maintain. It becomes possible to imagine him as a Western cowboy-type hero who, instead of reaching for his six-gun, kept his solicitors busy scurrying to write letters and issue writs on his behalf.

The dramatist's reputation in this respect was not something which sprang up overnight. As his works gradually became recognised and appreciated he began to assert his authority more and more over his companies, their stars, and his managers. This became the most remarkable feature of his domination of the theatrical world, which lasted for over thirty years. During the period nearly every great actor-manager, including Bancroft, Kendal, Toole, Hare, Wyndham, Alexander and Beerbohm Tree, worked for Gilbert in a way that none of them had been used to. It no doubt caused great hostility at first for men who were the masters of their own theatres to be subjected to Gilbert's prerogative requirements, as if they had been mere apprentices on the stage. They discovered, however, that Gilbert's innovations and creativity in the fields of stage management and direction were gifted with the same genius as his writing, and they began to accept the fact that the man had the temper and peculiar traits of some of his 'Bab Ballad' caricatures.

A number of the author's works hint at what the ideal organisation of a theatrical company should be, and its relationship with its controller, be he author, director or manager. In the Sullivan series he twice shows this, both in 'Thespis', the first, and, when his wheel of fortune was revolved fully, in 'The Grand Duke', the last. Gilbert tried to adopt his ideal, and was perhaps over-zealous in his treatment of his companies through the urgency of his task in creating exactly what he wanted. Francois Cellier, Sullivan's protegé, says that:

> Gilbert was by no means a severe martinet, but he was at all times an extremely strict man of business in all stage matters. His word was law. He never for a moment adopted the methods and language of a bullying taskmaster. Whenever any member of the company, principal or chorister, either through carelessness, inattention, or density of intellect, failed to satisfy him, he vented his displeasure with the keen shaft of satire which, whilst wounding where it fell, invariably had the effect of driving home and impressing the intended lesson.

As a dramatist he became conscious in the extreme of failure, and this might explain the extraordinary lengths to which he went to ensure not only that his words were spoken to the letter, but that his stage positions and directions were followed to the very inch, and that the comic gestures and business of the principal comedians were wholly his and not their interpolations. This rule he rigidly maintained, no matter how well-established or important was the principal whom he had engaged for the part. Gilbert had many conflicts which arose out of his attempts to press this view: one of his most famous and most successful pieces was presented at the Haymarket Theatre, in 1871, entitled *Pygmalion and Galatea.* The lead female role, and name part, was given to one of the finest actresses of the day, Madge Robertson (Mrs Kendal) who, as a well-known star, sought to interpret the part as she saw fit. This immediately brought her into conflict with Gilbert who, although he was determined to have the part performed his way, realised that as a leading lady of the theatrical world she should be treated with due respect. Consequently he began by making polite suggestions as to the interpretation of the role, but when these were ignored an argument soon developed. Gilbert would not risk losing the revenue that her popularity, as well as his piece, was bringing in, and so whilst during the day he contented himself by not speaking to her, in the evenings he took a stage box and whenever she came on stage he loudly criticised her performance.

The author's insistence on the way that this part was to be played led to other actresses having difficulties with him in many of the later revivals. He wrote to one, Janette Steer, threatening legal action:

> I must ask you to advance and kneel in front of Cynisca from her left, and not from her right - to throw yourself on your knees in front of her and (without making any exclamation) to fall at Cynisca's feet at the end of her speech, and not on any account to cross to Pygmalion, or indeed to do any business which was not arranged at rehearsal. If you do not comply with my wishes in these respects I give you notice that on Monday I shall apply for an injunction to prevent your playing the piece, or otherwise as I may be advised[2].

It was not merely the London productions that held the attention of Gilbert's gimlet eye. His own protegé managers who organised the authorised provincial company tours swiftly reported back any new material added to the work. Hesketh Pearson ably sums up the position:

> Provincial actors who toured his plays quickly discovered that they could take no liberties with an author whose eye was upon them from a distance of two to four hundred miles. If they did not pay his royalties promptly, they were threatened with legal proceedings; if they attempted to do his plays without his permission, they were injuncted; if they introduced 'gags' and vulgarities of their own, their contracts were terminated; if they did not give as many performances as they had agreed to give, they were served with a

summons. Gilbert possessed not only a keen sense of business but a still keener sense of other people's eye to business, and when he felt that he was being treated dishonestly the culprit was soon made aware of his feelings[3].

Nor was it ever a question of money. Gilbert would willingly ignore both cost and inconvenience in his efforts to maintain his rights, prove a point, or make his victim realise the magnitude of his wrongdoing. He would spend many times the sum he was seeking to recover in the attempt, and then have it sent to a particular charity he supported when it was won. It mattered little to him whether he had to go to law for the sake of professional pirates of his work, actor-managers who were too lazy or too forgetful to forward his share of the receipts, or amateur companies that had not taken the trouble to obtain a performing licence. He was seemingly as eager to take noisy neighbours to the local police court as he was to bring famous actors to the Court of Chancery. His various experiences with people in the theatrical world hardened his attitude towards their failings and weaknesses as human beings as well as professionals. Neither did audiences that withheld the expected reception to his favourite works, nor critics that failed to flatter, escape Gilbert's scathing comments which he made frequently, bluntly and publicly. He broadly outlined his views in the short play *Actors, Authors and Audiences* in which he attacks the theatre-managers' judgement in selecting pieces for presentation, the principals' spoilt demands for the emulation of their roles, the low comedian's introduction of unauthor-ised comic business that fails, and the audience that has no right to criticise if it can do no better.

One of Gilbert's chief concerns in the production of any of his pieces was the casting, not only of the piece as a whole, but also of the principal parts. He rebelled against a practice of his day that authors wrote their roles with certain performers in mind for them. Gilbert was totally averse to this, seeking to mould his actors to their parts and even going so far as to find relatively unknown and inexperienced men that would have no preconceived ideas of interpretation. Such was the way he and Sullivan created the company for their operas, managed by D'Oyly Carte. He then came back to the idea of personalising roles for Grossmith, Barrington and Rosina Brandram. The practical effect of this was to ensure that he had little or no trouble with the 'star snobbery' that was prevalent then, as now. This also enabled him to exclude from his work (which was prolific enough for this to have a serious effect on an actor's or actress's career) any performer with whom he had quarrelled, either professionally or socially. Thus John Hare, the Kendals and Henrietta Hodson, having had a brush with Gilbert, found themselves unable to appear in any of his work. The author's threat was simple, and was strengthened by the manager's knowledge that he would have no hesitation in obtaining a court injunction to support it - either that particular performer was replaced, or the show would be withdrawn.

Gilbert had a particular affection for his female choruses, and concerned himself not only with their professional training, but also their financial and moral well-being. He was rigidly firm in connection with any hint of scandal concerning these girls and any suspicion of backstage 'loose-living', and spared no expense in what he considered to be their best interests in both hunting down gossip-mongers and dissuading stage-door admirers. He expressed his kindness in different ways, and strangely won the loyalty and affection of his whole company vastly more than Sullivan, who was by far the more gentle character, or even for example D'Oyly Carte, their actual employer.

The events which involved May Fortescue, though perhaps not typical of all chorus-girl adventures, showed the considerable influence that Gilbert's benefaction now had: in fact through the dramatist's attention being focussed on her, she was later elevated from the chorus-line and became a successful actress[4] in her own right. During the run of *Patience* after it had been transferred to the Savoy, May Fortescue was one of a number of the girls that received letters of solicitation from members of the audiences, generally soldiers or young monied men. These letters invariably were taken to the green-room at half-time and distributed to the cast; the principals were allowed to have private guests in their dressing-rooms, although that was a practice that Gilbert unsuccessfully tried to prevent. When the author came across any of these letters he generally had their senders informed that they should leave the theatre quietly on pain of being thrown out. It came to his attention, however, that an officer in the Hussars was spreading a rumour that he was indulging in an affair with a chorus-girl, namely Miss Fortescue. Gilbert discovered the truth of the rumour and confronted the officer with such evidence as he had found, and in the presence of his long-suffering solicitor dictated a public apology which was duly signed:-

I,   , wish to express my unfeigned regret that on the 24th and 25th October, 1882, at the Raleigh Club, I intentionally allowed a member of that Club to infer that I had passed the night with Miss

Fortescue, a lady connected with the Savoy Theatre. I desire most unreservedly to withdraw this imputation against Miss Fortescue's character, to admit that I have not, nor have I ever had, any personal knowledge of that lady, and that except in her public capacity she is a total stranger to me. I desire further to acknowledge Miss Fortescue's forbearance in consenting to stay the action she has commenced against me on my signing this unqualified apology and retraction and agreeing to pay all her costs of and relating to the said action as between solicitor and client. I hereby authorize Miss Fortescue to make such use of this apology as she may be advised. Dated this 7th day of March, 1883.

A little over a year later there was more excitement concerning the same young lady. She was now playing a fairy in *Iolanthe* and, far from the male chorus counterpart, she had attracted the attention of a real peer. The young son of Earl Cairns, Lord Garmoyle, used to attend the show every night, and appear backstage often. He became engaged to May, but his family insisted that he should break off the engagement. Gilbert threatened to support his young chorus-girl in a suit for breach of promise, and consequently, to escape the scandal, the family settled out of court for the enormous sum of ten thousand pounds.

In support of his company Gilbert would often take their part in any conflict that arose with managers presenting his work - even to his own detriment: in the production of *The Mountebanks* the theatre manager, Horace Sedger, found it necessary to drastically economise and was forced to dismiss a large number of members of the chorus who had contracts for the run of the piece, without consulting Gilbert. The author not only immediately sent them a week's salary, but also offered his and Carte's support should they choose to bring an action against Sedger for victimisation. Thus it was that the man with the reputation of being a martinet, of being so obstinate that he should always get his way else legal threats would follow very quickly, received a note a few days later:

We shall remember with pleasure the kindness and consideration you bestowed upon us during the rehearsals, and could wish no better than always to be in your productions, to be ever under your kind surveillance.

'From your Mountebank girls.'[5]

BAR MUSICAL SOCIETY

Patron: Her Majesty Queen Elizabeth The Queen Mother
President: The Hon. Sir Fred Pritchard

WEDNESDAY, 6th DECEMBER, 1978, at 8.15 p.m.

in

MIDDLE TEMPLE HALL

by kind permission of the Treasurer and Masters of the Bench

TO CELEBRATE THE SOCIETY'S FIRST HUNDRED CONCERTS

THE D'OYLY CARTE OPERA COMPANY

will present

| JOHN REED | KENNETH SANDFORD |
| BARBARA LILLEY | MICHAEL RAYNER |

GEOFFREY SHOVELTON

CHORUS & ENSEMBLE

Conductor: ROYSTON NASH

Producers: LEONARD OSBORN & CYNTHIA MOREY

in a stage performance of

Gilbert & Sullivan's

TRIAL BY JURY

Burnand & Sullivan's

COX AND BOX

HER MAJESTY QUEEN ELIZABETH THE QUEEN MOTHER

has graciously intimated that she proposes to attend.

After the performance there will be a champagne soirée for which
separate tickets will be required

Tickets may be obtained by members of the Society for themselves and
their guests by application, preferably by letter, to Christopher Grundy,
4 Brick Court, Temple, E.C.4, at the following prices:-

Performance —

Floor of Hall —	£4 or £3 (all reserved)
Gallery —	£3 (unreserved)
Champagne Party —	£3

Members of the Society who are Barristers of less than 5 years' standing
or Students may obtain up to two £3 concert tickets at £1.50 each.

Dinner Jacket

Any member of an Inn of Court wishing to join the Society should apply
to Christopher Grundy, 4 Brick Court, Temple, E.C.4. The annual subscription to the Society is £1 if paid by Banker's Order, or £1.25 if not so
paid. The Society's financial year runs from the 1st June to the 31st May.
The subscription for each financial year is payable at the beginning of the
year, or on joining later in the year, but anyone joining between the 1st
January and the 31st May in any year is only required to pay 50p in
respect of that period.

DEBORAH ROWLAND
Chairman.

CHRISTOPHER GRUNDY
Hon. Secretary

Handbill advertisement for the Bar Musical Society's Centenary concert featuring the D'Oyly Carte Opera Company (See Preface.) *(photo: Jeremy Zeid)*

Exterior of the original Inner Temple Hall and Treasury in Crown Office Row both of which were destroyed during the Blitz. *(artist: Marianne Fountain)*

Interior view of the original Inner Temple Hall where Gilbert was called to the Bar on 17th November 1863. *(artist: Marianne Fountain)*

Line drawing of Clement's Inn as it was in Gilbert's day. *(artists: Steve and Marianne Fountain)*

Pump Court, Temple where Gilbert spent the greater part of his practice. *(photo: Jeremy Zeid)*

The Librettist—Gilbert in 1883. (*photo: Jeremy Zeid after a family original*)

Chapter 4

'Vulgar, coarse, offensive and indecent': 'The Wicked World'

Success came quickly to Gilbert as a developing young playwright. His early blank and pantomimic-verse pieces were surprisingly well received and in only a few years after 1866 his writing style was becoming known. He was closely associated with the earliest days of Hollingshead's Gaiety theatre, but then switched his loyalty and during the first half of the 1870s wrote a series of successful plays for the Haymarket theatre, then under the management of J. B. Buckstone, an experienced manager and well-known comedian. The first, *The Palace of Truth*, was moderately successful and introduced the Kendals to the author; they were to take the name parts in Gilbert's next drama, and the most financially rewarding non-musical play he ever wrote, *Pygmalion and Galatea*. With this work Gilbert's reputation as a dramatist became firmly established - he, especially, thought so, and consequently insisted on a raise in royalties from Buckstone. The manager became reticent, and this heralded a period of difficulty between them. The dramatist had his way and began work on his next piece for that theatre towards the close of 1872, which he presented to Buckstone with the demand of a guaranteed run of 100 performances, threatening to take it elsewhere, namely to the Prince of Wales's or Vaudeville theatres if he refused. Buckstone reluctantly agreed and this third work, entitled *The Wicked World* opened on Saturday, 4th January, 1873. Reception was mixed; however the manager found to his relief that it would fill the house, and to his surprise that it did so for a run of 200 nights. However he was to be dragged, either unwillingly or to revenge himself on his haughty author, into legal battle, which concerned the show, and which led to a bad feeling, between the collaborators, that was to last for many years.

Gilbert had begun to make enemies with the coming of his successes, and he made plain his antagonistic attitude towards what he considered to be the evils of his profession, with especially caustic remarks being reserved for drama critics and reviewers. The more influential of these soon took up the challenge and one, Enoch, of the *Pall Mall Gazette*, touched a raw nerve of Gilbert's when he reviewed this latest offering.

What had hurt Gilbert had been the original criticism of the piece. Correspondence that followed aggravated the bad feeling, and the critic was greatly delighted that his comments had hit home so hard. The author was clearly affected by what he thought was an unfair attack on him, and as Enoch became even more indiscreet in his opinion the dramatist waited for an opportunity to vent his anger in an action for defamation. The *Gazette* had carried the first advertisement for the play on Saturday 4th January, its first night. That first-night production was reviewed in the edition of Monday 6th January[1], and although a blunt attack, it certainly contained nothing of a libellous nature:

'The Wicked World'

A new comedy in three acts written by Mr. Gilbert and entitled "The Wicked World" has been produced at the Haymarket theatre. The dramatist has apparently derived his subject from a story bearing the same name which he contributed to "Hood's Annual" some two or three years ago. The incidents in the play are supposed to occur in the skyey kingdoms inhabited by fairies who from their elevated position in the clouds are enabled to watch and to condemn the proceedings of the mortal world hanging in the ether beneath them. At an early stage of the representation the spectators are informed that each dweller in fairyland has upon earth "a perfect counterpart in outward form", so perfect indeed that even the immortals are powerless to distinguish themselves from their duplicates. This "condition precedent" upon which the fable is based is sufficiently perplexing to the audience, but it has the

advantage of economising the strength of the company and enables
certain of the performers to quit the same as fairies and return in the
guise of human beings. The female fairies finding their state of
existence rather monotonously happy, resolve in exercise of certain
magical powers which they possess to summon to the skies "the
earthly counterparts" of two male fairies Ethias and Phyllon, who
have been dispatched by their king on some mysterious errand to
distant regions. The earthly Ethias and Phyllon are Gothic knights
of rude bearing and indifferent morality. They enter brawling and
blustering, and disgrace fairyland with their unchivalric conduct.
Indeed, as they frankly explain, they believe themselves in the
paradise of Mohammed, and view the fair creatures about them as
houris ministering to their employment. The fairies, however, with
one accord fall in love with these coarse roysterers. The introduction of mortal passion into fairyland and the miseries that
thereupon ensue constitute the chief argument of the drama . . .

As a story, "The Wicked World" displays considerable ingenuity, but it is essentially unsuited for dramatic purposes. Upon the
stage it wears the air of a laborious trifling, and its lack of action and
interest become oppressively manifest. The long speeches and
conversations of the characters are tedious, and weigh heavily on a
fable of so frail a construction, while they tend in no way to clear up
its obscurity or to render its many small complications in any way
intelligible to the audience. To relieve the more serious portions of
the drama, or in the hope of fortifying its unsubstantiality, the
character of a comic fairy has been introduced; but the sallies of
Lutin are not particularly humorous, while his observations upon
the nature and results of the earthly love are scarcely decorous. Mr.
Gilbert's fancy is agile enough, but his imagination seems cold and
inert. His fairies are unfairy-like, distinguishable in no degree from
the mortal characters using the same form of speech, expressing the
same modes of thought, and moved by the same impulses and
sentiments. The dramatis personae throughout are but shadowy,
inanimate creatures who never assert their individuality or attract
the sympathy of the spectators. The play is written in blank
verse, of a sufficiently fluent character if it be unillumed by poetic
thought . . .

"The Wicked World" has the advantage of zealous and pains-
taking representation . . . but provides few opportunities for acting,
and depends for success mainly upon declamation . . .

However in subsequent writing Enoch had become far too unguarded and began to describe the piece as coarse and indecent, and in places altogether unfit for public presentation[2]. Finding it fashionable to attack this upstart playwright, this relative newcomer to the theatrical firmament, Enoch extended his vocabulary with regard to the play, to include the words 'vulgar' and 'offensive'.

Gilbert lost no time in the issuing of a writ for libel and the case came on at the Court of Common Pleas in Westminster Hall before a judge and jury. The details of this action are obscure, though it is well known that the appearance in the witness-box of Buckstone caused both great hilarity in court and great discomforture to Gilbert, since whilst an array of theatrical stars appeared for the plaintiff dramatist, his own manager gave evidence on behalf of Enoch, the defendant[3].

John Baldwin Buckstone was described by Hollingshead as 'the last of the natural, juicy, genuine low comedians[4]. The two men were at odds with each other over their respective policies as theatre managers with regard to the relationship between theatres and music halls, and their respective rights of presentation. Both men were leaders of groups of managers advocating different positions. Buckstone was a strong supporter of the Stage-Play Act which prohibited 'stage-plays' being produced in music halls, and which was enforced by Webster and Wigan's Anti-Music-Hall Crusade. Hollingshead was actively opposed to this movement, having fallen foul of it when, as manager of the Alhambra music hall, he produced a pantomimic ballet, was prosecuted under the act and fined £240 by Marlborough Street magistrates, which was upheld on an appeal by him to Quarter-Sessions.

The jury, after being greatly entertained, rejected the defendant's plea of justification and found as fact that the play was neither vulgar nor offensive, coarse or indecent. However they also found that Gilbert had failed to prove libel, and returned an overall verdict in favour of Enoch; consequently Gilbert had to pay £60 in costs. Naturally enough Gilbert's relations with Buckstone became incredibly strained after this, and shortly afterwards came his first failure at the Haymarket, a play entitled *Charity*. It was to be two years before Gilbert's work returned to the Haymarket, in the form of his most successful comedy, *Engaged*, and in the meantime he wrote his two sentimental works *Sweethearts* for the Prince of Wales's, and *Broken Hearts* for the Court theatre. Also by that time *The Sorcerer* was running at the Opera Comique, and his ties with Sir Arthur Sullivan and D'Oyly Carte were gradually evolving.

As a direct result of the criticism of *The Wicked World* came the burlesque on the same theme, set with a topical political background, *The Happy Land* which, as later will be seen, caused the displeasure of the Censor and the Lord Chamberlain's Office[5]. The dramatist had suffered his first set-back. He had become aware that his methods and immodest opinions were not necessarily endearing him to everyone within shouting distance. Any modification, however, was not to be within his character, and the first legal tussle with his critics can be seen as merely the Act I prelude to a very Victorian melodrama.

Chapter 5

'Persecutions suffered': The Hodson quarrel

By the mid-1870s, the devotees of the theatrical world and members of the profession were being treated to a marvellous new form of free entertainment. Nor was it to be seen on any London stage, but in the press; at the various clubs frequented by the theatrical fraternity, actors and writers, and socialities revelled in the latest gossip concerning the various well-publicised arguments of the brilliant but hot-tempered 'playwright', Gilbert. The most famous and longest of these was a quarrel drawn out over three years with a highly popular actress of the day, Henrietta Hodson. For Gilbert it was an 'oh, so all-but!' legal confrontation, and he backed away from his usual recourse to law twice, on discovering that Miss Hodson was quite as strong-willed as he, and that she had powerful allies.

Henrietta Hodson was an exciting and provocative actress with Irish blood and a fiery temper. In her day she was a romantic and liberal figure, having started her career touring, in the North and Scotland, in repertory with another penniless unknown actor friend - Henry Irving. She was born in a theatre pit on an improvised bed after an evening performance at the Bower Saloon, Lambeth, the daughter of well-known Irish music-hall comedian, George Hodson. At the age of seventeen she was on the stage professionally, but left it in 1863 to marry a Mr Walter Pigeon. Returning three years later she became successful on the West End stage at the Prince of Wales's Theatre and

48

later the Queen's, Longacre[1]. In 1868 she ran away with the radical MP for Windsor, Henry Labouchère, the founder and editor of the satirical *Truth* magazine, who married her on the death of Pigeon, a few months later. He also bought out the other lessees of the Queen's and became sole proprietor in order to further her career. In October 1870 the Royalty Theatre was opened with Mrs Labouchère as manageress. Her brush with Gilbert occurred between January 1874 and January 1877, a year after which she retired from the stage and became one of the best-known London hostesses. She helped persuade Lillie Langtry to go on the stage in 1881, and the following year accompanied her on an American tour, but returned quickly after a violent quarrel with the new star.

The argument with Gilbert originated in a fit of pique by both parties and escalated to ridiculous proportions, urged on to a large extent by the *Theatre* magazine[2], and of course, Labouchère's *Truth*. It is of interest mainly due to the incredible chronicle of events, recorded, printed and circulated by both Hodson and Gilbert in the form of pamphlets giving their respective versions. The whole affair started with disagreements at the rehearsals of Gilbert's play *Ought We To Visit Her?* at the Royalty Theatre in January, 1874, where Henrietta Hodson was manageress and starred in the production together with Charles Wyndham and the comedian, J. L. Toole. After this dispute one thing led to another and Gilbert invoked a lock-out against the actress by preventing her from appearing in any of his plays. She claimed that he was persecuting her, and indeed he succeeded in stopping her from playing in his roles in *Ought We To Visit Her?* at the Prince of Wales Theatre, Liverpool, 1875; *The Princess*, St. James' Theatre, July 1876 and *Dan'l Druce*, Theatre Royal, Haymarket in October 1876. Eventually when Buckstone hired her to play in a revival of Gilbert's *Pygmalion and Galatea* in November of that year, she claimed that the author had persuaded him and Henry Howe, the stage manager, to deprive her of the leading role, which she was under contract to play and which she felt her experience merited, and to place her in a secondary role with Marion Terry as principal. It may well have been that pressure from the theatre's financial sponsor, the printseller Graves (who wanted a girlfriend to take the lead), had had some effect.

In January 1877 and soon afterwards two letter pamphlets appeared in London in various circles of people associated with the theatrical world. The first was entitled 'A Letter from Miss Henrietta Hodson, an Actress, to the Members of the Dramatic Profession being a Relation of the Persecutions which she has Suffered from Mr. William Schwenck Gilbert, a Dramatic Author'; the use of Gilbert's unusual middle-name was deliberate and employed as often as possible. The second was entitled 'A Letter addressed to the Members of the Dramatic Profession in reply to Miss Henrietta Hodson's Pamphlet by W. S. Gilbert.'

The Hodson Pamphlet began:

> I beg to lay before the members of the profession to which I have the honour to belong the following statement of the behaviour of Mr. William Schwenck Gilbert towards me, leaving them to form their own conclusions respecting it. I have been on the stage for a number of years, and have been brought into contact with authors, managers, actors and actresses. My relations with them have always been most friendly. Mr. Gilbert is the one single exception; and he has made so many assertions in respect of me so entirely at variance with fact, and misrepresentation has become with him so confirmed a habit, that I am obliged, in self-defence, to submit to those whose good opinion I desire to retain this relation.

Gilbert introduces his accordingly:

> Miss Henrietta Hodson has thought proper to print and circulate among the Members of the Dramatic Profession seven-hundred-and-fifty copies of a pamphlet, in which she professes to describe certain "persecutions" which she claims to have suffered at my hands. I referred the matter to two eminent counsel, and, acting under their advice, I publish the following reply to Miss Hodson's charges.

It is not difficult to appreciate how diametrically opposed the contents of the two letters were, each relying on things said or written to third parties as evidence of the misconduct of the other, but they should be read in the context of an indictment and a reply:

> Hodson: I had known Mr. Gilbert for several years. In 1874, I saw a great deal of him, as I was then the Lessee of the Royalty Theatre, and he wished to write a play for me.

> W.S.G.: In 1873, at the very earnest request of Miss Hodson, who was at that time manageress of the Royalty Theatre, I dramatized Mrs. Edwardes's novel, *Ought We To Visit Her?*

Hodson: The rehearsals commenced, and all went smoothly until
the day before the appearance of the play. I was con-
gratulating myself that I had managed not to have a
single quarrel with my quarrelsome friend, by carrying
out his suggestions without even discussing them…
The last rehearsal was going on when suddenly Mr.
Gilbert jumped up, and commenced pulling his hair
and dancing like a maniac. "Look," he said, "at that
man reading a newspaper;" and he pointed to Mr.
Bannister, who was rehearsing the reading of a newspaper on the stage. "Do pray," I said, "let the rehearsal
go on quietly, and if anything goes wrong, make a note
of it, and we will go all over it again." On this, he put
on his hat, and, without a word, walked out of the
theatre. This was followed by many letters telling me
that he would not allow *Ought We To Visit Her?* to be
played, and by a threat, after it had appeared, that he
would bring an action against me for the payment of
certain fees, which he subsequently admitted were not
due.

W.S.G.:   The rehearsals, generally, had resulted in disagreements
between Miss Hodson and myself, and at the last
rehearsal a dispute took place between us, of which I
will say no more than it had the effect of making me
extremely angry. I immediately left the theatre and,
under the influence of strong excitement, I described
the occurrence to a lady - a friend of Miss Hodson's - in
words which, on reflection, appeared to me to be
stronger than the occasion warranted.

Hodson: Shortly after this, I discovered that, whilst he had profes-
sed to be on the most friendly terms with me, he had
been abusing me to my friends, and telling them that I
was in the habit of making use of bad language during
rehearsals. On this I went to my solicitor, who wrote to
him, [on 3rd February 1874]:
Sir, - Miss Hodson has this day consulted us with
reference to what has recently come to her knowledge,
that you have been going about and circulating
slanders reflecting upon her character of a very

198560

disgraceful description. Your conduct towards this lady is
of a most unmanly character... she is prepared to
defend herself in a court of law ... you do not hesitate
to state to Miss Litton and others that this lady is
guilty, in her position as manageress of a theatre, of
using disgusting and obscene language, and otherwise
so grossly misconducting herself as would render her
utterly unfit for such a position if such statements were
true. Miss Hodson, however, is determined not to
leave her reputation in the hands of a man, who is
capable of such disgraceful conduct, and she has given
us very definite instructions, unless you are prepared
forthwith to sign such an apology as we should settle
on her behalf, to bring an action against you and to
place your conduct before a jury.

On the following day Gilbert wrote to that friend of Henrietta
Hodson's, Marie Lytton: 'As I am certain she must be acting under
some misapprehension, I shall be much obliged if you will kindly let me
know what you said to Miss Hodson in reference to our conversation
concerning her, that could possibly bear the interpretation "obscene
and disgusting language". On 3rd March he signed the apology drafted
by Miss Hodson's solicitors, but asked that it should not be published; it
amounted to a complete surrender on Gilbert's part, and he must have
been very frustratedly outmanoeuvred signing:

> ... I hereby desire to state in the fullest sense, that in the use of the
> language in question, I never intended to make the least imputation
> upon your character as manageress of the Royalty Theatre. And I
> also desire to state that I have never attributed to you the use of
> language inconsistent with your position as a lady. I further desire
> to express to you my sincere regret that, in a moment of great
> excitement I should have used words that offended you, and I trust
> you will accept this retraction.

Gilbert had cause to bemoan, for the lady gave him back a good dose of
his own medicine:

> ... although I had mentioned the matter to no-one but the lady in
> question Miss Hodson thought fit to distribute, not only to her

personal friends, but to all the leading members of the dramatic profession in London. In taking this extreme course, . . . it was an act which seemed to place all friendly relations between Miss Hodson and myself out of the question. I may add that the letter [of apology] eventually appeared in the columns of *The Hornet*.

This then, was the basis of the argument which continued over the following three years, as is told in detail by the parties' respective pamphlets:

Hodson: Some time afterwards, the manager of the Prince of Wales' Theatre at Liverpool offered me an engagement to play *Ought We*. I sent Mr. Blackmore, the agent to ask upon what terms I could have the piece. He telegraphed to Mr. Gilbert, who went to Mr. Blackmore's office, and said, "She shall not have the piece, if she pays me £100 per night for it."
　　　When, later on, I was engaged at the St. James's Theatre, it was intended to produce Mr. Gilbert's play called *The Princess*, in which I was to play the heroine. He said he would not allow me to play in that, or in any other piece of his.

Gilbert: When Miss Hodson applied to me, immediately after the publication of the letter in *The Hornet*, for permission to play in *Ought We* in Liverpool, I declined to hold any communication with her ... In point of fact it was a matter of indifference to me whether Miss Hodson did or did not play in my pieces, so that I was not called upon to enter into any personal relations with her. Of the proposed revival of *The Princess* ... it did not come to my knowledge that it had been in contemplation to revive it until I read Miss Hodson's pamphlet.

In July 1876, Henrietta Hodson was engaged as the leading lady of J. B. Buckstone's company at the Theatre Royal, Haymarket. The continuing problem arose when a revival of the author's *Pygmalion and Galatea* was planned. At first Buckstone suggested that Hodson should play the second part rather than the lead, in order to appease Gilbert, but was eventually forced to write to the actress on 23rd November:

I have a letter from Mr. Gilbert in which he states that from certain differences, the nature of which he could give at length, it is impossible that he could allow you to appear in any play written by him. This is a most embarrassing position to place me in...

Henry Howe, the stage manager, wrote the next day to confirm that he had seen the letter which as he recalled it stated:

Miss Hodson's conduct to me has been so gross that I will never allow her to appear in any play of mine.

and a friend of the actress, F. A. Marshal, reported to her that in conversation at the Criterion Theatre, in answer to a question, Gilbert had said, 'Do you think after the way in which she behaved to me I would let her play any part in one of my pieces?' Consequently a solicitor's letter was again forwarded to the dramatist charging him with his continuing transgressions towards her and threatening proceedings for slander.

Gilbert ignored that letter but produced a copy of the communication he had sent to Buckstone, sent a copy to his adversary, confirmed it with the Theatre Royal manager and also showed it to Marshal who wrote two letters of apology recognising his error, and the injustice he had done Gilbert. Buckstone wrote to Miss Hodson supporting Gilbert's explanation and offering to supervise a reconciliatory meeting, but this piece of correspondence was not to be seen in her own pamphlet. Eventually Gilbert allowed her to remain in the production and Marion Terry even offered to relinquish the lead in her favour, which generous sacrifice was refused. Gilbert also wrote to Howe asking that the stage manager should try and keep him under more control should his temper quicken during rehearsals.

Miss Hodson claimed that Howe wrote to her saying, 'I sincerely congratulate you on your triumph over Gilbert. The entire profession owes you thanks for your pluck in putting down this tyrant'. Howe very quickly sent a letter to Gilbert on 25th April 1877:

I have read in a pamphlet issued by Miss Hodson a quotation said to be taken from a letter of mine to her, in which she asserts I made use of expressions I wish to contradict. I am as certain as it is possible for anyone to be that I never wrote in the form she puts it. I did congratulate her on being in the cast of *Pygmalion* and that all was amicably settled.

Finally, serious doubt was cast on the credibility of her pamphlet when she wrote to Gilbert on 3rd March claiming that this letter, and one written to her by Buckstone on 18th February terminating her contract on the grounds of not needing her services for the following season and her being too expensive, were forged by the author:

> You are fully capable of either having dictated it to him or of having forged it to suit your own purposes.

The *Dictionary of National Biography* clearly took her side, however, when it recorded after her death, that:

> Miss Hodson won lavish praise in January, 1874, for the naturalness of her acting in the new comedy *Ought We to Visit Her?* although the conduct of one of the authors, W. S. Gilbert, at the rehearsals was highly distasteful to her.
> After other engagements she played in January, 1877, Cynisca in a revival of Gilbert's *Pygmalion and Galatea* at the Haymarket, and during the rehearsal had a fresh dispute with the author, whose dictatorial control she attacked in a pamphlet-letter addressed to the profession[3].

Throughout the period of the argument Gilbert was trying to suppress the editorials in Labouchère's *Truth* in which Miss Hodson's husband attacked the playwright as much as he could. However on passing the question to counsel he was told:

> I do not advise Mr. Gilbert to notice the attacks made upon him in the pages of *Truth*. The articles and notices before me show clearly enough that the writer is an adept in the art of offensive comment and criticism and that he has done his best to annoy and insult Mr. Gilbert. But I am of the opinion that proceedings by way of criminal information against the publisher and proprietor of the paper would not be successful.

The *Theatre* magazine closed its final report of the incident, again favouring Henrietta Hodson, in its issue of 5th June 1877, by voicing the opinion that:

Mr Gilbert has yet to learn that he is a servant of the public and amenable to public opinion, and Miss Hodson must be congratulated on the courage she has shown in appealing to her profession against him.

Perhaps it was this defeat when going to arbitration, instead of using the full force of the law, that made Gilbert take a strictly formal legal recourse in nearly all the subsequent arguments in which he found himself during the rest of his life.

Part II

'I don't think we quite understand one another'

Chapter 6

'Consider the moral, I pray': Trial by Jury

At a little after 10.20 on the evening of 25th March 1875, the curtain went up at the little Royalty (Soho) Theatre in Dean Street, Soho, on the third and final production of the evening, the new 'dramatic cantata', *Trial by Jury*. The audience were astounded to see an exact replica of a courtroom, complete with wood panelling, bench and royal arms. Little could that audience possibly have realised or appreciated that what was being literally ushered in before them was not only a completely new plane of theatrical realism in set and properties, but the practical beginning of the greatest partnership in the history of musical entertainment.

Principally, however, it was this realism in the piece that caught the imagination of the public and critics alike. It was fresh and fast-moving, with witty lyrics that made the standard burlesques of the day, including the two pieces that were billed together with it earlier in the programme, rather staid and quite dull by comparison; and it was daring. The concept of parodying a breach-of-promise action with such accuracy was much more revolutionary in the stagecraft of the time than Gilbert is now given credit for. His eye for detail and Sullivan's delightful melodies made each character stand out; Counsel and Usher, Plaintiff and Defendant, and of course the Learned Judge, whose most famous song displays to the full Gilbert's masterly lyrics, no less equalled by Sullivan's huge musical joke in spoofing a Handelian

59

anthem for his entrance. With this in mind, and who the creators were, it becomes less surprising that this tiny piece, really a half-hour programme-filler at a small and unfashionable theatre in a very poor district of London, attracted the attention and critical acclaim that it did, word quickly being passed around. *The Times* critic wrote:

> It should be added that the various costumes are exact, without caricature, and that - the appearance of the Plaintiff with a troop of bridesmaids in bridesmaids attire excepted, - everything is precisely what might be witnessed on such an occasion in the court at Westminster[1].

Trial by Jury was clearly conceived from the one-page illustrated sketch that appeared on page 54 of the Easter edition of *Fun* magazine, 11th April 1868. This was Gilbert's original attempt at a parody of the action for breach of promise, a legal suit that existed in England until 1970[2], and that was not then an uncommon thing, quite likely to be seen among the copious law reports that nearly every daily journal maintained. Gilbert had entitled the two-column skit 'Trial by Jury - an Operetta' and in content, rather than in format, it closely followed what was becoming a little collection of legal 'Bab ballads' reflecting the barrister's knowledge of the oddities of legal terms and procedure. From the enlargement of this tiny chrysalis was to emerge the final polished gem, so loved then and today.

The fact that *Trial* came to be performed at all was chance, as was the decision to try to persuade Sullivan to write the music, as indeed was obtaining the use of the Royalty, Soho, at that time. So many factors that affected the final result, the creation of an institution in the entertainment world, were governed by the hand of fate, that to look at them without any hint of fatalism would be naive in the extreme. How did Gilbert come to write a piece at all for musical adaptation, having concentrated on farces and burlesques for four years; and why this particular plot? Why Sullivan, when he was known to be reluctant to write for the musical theatre, had success-fully played down his association with *Thespis* in order to concentrate on his aspirations towards a higher plane in musical composition, and was no particular friend of Gilbert. Of all places - leaving aside its poor location - why the Royalty Theatre in Dean Street, which was then leased to none other than Gilbert's bosom friend of the period, Henrietta Hodson?

Towards the end of 1873, Gilbert had been approached by composer Carl Rosa to write a piece in which a fairly well known singer of the day, his wife, Parepa Rosa, could be given the lead. Carl Rosa would set the music. As later became very clear, the dramatist was positively miserly in his creativity and would squeeze his singular ideas dry again and again if he thought they were good enough, or could be sufficiently well disguised. He must have had the law in mind as a theme, and found the little sketch of the breach-of-promise action a very sound base upon which to build, with a creditable plot and the opportunity to introduce onto the stage the courtroom scene of which he was so fond, but liked to joke with. However, tragedy struck and the project was shelved owing to the sudden death of Madame Rosa. Her husband had been a friend of Sullivan's when they were both students in Leipzig and again, by chance, the piece became set by the latter, rather than Carl Rosa.

Carte was the man. Richard D'Oyly Carte, thirty-one, lecture and concert manager and agent, Craig's Court, Charing Cross Road, and aspiring impresario-to-be. He wrote and conducted music for operettas, lived in the musical world and loved the theatrical world. Brains, a commercial cunning and a knowledge of the market made him the perfect catalyst to draw Gilbert and Sullivan together. He had admired *Thespis* but could not then have been sure of the potential in commercial terms. Now in 1875 as general manager for Selina ('Dolly') Dolaro, who had taken Henrietta Hodson's Royalty Theatre for that season, he was entrusted to commission a short piece to fill the last hour of the programme. Some authorities say that he approached Gilbert; others that Gilbert had called into his agency anyway or had attended the Royalty one night - the result being the 'impresario' needing a short piece and the dramatist having the very thing, ready written, and certainly something not to be wasted!

Who can say whether Carte had a flash of genius, or whether he had planned the encounter and was awaiting his opportunity? He persuaded Gilbert that not Rosa, but Sullivan, was the only man that could do justice to the lyrics; he must have foreseen too, that the piece itself, rather than his persuasion, would sell the idea to Sullivan. Three weeks later *Trial* was ready for performance.

The tremendous reception reflected both artists' work and enthusiasm for the piece; and no less justice did the company do the work, with the 'Learned Judge', Sullivan's elder brother Fred, causing a sensation, having been made up to look like the current Lord Chief

Justice, Sir Alexander Cockburn. W. S. Penley, later the original 'Charley's Aunt', scored a big hit as the Foreman of the Jury, and naturally so did the beautiful Plaintiff, Nelly Bromley. The gay little show was destined to run continuously in London for 300 performances, over two years, and at three theatres.

Cockburn himself had gone to see the piece at the invitation of Sullivan who was a fairly close friend; this was in return for an invitation that the Lord Chief Justice had given the composer, when he was involved heavily in the most famous lawsuit of the day, the series of cases involving the Tichborne Claimant. Sir Arthur related the incident to his biographer, Lawrence:

> Although he was very fond of me personally, and very fond of
> music, he did not like the notion of our *Trial by Jury* at all, as he
> thought the piece was calculated to bring the Bench into contempt!
> He went to see the piece once, remarking afterwards that it was
> very pretty and clever, and 'all that sort of thing', but he would not
> go again for fear he should seem to encourage it.
>
> I used to go and sit on the Bench with him, however, at the time
> of the trial of the Claimant, and occasionally I would sleep at his
> house overnight, so that I might be in time in the morning to drive
> down with him to the Court. The incidents of the trial and
> Cockburn's masterly summing-up are, of course, matters of history,
> but I was greatly struck by the effect of the adverse verdict on the
> Claimant. He was, as you know, a big burly fellow, but at the
> moment the verdict was given he seemed in some unaccountable
> manner to decrease instantly in bulk, so that his clothes appeared to
> hang loosely about him. I certainly never witnessed a more curious
> sight[3].

A word of explanation must be offered, since the newspapers quickly caught on to the association, and pictures began to appear depicting the real parties in the Tichborne cases in the context of the set of *Trial by Jury* with appropriate captions; for example in *Entr'acte* magazine, as late as 22nd August 1885[4].

In 1870 an Australian butcher by the name of Arthur Orton appeared in England and claimed to be the long-lost heir to the Tichborne estates and fortune. In one of the longest civil trials in history, Tichborne v Lushington, which lasted from 10th May 1871 until 6th March 1872, it was decided that the man was a fraud, and further that he had committed perjury in giving his evidence. He was indicted to stand trial on twenty-three charges of perjury, and the great importance of the case led to an order for it to be tried 'at the Bar', which meant that it would be heard before three judges and a jury, and presided over by the Chief Justice of the Queen's Bench Division, Alexander Cockburn. Sitting together with Mr Justice Lush and Mr Justice Mellor, the case of R. v. Thomas Castro alias Arthur Orton opened at Westminster Hall on 23rd April 1873 and lasted for 188 days; sixty-six were taken up by counsel's speeches and twenty by Cockburn's remarkable summing-up to the jury. To add to the sensationalism of the case, the Claimant's counsel, Dr. Kenealy Q.C., was considered to have conducted the case in such an improper way that the Benchers of Gray's Inn disbarred him. It was evidently considered that he must have known of his client's perjury and abetted the deceit practised upon the court[5].

In September 1879, Kate Field of *Scribner's Monthly* magazine had interviewed Gilbert during which he spoke of *Trial by Jury*:

> On the occasion of the first dress rehearsal, every man in the cantata appeared made up for Dr. Kenealy! The stage swarmed with the Tichborne champion, much to the disgust of every individual actor who thought he had conceived an original idea.

At that time the disbarred counsel was even more of a popular figure, having stood as an independent candidate for a by-election at Stoke-on-Trent earlier in the year, where he won the seat against both party candidates, and so was very much a newsworthy figure.

Authorities differ as to whether the set was based on Clerkenwell Sessions House, or the Court of Exchequer at Westminster Hall. Although the *Fun* sketch is headed 'a Court at Westminster' the operetta merely says 'a Court of Justice'. The Defendant on entering asks whether it be the Court of Exchequer. Both are possible, the Sessions having statutory jurisdiction to try the case, the Exchequer Court having equitable jurisdiction, and Gilbert practised in both. The procedure adopted is confusing however: trial would only actually be by jury in the Sessions House (or at the County Court) whereas a judge would not sit at petty sessions, only either at Quarter Sessions or in the Exchequer Court. Considering the original set, however, it seems most likely that what Gilbert envisaged was a Quarter Session at Clerkenwell despite the Defendant's line; and more especially since trials by juries of this nature were confined to County Courts of Quarter Session with unpaid County Justices, Borough Courts or Quarter Session with Crown-appointed, salaried Recorders, Circuit Courts of Assize held by 'Judges of the Superior Courts of Common Law, Queens Counsel or Serjeants, or the Central Criminal Court' (a Gilbertian favourite) where Superior Court Justices, the Lord Mayor and Aldermen of the City of London, Common Serjeant, Common Recorder or Judges of the City Court presided.

From that one-page sketch had emerged a delightful operetta, the plot and lyrics of which closely followed the procedure that was to be expected in any court of the day. The highlight of the piece, the Judge's song[6], is a perfect satire on the state of the Bar and advancement within it - and in an age of no legal education for the profession that was far closer to the truth than certainly the Lord Chief Justice would have cared to admit! However the real importance of this short, vivacious Easter novelty, which continued by public demand for a further two Easters, was the brilliant artistic unity of the piece, bringing to Sullivan the kind of money he wasn't used to, and to Gilbert the lavish critical praise that he needed to thrive on. The only question remains, would the success of the piece have been so spontaneous had it been couched in an object of satire other than the law, or was it the topicality and everyday nature of the basic plot that scored the great hit? Of course the music, and lyrics, speak for themselves.

Chapter 7

'When the balls whistle free:' The rise and fall of the Comedy Opera Company

As soon as it was recognised that *Trial by Jury* was a triumph, holding audiences waiting impatiently whilst the earlier curtain-raisers and even main pieces were dispensed with, D'Oyly Carte faced a dilemma. Theatrical wizard though he was as an impresario, he knew that it needed few brains to see that anyone who could harness the impetus created by this major success and develop it would surely be on to a money-spinner of vast proportions. He also realised that financially he was in no position to start building the foundations of his dream of popular English-based opera and operetta; he had no company, no independence as a producer-manager, no immediate backers, and no theatre. He did, however, have rivals, and he knew that this opportunity would all too quickly pass him by unless he could make a move before any other monied theatrical interests caught on to the idea.

Carte's principal danger was John Hollingshead, owner and licensee of the Gaiety Theatre, which although only a little over seven years old, was already recognised by London playgoers as the home of musical comedy. Gilbert was a close friend of Hollingshead and between them they formed a mutual admiration society - the dramatist admiring Hollingshead's rigid control over the managerial affairs, and the latter appreciating and utilising Gilbert's revolutionary concepts in stage movement and management. Gilbert was commissioned to write a piece for the opening of the Gaiety on 21st December 1868, entitled *Robert the Devil* which ran successfully as a Christmas season piece. At the Gaiety, Hollingshead offered nightly a programme containing operetta, drama, 'extravaganza' and ballet; he kept a tight reign on productions and built up a repertory company that specialised in the most popular opera and operetta of the day: Offenbach and Halevy, Von Suppe and Donizetti. Carte's main concern was focused on the fact that it was Hollingshead and not himself who had first brought Gilbert and Sullivan together (although Edward German-Reed of the Royal Gallery of Illustration in Lower Regent Street had tried without success in 1870). On 23rd December 1871, *Thespis* opened at the Gaiety and had a run of 64 performances, at least as many as Hollingshead would have anticipated for a Christmas show. However, to Carte's good fortune the idea of a more permanent working relationship between the two lapsed for, whilst the critics were generally appreciative of the quality of the work, it was stated (at some length in the *Daily Telegraph* and the *Sporting Life*), that the plot was too intellectually overpowering for the type of audience to be seen at the Gaiety, especially over Christmas, and Hollingshead must have realised this as well[1]. Carte also knew that Sullivan had afterwards decided against writing any further for the musical theatre, and it was only Hollingshead who persuaded him to return to that creative sphere, in 1874, when he wrote his incidental music to *The Merry Wives of Windsor*, again for the Gaiety.

In the face of his potential difficulties Richard D'Oyly Carte quickly made plans for the establishment of a company to follow upon the success of *Trial*, principally by retaining Gilbert and Sullivan as a writing team. This was also an attempt to generate sufficient interest in 'home-grown' operetta in order to start a new artistic movement, and consequently invitations were sent to all the leading English composers of the period, including Francis Burnand with Alfred Cellier, and James Albery with Frederic Clay, for them to tender contributions (none of which, however, materialised). Carte had approached the music-publishing firm of George Metzler, which had published the score and libretto of *Trial*, as his initial backers. The stake money for each director was to be £500, and with the interest of several people gained, the Comedy Opera Company Limited was incorporated under the provisions of the Joint-Stock Companies Act 1862, in November, 1876.

The picture now becomes confused in the various authoritative works on Gilbert and Sullivan. Most writers agree that there were four directors besides Carte himself, who initially was the general manager and then became managing director when he eventually could raise his stake money in May 1878; one contemporary account states that there were five. All are agreed on only one name, that of George Metzler. Percy M. Young, in *Sir Arthur Sullivan*; Reginald Allen, in *The First Night Gilbert and Sullivan*; and the D'Oyly Carte Opera Company's Centenary Programme name Frank Chappell, described variously as a partner or employee in Metzler's, as a director; Isaac Goldberg, in his authoritative *Story of Gilbert and Sullivan*, says it was William Chappell, Frank's father and famous musicologist, which would seem to be more likely but for contemporary accounts. The next inexplicable divergence is still more fascinating: Allen and the Carte Centenary Programme name Collard Augustus Drake, the former as secretary of the company and an associate of Metzler, the latter as a member of the pianoforte-makers firm of Collard; Young calls him A. D. Collard and Goldberg thinks that this third director was Charles Lukey Collard, also of the piano business. There is general agreement, however, that the fourth director had a monopoly over the water-cart street sprinklers in London, and he is variously called Edward Hodgson Bayley, 'Water-Cart' Bailey or Bailey-Generalli. The fifth is mentioned only in one source, an intriguing hint, in the London *Figaro* of 1st June, 1878:

The directors of the Opera Comique are Mr. Metzler, Mr. Frank Chappell (a member of Mr. Metzler's firm), Mr. Drake (known to amateur flute players as Mr. 'Collard', and who is connected with the firm of Metzler's in the production of a new music easel), Mr. Bailey, and a Mr. Wilson.

It is understood that in order to increase the average intellect of the Board of Directors of the Opera Comique, Mr. D'Oyly Carte has just been made a director.

Carte now needed two things: sufficient money to tempt Gilbert and Sullivan, and a theatre to bring in a return on the investment. Early in 1877 he had written to an unidentified nobleman to solicit about £6,000, describing his involvement with Gilbert and Sullivan. The peer was probably Lord Kilmorey who owned the Opera Comique and responded to a request by Carte for a short-term lease, but granted it to him personally and not to Comedy Opera Company. Carte also found himself in adequate funds to put forward a proposition tempting enough to secure the services of both author and composer, and he received a letter from Sullivan to that effect dated 5th June, stating:

> Gilbert and myself are quite willing to write a two-act piece for you on the following terms:
> 1. Payment to us of two hundred guineas (£210) on the delivery of the MS. words and music - that is to say before the piece is produced.
> 2. Six guineas a performance (£6.6s.) to be paid to us for the run of the piece in London, from this will be deducted the two hundred guineas paid in advance so that the payment of the six guineas a performance will not really commence until about the 33rd or 34th performance.
> 3. We reserve the country right, your right to play it in London on these terms only to extend to the end of your season.
>   The piece would be of a musical comedy character and could be ready for performance by the end of September. If this outline of terms is agreed to, we could prepare a proper agreement upon this basis.

The actual contract and memorandum of agreement was drawn up and signed a month later and included a time schedule:

> The said Arthur Sullivan and W. S. Gilbert undertake to deliver the manuscript (words and music) in instalments as completed in sufficient time for the production of the piece on Monday, 29th October, 1877, the whole of the manuscript to be delivered not later than the 15th October, 1877. The said R. D'Oyly Carte undertakes to produce the said opera on or about the 29th October, 1877.

The well-known history of the Comedy Opera Company was one of frenzied conflict between the Board of Directors and the triumvirate of Carte and his two writers. The businessmen had put up a considerable amount of money for their directorships and even those from the music world were eager, and quite understandably so, for a speedy return on their investment. That investment represented to them no more than any other business arrangement in a growth economy; they cared little for Carte's dream of a new artistic movement and were sharply aware that in presenting a young and untried, almost unknown, manager with such means as they had, their end-result would be by no means an automatic return. They were constantly nervous and on occasion almost apoplectic in their anxiety, and a constant stream of correspondence arrived at Carte's office, making requests, offering instructions or giving orders. Carte was fighting for his independence and knew that he was only relatively safe for as long as the profit kept coming in for his backers. They, for their part, realised that he was the personal licensee of the Opera Comique and their only contact with Gilbert and Sullivan; only he had the ear of the anonymous nobleman sponsor. They therefore uneasily but noisily suffered for the sake of their wallets until the position looked desperate to them, which it did periodically and frequently.

Gilbert and Sullivan had reserved in their contract the right to select and train personally their entire company, and Carte readily concurred. However, the board either didn't at the time fully realise the implications or decided to ignore that part of the agreement; under the circumstances it is not difficult to understand their qualms: in *The Sorcerer* not only did Gilbert wish to introduce the character of a clergyman into comic opera; for the name part he wanted to employ a drawing-room entertainer and lecturer, vastly more at home in Sunday amusements at the Y.M.C.A. than on a professional stage as a principal in comic opera. They had good reason to feel that this man was not capable of performing a Sullivan role, and quickly telegraphed to Carte, 'whatever you do, don't engage Grossmith', an instruction which Carte promptly, and, as it turned out, happily ignored.

Thus started the intimations of a great game which was to last until the collapse of the 'Company' in the Royal Courts of Justice, and in the depths of Shoreditch. *The Sorcerer* opened on 17th November 1877, and began a run of six months, the directors beginning a careful scrutiny of the weekly box-office takings. Gilbert was particularly pleased with the enthusiastic reception of his work by the public and began working on the scenario of his next piece before it was even commissioned him. The directors were nervous to a traumatic degree, and that did not help Carte's management at all: in a good week they were not only happy with *The Sorcerer* but quite prepared to discuss and eventually commission the work needed to follow it up. However even if the bookings dropped only slightly they at once pressed Carte to issue a fortnight's closure notice and pull out of the entire venture. Their general manager had a hard time resisting these demands when they came. After agreeing the next work on the same terms, a subsequent bad patch at the

Opera Comique sent them scurrying to Carte to demand a reduction of the guarantee on the run of the new piece. Gilbert rejected that demand absolutely in early January 1878, and Sullivan wrote to Carte from Nice on 5th February:

> Don't be under any apprehension about the 'Company'. They can do nothing without us, and I certainly shall not deal with them unless through you. And I shan't deal with them at all unless they make up their minds to settle your business quickly.
>
> They ought to have done it long ago.

H.M.S. Pinafore, having been launched on 25th May 1878, was becalmed for a summer, nearly broken up in a prolonged squall a little over a year later, and a prize crew employed on another vessel to take business away from the mother ship sank without trace at the Standard Theatre, Shoreditch, some time in 1880. It is paradoxical that it was the success of *Pinafore*, rather than its early failure, that heralded the collapse of the uneasy relationship that was the Comedy Opera Company. Despite the brilliant society opening and general critical acclaim, receipts from the new production fell quickly away during the long hot summer of 1878, and the directors' murmurings of closure were dispelled only by reference to the minimum guaranteed run of the piece of 100 performances in the contract. D'Oyly Carte was himself concerned with the receipts and had to issue a notice to the press to resist rumours that the show was being run at a disastrous loss. From September Carte knew that the directors could and would post closure notices; out of his desperation and their loyalty, the cast agreed to take a cut of one-third in their salaries. The nobility of this action was sadly not reciprocated by that of the directors, a few months later, when they did not even thank the cast either at the time or at the duration of the artists' contracts with the 'Company'. To add to his problems, just as the show was beginning to move out of the financial doldrums, Carte received a letter from Sullivan dated 12th September accusing him of giving short measure to his music:

> I regret to say that on my visit to the Theatre last Tuesday I found the orchestra both in number and efficiency very different to what it was when I rehearsed the 'Pinafore'.
>
> There seemed to be two second violins short and the whole band is of very different quality. I beg to give you notice that if the

deficiencies are not supplied by Saturday and the efficiency of the orchestra increased by engaging better players both of the wind and stringed instruments I shall withdraw my music from the Theatre on Monday night.

You know perfectly well that what I say I mean. Kindly inform the Directors of this and oblige.

Carte was quick to appease the composer, especially since it was he alone that had helped business to pick up by conducting an arrangement of selections from *H.M.S. Pinafore* at the Covent Garden Promenade Concert on 19th August. It was only after this that the opera began to generate the interest and success that it has maintained to this day.

Whether the Company directors were short-sighted to a man, or whether their temperament and business instincts told them to take as much as they could and run, they determined, once their profits were rapidly mounting, that it was the piece *Pinafore* (not the team of Gilbert and Sullivan, and certainly not their recently appointed managing director, Carte), that was the money-maker. In the face of Carte ignoring their instructions as often as they gave him any, it was firmly resolved by them to dispense with his services, and those of his extremely expensive writers, as soon as possible, and take over for themselves the day-to-day running of the show. Their action was not a rash decision based merely on the profit motive, but as events were to show, the results of a carefully considered plan, developed in an atmosphere of festering antagonism towards the outwardly responsible and thus successful trio who consciously or unconsciously disregarded them. The opportunity for a power struggle arose out of the arrangements for the continuation of the leasing of the Opera Comique. It should be made clear, however, that by now Carte welcomed any opportunity to be rid of his gentlemen albatrosses, since he could now stand financially independent. Suddenly 'Gilbert and Sullivan' opera now seemed a safe enough investment for Carte to force the issue, wind up the Comedy Opera Company and ditch his fellow directors overboard; consequently on 27th November a new arrangement was decided upon between the directors and Carte whereby they were to receive the net profits of the show for such periods as Carte could negotiate a renewal of the lease of the theatre; after which he would have the sole right to deal with the landlord, author and composer and hire the cast.

The lease of the Opera Comique was due to expire at the end of December 1878, and by an agreement Carte made with Lord Kilmorey's agent, the Earl of Dunraven, the show was to close after the last performance on Christmas Day for the theatre's drains to be relaid in accordance with new sanitary regulations being imposed on the owners by the 1875 Public Health Act. Thus the actors had to be laid off during what would normally have been their busiest working period. In some recompense Carte was granted a renewal of the lease from 1st February for six months, which in turn meant that as far as he was concerned the directors of the Comedy Opera Company would have no further control over him, if they had ever had any, or the show as of 1st August 1879. The profits continued to be amassed, especially as press reports reached London of the *Pinafore* craze that was sweeping America. The directors who only a year before were determined to opt out of the venture were now going to have a hard struggle to hang on to any rights that they then had; this was brought home to them on 8th July when Carte gave them notice that they would have no further rights in the opera as from the end of the month.

Carte had planned to go to America to seek out the pirate productions of *Pinafore* early in the month. With a reaction from the directors obviously in the offing he had to make a decision whether to go or not, and by a strange coincidence bumped into a old friend, Michael Gunn, while walking in the Strand. Having talked over the problem Gunn offered to put up any capital that might be needed initially if the directors started any trouble, and Carte installed him as assistant manager, armed him with his power of attorney and set off for New York as planned.

The directors acted, and much faster than Carte or Gunn had imagined they would. They were to have all the takings until the end of the month anyway, but wanted to cut off any funds due to Carte in the meantime so as to command a stronger position when the showdown arrived. Consequently, the opening shot was fired on the 15th when the directors made an ex parte application for an injunction to restrain Gunn from taking any of the receipts into his possession, and for the appointment of a receiver to be made. On the following day the Master of the Rolls, Sir George Jessell, granted an interim injunction and the directors' treasurer, J. H. Jarvis, was appointed receiver. The directors, well pleased with their initial success, returned to court a week later to have the injunction made permanent and try and extend its terms to keep Gunn actually out of the theatre, claiming in their supporting affidavit that they had dismissed him for inefficiency. Meanwhile they had passed a resolution removing Carte as their managing director and general manager, and posted a notice to that effect at the theatre on the 21st. However the eloquence of their two leading counsel, Chitty and Southgate, failed to persuade the court, and the representatives of the Defendant Davey, Q.C., and Stiff Everitt were not even called upon to defend the motion. Sir George, sitting as a Chancery judge in chambers, threw out their application on the grounds that the directors had no authority to take away Carte's power of attorney from Gunn, and that Carte, rather than the Company, was the personal lessee from the Earl of Dunraven of the Opera Comique.

Under a week remained before the directors were to lose their rights in the opera, and swift action was called for if they were to save anything. They knew that the law would not help them, or certainly not within the week. Rightly or wrongly they believed that if the show wasn't theirs, the costumes, scenery and properties certainly were. Metzler, however, wanted no part of anything which might be illegal and he opted out of the C.O.C.'s drastic plan. The week passed and Bailey drew up the details.

As the lease drew to a close on the 31st, the 374th performance of *H.M.S. Pinafore* started, with no little trepidation. The cast had heard rumours that there might be trouble but the day had passed quietly enough, as did the first act. The house was full and warmly receptive. At a little before a quarter past ten several horse-drawn vans belonging to Bailey drew up outside the stage door and he, Collard and Chappell stepped down together with a large group of men[2]. Accounts vary, as before, but between twelve and fifty dock-workers and labourers from the East End had been hired by the Comedy Opera Company to create a sufficient disturbance in the front of the house for the directors and staff to remove the props and as much of the set as they could carry off. They quickly forced their way through the stage door and past the green room. To get to the stage itself they had to descend a small flight of stone steps that led to a door opening into the wings. Just as they were doing so Richard Barker, the stage manager, opened the door to come up. He was immediately knocked down and pushed over the handrail by the stairs. The chorus, waiting for an entrance, were startled by the sudden appearance of several rough-looking men moving quickly in the wings and amongst the flaps, and when Bailey shouted from behind them, 'Come on my boys, now's the time!', there was a commotion amongst the women. One of the men started to scale the ladder up to the flies shouting 'fire' as he went. By now eight or nine men appeared on stage and the 'sailors' knew a determined effort would have to be made to repel the boarders. Frank Thornton, a member of the chorus, went forward into the stage-box and attempted to calm the audience, as did Alfred Cellier from the pit where he was conducting but to no avail: they couldn't be heard above the noise. After a few minutes the main curtain was brought down and George Grossmith appeared from behind it; he shouted to the audience exactly what was happening, and the rush to the exits was stemmed - the house returned to their seats and anxiously awaited the outcome of the battle going on before them, and the arrival of the police who had been sent for. The constabulary arrived in force; the boarders were repelled, and the press reported the following day an 'hour-long fracas at the Opera Comique'. The performance was concluded, and both cast and audience returned home wondering what could possibly happen next.

The first day of August was a day of frantic activity for both sides. Gunn was busy at the theatre sorting out the damage and packing away the costumes which were indeed the rightful property of the Comedy Opera Company, and had to be delivered up to them that day as Carte had instructed. Gilbert had sent a member of his firm of solicitors, Lewis and Lewis, down to Bow Street Police Court to take out summonses from Mr Flowers, the magistrate, against all the directors, including Metzler, for causing or permitting a riot at the Opera Comique, and for common assault on Richard Barker. A hearing date was set for 5th August. The directors, having decided to mount an alternative production, were desperately trying to get together a scratch company and set for the theatre they had hired, the Imperial, attached to the Royal Aquarium, Westminster. Gilbert had anticipated that they might try to rival the show, and as soon as he heard which theatre they intended to use he sent Ince, Q.C., with Stiff Everitt down to the Rolls Gardens off Chancery Lane to apply for an injunction from the Master of the Rolls to stop the Comedy Opera Company producing *Pinafore* at the Royal Aquarium, in any other London theatre or indeed, anywhere else. The directors in turn realised that Gilbert was certain to adopt this course and had dispatched counsel in anticipation to prevent Gilbert and Carte from presenting only one side of the story at an ex parte hearing. He propounded unsuccessfully the view that Gilbert and Sullivan had agreed to deliver to the Company a two-act opera and, having done so, their rights in the actual production of the piece terminated with the end of the guaranteed run. Sir George commented on the fact that the applicants had not come to court in person, although there was no reason why they should have done so, but allowed the injunction on the evidence in the affidavits. Gilbert's triumph, however, was premature as the directors, planning to open at the 'Aquarium' that evening, had instructed their counsel in exactly what to do should this event occur: he raced through Hare Court into Lincoln's Inn and arranged for the Lords Justices in Chancery to hear an appeal as a matter of urgency, when they returned from luncheon. Lords Justices James, Brett and Cotton decided that the point was an arguable one and that Gilbert did not have a prima facie case; due to the nature of the loss and inconvenience that the directors would be put to, they overruled Sir George Jessel and lifted the injunction. In consequence, two '375th' performances of *Pinafore* took place that evening, the old cast in new costumes at the Opera Comique, and the new cast in old costumes at the Imperial.

The leading theatrical newspaper of the day was the *Era* magazine which was published every Thursday. Whilst it had not been able to catch the riot at the theatre as it had occurred on a Thursday, the paper had a field day afterwards in letters and reports which lasted throughout August:

Comedy Opera Company v Gunn   *August 3rd, 1879*
To the Editor of the Era
Sir, The continuance of Mr. Jarvis as receiver on the hearing of the motion for injunction seems to have been misconceived by some persons, and our client thinks it desirable that it should be explained that no opposition was offered whatever by the counsel employed on his behalf to this course as practically it made little or no alteration from what has always been the practice at the theatre, since Mr. Jarvis has always in his capacity as Treasurer been in the habit of collecting the receipts and paying them into the bank without any interference. Mr. Jarvis made an affidavit on behalf of our client stating this, but it was not even read to the Court, owing to the fact that the Defendant's counsel was not called, the Master of the Rolls deciding in his favour, as appears by your report, without any explanation on his part. It is only fair to say that if they had been necessary he was prepared with ample evidence in support of his contention and in opposition to the subject of the action. More than this we are not at liberty to say at present as the case may still be said to be sub judice. We shall feel obliged by your insertion of this,
  Your obedient servants,
  Beyfus & Beyfus, Defendant's Solicitors,
   69, Lincoln's Inn Fields, London WC. 30th July, 1879.

'H.M.S. Pinafore in Chancery'   *August 3rd, 1879*

Mr. Ince, Q.C., with whom was Mr. Stiff Everitt, applied on
Friday afternoon to the Master of the Rolls on behalf of Mr. W. S.
Gilbert and Mr. Arthur Sullivan, for an injunction to restrain the
Comedy Opera Company from representing at the Aquarium
Theatre, or any other theatre in London or elsewhere, the opera-
bouffe or comedy opera of H.M.S. Pinafore. The Defendants
contended that they had an agreement with Messrs. Gilbert and
Sullivan under which they were entitled to perform the piece, and
they put in the minute-book of the company, in which an agreement, dictated by Mr. Gilbert and written by Mr. Drake, the
Secretary, appeared, whereby Gilbert and Sullivan agreed to write
a new two-act comedy opera and deliver the same to the opera
company by 31st March, 1878, at a dead rent of eight guineas a
night and a guaranteed run of 100 nights. There was another licence
for acting in the country.

The 100 nights for London expired last December when a new
agreement was come to. The company contended that they became
owners of the copyright. His Lordship, after looking at the agreement, said the agreement for 'Pinafore' was not quite clear, but the
agreement with reference to the 'Sorcerer', which was linked with
it, threw some light upon it. He had a very strong opinion with
regard to the conduct of the opera company. He might be wrong,
but it appeared to him that it was a dishonest attempt to take
advantage of the wording of the agreement. That view might be
entirely erroneous therefore he only gave it as his present impression. He had seen the agreement as to the 'Sorcerer' and the
subsequent agreement in the company's own minute-book as to the
country tour. He could not give any final judgement, and before
doing that he should very likely require the gentlemen themselves to
learn what they understood by the agreement. If Mr. Gilbert was
not committing perjury in his affidavit there was the very strongest
evidence in favour of his version. He had treated the matter as an ex
parte application but if it could be shown that he had formed an
erroneous opinion of the case or evidence to that effect, he should
dissolve the injunction, which he now granted on an undertaking by
the Plaintiffs to be answerable in damages.

Later in the day the Defendants appealed from the decision of the
Master of the Rolls to the Lords Justices sitting in Lincoln's Inn.
Their Lordships held that there was a doubt as to the terms of the

contract. They could not say whether the licence was for a definite period or whether the 'run' had already come to an end. The letters produced before them, but not produced before the Court before, showed that the Defendants had given a distinct notice of their claim as far back as the 9th July. This was a case for argument and on the balance of convenience and inconvenience their Lordships thought that an injunction should not be granted. They therefore dissolved the injunction, with costs of the appeal.

The 'Scene' at the Opera Comique   *August 10th, 1879*
At Bow Street Police Court on Friday Mr. Alfred Beyfus applied to Mr. Flowers, on behalf of Mr. Barker of the Opera Comique, Strand, for assault summonses against Mr. Drake and Mr. Bayley, Directors of the Opera Comedy Company [sic] and late occupants of the Theatre. He requested that the summonses should be served immediately on the gentlemen named, who, he said, accompanied by a gang of roughs, forced their way through the stage door of the Theatre, shortly after ten o'clock on Thurday night, during the performance of the comic opera H.M.S. Pinafore, and endeavoured to take forceable possession of some of the 'properties' etc., including the big guns used in the representation, and thereby causing a panic in the house. It was obvious that, apart from the question of ownership, no-one could legally enforce a claim, real or imaginary, in a way likely to endanger the peace and safety of the public, and there was no telling what might have been the consequences of the panic excited in the crowded Theatre on Thursday evening if it had not been for the presence of mind and promptitude of the leading artists of the establishment, who addressed the audience to assure them that no 'fire' had broken out and induced them to return to their seats. Mr. Beyfus described the nature of the assaults on Mr. Barker who was thrown downstairs and seriously injured, and asked that the summonses might be returnable immediately, to prevent the recurrence of a scene alike dangerous and discreditable, and which would have culminated in a riot but for the interference of the police. The summonses were granted.

Disgraceful Scene at the Opera Comique   *10th August 1879*
On Thursday evening the 374th representation of H.M.S. Pinafore was marked by a disgraceful incident. The Theatre had been conducted by the Comedy Opera Company (Limited); Mr. D'Oyly

Carte acted as manager on their behalf. Their tenure of the Theatre expired on Thursday evening, and, as had been announced in the daily papers, Mr. D'Oyly Carte proposed to continue the representations on his own responsibility, retaining the present company so that the performances might proceed without any break. As the performance of H.M.S. Pinafore was drawing to a close on Thursday evening a loud cry of 'Fire' was heard raised by someone in the flies, followed by a scuffling and a tumult. Several of the performers were evidently alarmed, and a feeling of insecurity rapidly ran through the audience, who began hurriedly to leave in large numbers. At this juncture Mr. George Grossmith jun., with commendable presence of mind assured the auditory that it was only a case of the disputed possession of scenic effects, and the performance proceeded, after a fashion, to its close. Mr. Barrington then came before the curtain and announced that a determined effort had been made by a large gang of roughs, acting under inspiration, to stop the performance and seize the scenery. Fortunately, however, the resistance had been sufficiently energetic to effect the expulsion of the storming party, and the curtain would rise for 'After All' as usual. From the time of Mr. Grossmith's remarks to those of Mr. Barrington the disorder increased to such a pitch that it was evident a serious riot was in progress. Several of the Ladies of the company were fainting. Mr. Barker was thrown violently down a steep flight of stone steps, and the foreman fireman was hustled and trodden underfoot. Eventually all the doors to the Theatre were closed and a strong force of police were summoned behind the scenes, when order was once more restored. After a considerable interval the curtain rose, and the remaining item on the programme was proceeded with.

The Fracas at the Opera Comique   *August 10th, 1879*
Mr. Beyfus, Solicitor, of Lincoln's Inn Fields, applied to Mr. Flowers at Bow Street Police Court on Monday for a postponement of the summonses taken out on the lst inst. against Mr. Drake and Mr. Bayley, Directors of the Comedy Opera Company, the hearing for which had been appointed for two o'clock. Mr. Beyfus read a medical certificate which had been forwarded to him, to the effect that the injuries sustained by Mr. Barker, the agent representing the Proprietors of the Theatre, would make it quite impossible for him to attend personally to support the charges of assault. Indeed they

were of so serious a nature that it was not improbabale that the case would eventually assume a far graver character, and that at least two other of the Directors would have to be included in what there is every reason to fear would become a criminal prosecution. The medical certificate was shown to the magistrate, and the summonses were allowed to stand over for a week.

Later in the day Mr. Poland, addressing the Court, stated that he attended on behalf of Mr. Drake, one of the gentlemen who had been summonsed, and his friend Mr. Besley was also in attendance, as the representative of the other defendant. They had come with all their witnesses to meet the charges made against them, which they were very anxious to do, and it was a great disappointment for them to learn now, for the first time, that the inquiry had been postponed until next week. Only one side of the case had been placed before the Court, but they were anxious that his Worship should hear the other side with as little delay as possible.

Mr. Flowers said the adjournment had been allowed on the production of a medical certificate showing the inability of Mr. Barker, the complainant, to attend owing to the injuries he had sustained. Of course the case must have been put off under the circumstances, and a promise was given that notice should be given to the other side if possible. It was rather difficult to get to people, he knew, on Bank Holiday, but if no reasonable attempt had been made to comply with the condition the fact would be considered when the hearing took place.

Mr. Besley said he should like to have seen the medical certificate and to have learnt the precise nature of Mr. Barker's complaint. As H.M.S. Pinafore was just now sailing in troubled waters, it might merely have been an attack of 'sea-sickness.' At any rate he could only say that his client took part in no assault, nor was he present when any assault was committed on the complainant, as he should abundantly prove by witnesses when the case came on, if it ever did come on, for hearing. He begged also to add that no intimation had been given him of the intended application to postpone the case.

At Bow Street on Wednesday Mr. Beyfus applied for assault summonses against Mr. Cecil Chappell, Solicitor, and Mr. Frank Chappell, Musicseller, Director of the Comedy Opera Company, and also for summonses against Messrs. Chappell and Mr. Drake and Mr. Bayley, and two other Directors for creating a riot in the Theatre on the night of the 31st July, during the performance of H.M.S. Pinafore.

Mr. Beyfus stated that these additional summonses had been taken out less on account of his client Mr. Barker (the agent of the Proprietor) than in the interest of the public, whom it was his duty to protect from a recurrence of an outrage which had seriously endangered their safety. He felt bound to state this owing to a statement which he had read in the papers that Mr. Barker, notwithstanding the injury he had suffered in the affray, did not intend to continue the proceedings any further - a statement which had no foundation whatever.

All the four summonses were granted, and made returnable for the day already appointed to investigate the case.

Disturbance on Board "H.M.S. Pinafore"   *August 17th, 1879*
On Tuesday afternoon, at Bow Street Police Court, Collard Augustus Drake, 3 Bedford Square; Edward Hodgson Bayley, 42 Newington-Causeway; Cecil Chappell, Solicitor, 26 Golden Square; and Frank Chappell (Metzler and Co.), 36 Great Marlborough Street, appeared before Mr. Flowers, to answer summonses for assaulting Mr. Richard Barker, and creating a disturbance at the Opera Comique Theatre, on the night of the 31st ult.

Mr. Montagu Williams and Mr. Selfe conducted the prosecution; Mr. Besley appeared for Bayley, Mr. Grain for Drake, Mr. Oppenheim for C. Chappell and Mr. Maddison for F. Chappell.

Mr. Williams said that the four defendants were charged, first with assault, and, secondly, with the more serious offence of rioting. The defendants Drake, Bayley, and Frank Chappell were Directors of the Opera Comedy Company. It appeared that sometime since, the Earl of Dunraven became possessed of the lease of the Opera Comique Theatre, and he sublet the Theatre to Mr. D'Oyly Carte. For the purpose of subsidising Mr. Carte with money a company was formed. There was an agreement with Mr. Carte to have the Theatre from the 1st of February to the end of July, and he was the real tenant, the company only being allowed to carry on what had really been a prosperous venture. The company were to have the profits for that time, and after then Mr. Carte was to receive them for himself for a period of seven weeks. The 31st July was the last night on which the company were to receive the takings, on the following night Mr. Carte having full possession. A usual covenant in theatrical leases prevented "properties" and scenery being removed from a Theatre without the consent of the

ground landlord and the same covenant was in this lease. The
Opera Company commenced business with a successful opera
entitled The Sorcerer by Messrs. Gilbert and Sullivan. When that
finished its run there was no attempt to claim properties. Subsequently another piece by the same authors, H.M.S. Pinafore, was
produced, and was a source of great profit to the limited company,
they receiving, he believed, £16,000. On the 31st July this term
ended, and Mr. Carte claimed to go on for seven weeks, engaging
the services of Messrs. Grossmith and others, who had earned well-
deserved celebrity in the chief characters. This being disputed, the
Master of the Rolls decided that Mr. Carte was the Lessee, and that
any business the company had must be through that gentleman.
That judgement now stood. The company then determined to start
H.M.S. Pinafore from another harbour into another sea - viz. The
Imperial Theatre. This would prevent Mr. Carte having the full
profits that would accrue if only one ship was sailing. An injunction
was on this sought by the authors, Messrs. Gilbert and Sullivan, to
prevent it being played, and this was granted by the Master of the
Rolls, whose decision was, however, reversed on the same day by
the Lords Justices. Thus, they had licence to go on with the performance; but if it could be stopped at the Opera Comique then all
those wishing to see the Pinafore would have to go to the Imperial.
On the last night the Directors had any share in the takings they
hired a band of ruffians (he would call them nothing else) and
proceeded to the stage door. It was a mercy that there was no loss of
life as they forced their way onto the stage. Mr. Barker, the locum
tenens of Mr. Carte and Lord Dunraven - who was acting for Mr.
Carte in his absence - heard a disturbance by these people endeav-
ouring to force their way to the stage. Mr. Barker was knocked
down and injured and there was a perfect riot, and panic ensued.
Mr. Grossmith addressed the audience to allay the panic, a cry of
'Fire' being raised, and many ladies were carried fainting from the
Theatre. The gas-room was taken possession of, and had the
slightest mistake been made in the turn of an elbow the consequences could not possibly be foreseen. Mr. Cecil Chappell and Mr.
Bayley met Mr. Barker, and the former asked to take some article to
show their right. Mr. Barker refused, and Mr. Chappell then said
that the riot must proceed. Subsequently the "supers" who formed
the crew of H.M.S. Pinafore cleared the Theatre. If the defendants
had any claim there was a law to vindicate their rights, but to

attempt to assert them in the manner they had done was a riot of the worst description, and he would ask the Magistrate to commit them all for trial.

Mr. Richard Barker, of 299 Strand, examined by Mr. Selfe - I am the agent for the Earl of Dunraven at the Opera Comique Theatre, and hold the Lord Chamberlain's licence. The Earl of Dunraven let the Theatre, through me, to Mr. D'Oyly Carte. In consequence of that lease Mr. Carte took possession of the Theatre and produced a new piece. That lease terminated on the 31st July. Previous to that date a piece called H.M.S. Pinafore had been produced by Mr. Carte. I knew there was a company in existence, as they had a Board Room at the Theatre. Three of the defendants - Mr. Bayley, Mr. Drake and Mr. Frank Chappell, were members of the company acting with Mr. Carte. I acted as Stage-Manager for Mr. Carte besides being Lord Dunraven's agent. I saw the three defendants frequently about the Theatre.

Did you know the position that Mr. Cecil Chappell occupied?

I have ascertained that he was the Solicitor to the company. Mr. Carte went to America and Mr. Gunn was appointed his locum tenens. He was so acting on the 31st July. On that evening I was at the prompt entrance, and received a communication that I was wanted. I went up the stairs to the stage entrance in Wych Street. While I was speaking I saw Mr. Bayley and Mr. Drake coming in through the outer stage entrance. There was a crowd of people. I should think a dozen.

What took place? - Wilkinson, the clerk to Mr. Carte, took me by the arm, and asked me if those people were to come in. I replied, "Certainly the Directors, but no-one else." I then heard a voice exclaim, "Now then, boys - now's your time!"

Did you say anything to them before that about interrupting the performance? - Yes, I said, "For God's sake don't make a disturbance during the performance." The second act was then being proceeded with. I heard no reply to me, but a rush took place, and I was thrown down inside the inner door. I got up, and in doing so turned my back to the crowd.

What took place then? - I received a violent push or blow that precipitated me very nearly to the bottom of the steps. I did not see any of the defendants near as I had my back to the people. I fell partially on my back and my left side. I have been under medical treatment since.

Did you get up? - Yes, I then went on the stage and there saw
Williams, one of the stage carpenters, whom I sent for the police.
After that I saw Mr. Frank Chappell. He was then on the right hand
side of me on the stage.

Were there any other intruders on the stage at the same time? - I
did not see any. Mr. Frank Chappell said, "I am sorry you are hurt,
Barker," and I replied, "I am afraid I am severely."

Was there at that time any disturbance going on in the Theatre? -
Yes, behind the scenes. I did not hear any speech made from the
stage. I saw Mr. Cecil Chappell and Mr. Bayley on the stage, and
went with them into my private room.

What took place? - When I got upstairs Mr. Cecil Chappell asked
me if I would deliver up the scenery and the properties. I told him,
"Certainly not," and said that I looked upon them as trespassers in the
Theatre.

The Magistrate - was that to all the Directors? - No, only the two in
my room. Mr. Chappell then asked me if I would give up a bucket
that he might take away under protest? I replied, "If you bring in a
mob of a hundred roughs and knock me to pieces I shall protect the
property of the Earl of Dunraven, my employer." Mr. Bayley then
rose and said, "It must go on."

Could you from your room hear whether there was a disturbance
below? - No. Mr. Bayley and Mr. Chappell went downstairs, and I
followed. I met the fireman (Blake) on the landing, and I said to him,
"Let us go through to the front and see if the audience are quiet." I
went through and found the performance going on. After that I went
to the stage, at the prompt entrance of which the gas supply of the
house is situated. There were eight or nine people there who had no
business, and my men were attempting to put them out. There was a
disturbance. The gasmen eventually, with the aid of the "supers"
who were acting as marines, put them out. I saw a man attempt to
strike someone with a stick while going up the stairs. The stick was
taken from him.

Cross-examined by Mr. Besley - I have been in the Theatre about
five years. My first engagement was as agent for the Earl of
Dunraven. I have fulfilled dual engagements in that period. I was
Stage-Manager to Mr. Morton and Miss Amy Sheridan. For two
years preceding November, 1876, I was away from London. I have
an old inventory that was handed to me five years ago of fixtures and
fittings. I made an inventory for myself of scenery and "properties."

Within your knowledge have not scenes been taken from the Gaiety Theatre? - We have borrowed from one another.

Would you deny that scenery, dresses and music have been brought into the Theatre and taken out again? - Yes; we store scenery under a railway arch. Mr. Hollingshead would frequently lend us a scene if we wanted one. The board-room is up some steps from the stage entrance, above the level of the street. I was aware of Mr. Carte leaving England. It was about eight weeks ago. I was acquainted with the agreement of the 27th November, 1878. That was an underlet by Lord Dunraven to Mr. D'Oyly Carte.

Were you not aware of Mr. D'Oyly Carte being a servant of the Comedy Opera Company? - I know nothing of his arrangements. I may have heard from him that he received a salary from them. I assume there was an agreement with Mr. Carte, as I do not think he would do his work for nothing. I think the board-room was opened at the Theatre in February last. I have occasionally seen Mr. Bayley going upstairs. The company had possession of the board-room. I knew nothing of the payment of the outgoings, as that had nothing to do with me. I drew a salary of £10 per week from Mr. Jarvis the treasurer, since the 1st of February last.

Was that paid you on the Saturday previous to the disturbance? - Yes, I have always had my salary. I have been paid since by Mr. Jarvis up to last Saturday. I do not know who put the properties in. After the disturbance (on August lst) I returned some dresses to the Comedy Opera Company. Those were the whole of the dresses used by the actors in the Pinafore.

Was it within your knowledge that Mr. Jarvis was appointed treasurer of the Comedy Opera Company? - I knew he was appointed by the Master of the Rolls receiver in the cause "Comedy Opera Company v Gunn." That was some weeks before the end of July. I knew there was some question about the right of performing the Pinafore going on, but there was no negotiation for Messrs. Gilbert and Sullivan to take the Theatre from Lord Dunraven. I heard that the Comedy Opera Company had been to the ground landlord about taking the Theatre. On the afternoon of July 31st Mr. Gunn read a letter to me.

[Letter read from Mr. Drake to Mr. Gunn asking for the return of all properties, scenery, band parts etc. after that evening's performance.]

Cross-examination continued: There were very few properties in the opera. The performance of Pinafore closed at twenty-five minutes past ten o'clock. It was a few minutes after ten when the men came. I can assert most positively there were more than twelve men intruded. I did not hear Mr. Bayley say that the men would come in and wait. At the time the entry was effected there were five of my men on the stage, in addition to the actors. The remainder of the carpenters would come in time to strike the Pinafore scene.

When you fell was it not caused by some of your men coming into the Theatre? - No, they were not in. At the door the steps are only about two feet wide, and I was thrown from the top to about the fourth or fifth step from the bottom. I was injured. I did not "skip" up to my room afterwards but moved with great difficulty. I was not assisted to my room. In reply to Mr. Frank Chappell, I said I was afraid I was seriously hurt. In my room I shut the door, and it was perfectly quiet. Mr. Bayley and Mr. Chappell were never, so far as I know, within sight of the audience. When they came into my room Mr. Chappell asked for the properties. Nothing was said to me about putting a finger on them for the purpose of ejection and they would go. They did not say that the mountings had been paid for with their money.

May I take it you were aware of the dispute as to the agreement between Messrs. Gilbert and Sullivan and the Comedy Opera Company? - I knew there was a dispute as I read about it in the newspapers.

By Mr. Grain - I saw Mr. Drake on the stage. He looked very much alarmed at the close of the affair. I did not give the defendants the dresses that belonged to them that night. I gave directions to have them put together, but Mr. Gunn, in consequence of the mob outside, refused to let them go, and said they should be sent in the morning. After the disturbance was over inside the Theatre someone came back for the dresses. I never refused to allow a Director to pass to the Board-Room. I put my hands up involuntarily when I asked them not to make a disturbance. It was no good my trying to stop such a crowd. A suggestion was thrown out that I was a servant of the Opera Comedy Company. I was engaged by Mr. Carte and not by the Directors. The mob intruded into a place where the public have no business.

By Mr. Oppenheim - I am still agent for Lord Dunraven. My duties include letting the Theatre, the collecting of rents, and generally looking after the property. I received the rent both from Mr. Carte and from Mr. Gunn (in his absence). It was always paid by cheque. At the time the first lease was granted by Lord Dunraven to Mr. D'Oyly Carte none of the scenery or properties of the Pinafore were in existence. I do not know of my own knowledge that the whole of the scenery and properties were paid for by the Comedy Opera Company. When the letter was read to me about the scenery and properties on July 31st I said that as agent for Lord Dunraven I should not let them go. As agent I subsequently refused. I know nothing about the band music. That comes under the orders of the orchestral conductor. I do not know whether the same music is used now. The scenery used is the same. All the dresses used in the piece were sent back the next day. The interview in my room lasted about four minutes. I did not say anything about the dresses, but I said they were all trespassers. The mob came to the Theatre shortly after ten, and left it five or six minutes after the curtain fell.

Did you direct the "supers" who were acting as marines to turn them out? - I did not, I saw them doing so and I said, "Out with them, my boys." I did not see the "marines" use their muskets or bayonets. I was looking at them for about three minutes.

Do you mean to say you did not see the bayonets, or they did not have them? - I did not see the bayonets. The marines left the stage before the curtain fell, which was contrary to the usual rule, but it was not me that called them. I know nothing about them coming through a fanlight.

At this point the case was adjourned until Friday, Mr. Williams, on the part of the prosecutors, deprecating any wish to make it a "weekly advertisement."

A gentleman, who handed his card to the Magistrate, applied to Mr. Flowers on Wednesday for a summons against the Comedy Opera Company to compel them to show cause why they had refused to permit an examination of their account books by the shareholders of the Company. He stated that he was himself a shareholder, and he believed that the present action of the Company was illegal, besides necessitating an expenditure of money which he regarded as wholly reckless and unjustifiable. Mr. Flowers said the parties would be at court on Friday, and the gentleman might like to take the opportunity of seeing them on the subject.

On Friday the defendants again appeared,

Mr. Collette, Solicitor, said that a gentleman complained a day or two ago in court that he had made an application to see the books of the Comedy Opera Company, and had been refused. This gentleman was Mr. Allen, and he [Mr. Collette] wished to state that he held in his hand a reply to Mr. Allen's application, written by

Mr. Drake, and posted on the 26th ult. informing Mr. Allen that the offices of the company were in the course of removal.

Mr. Allen, upon this, got into the witness box and declared that he had never received such a letter or he would not have made the statement he did.

Mr. Montagu Williams then addressed the Magistrate, and said that, with permission, he would withdraw the summons. He was very glad to say that since the last hearing the parties had met, and had agreed to compensate Mr. Barker for the injuries he had received, and he believed that by putting their heads together in a friendly spirit there would be an end to all litigation as to H.M.S. Pinafore. The defendants while expressing regret to Mr. Barker that any riot or fracas took place, assured him that there was no intention on their part, when they went to the Theatre, to commit a breach of the peace. Mr. Cecil Chappell had taken the opinion of eminent counsel as to their rights, and undoubtedly did not intend any disturbance; but the hot blood of some of those accompanying appeared to have grown hotter, and hence the noise that ensued. Under all the circumstances he would now ask leave to withdraw the summons.

Mr. Oppenheim, on behalf of Mr. Cecil Chappell, disclaimed the slightest intention on the part of that gentleman to make any disturbance, which was proved by his asking to be allowed to take away some small article under protest.

The learned Magistrate, in allowing the withdrawal of the summonses, said he thought perhaps the less said the better. The rights of people could always be enforced in a court of law, and in this particular case even the Court of Chancery could not be blamed for delay, as though an injunction had been granted in the morning, it had been set aside the same afternoon. He would accept that the defendants were sorry for what they did, and allow the plaintiff to pursue the course suggested, and withdraw the summons.

Mr. Editor   *August 17th, 1879*

Sir - Will you allow me to state that I am not (nor in any way connected with) the Mr. Drake summoned at the Bow Street Police Court in the Opera Comique case? There appears to be an erroneous impression amongst the Profession, greatly to my detriment.

Yours obediently -   Horatio Horace Henry Drake
                                                                    (Bill Inspector)
Opera Comique, Strand, London WC.   August 13th 1879

One director, Collard, continued to personally threaten Carte and his performers with litigation involving vast sums in damages, but the intimidation had no effect and anyway the Company was forced to settle out of court a sum in compensation for Barker's injuries, and to publicly apologise at Bow Street for the disturbance they had caused at the theatre. Despite the huge and free publicity both productions were getting due to the court cases, the Comedy Opera Company was by now in financial difficulties - they progressively moved to smaller and hence cheaper theatres; first to the Olympic in Wych Street - the same street as the Opera Comique - in a bid to gain an amount of business by the publicity given merely to such a location; and finally to the suburban Standard theatre at Shoreditch, where both production and Company were to disappear. Consequently the money in the possession of Jarvis, the receiver from July 15th to 31st, about £1,100, would prove useful in the extreme and on 9th October they entered a motion in the High Court, and subsequently Gilbert a cross-motion, that each side respectively should be paid the money. The judge threw out both motions on the ground that the main issue, that of the rights in *Pinafore*, had to be disposed of first.

Another problem which the Comedy Opera Company production faced was the lack of an original score of the music which Sullivan would not give up; nor could he be made to. On 6th August, Gilbert had written to him in the South of France concerning the events of the week before, and some little time later Sullivan wrote to John Hollingshead:

You once settled a precedent for me which may just at present be of great importance to me. I asked you for the band parts of the Merry Wives of Windsor, for performance at the Crystal Palace, and you sent them to me and said, 'They are yours, as our run is over, only you will let me have them whenever we want them won't you?'

I kept them and some time afterwards you sent to borrow them for a performance in Manchester. I sent them to you at once, and I think you have them still. Now will you please let me have them, and the parts of Thespis, at once. I am detaining the parts of the Pinafore, so that the directors shall not take them away from the Comique tomorrow, and I base my claim on the precedent you set.

They will probably fly at me in a court of law and I want to be able to say, 'Mr. Hollingshead paid for the copying of the pieces I did for him, but returned the parts to me when the run was over'. So if you will give them to Michael Gunn any time tomorrow before the evening, he will hold them for me.

I shall be much obliged if you will do this, My Dear John, as your name is weighty in a court of law[3].

In an act almost of sheer spite the directors discovered a sum of £150 owing to them from Carte and as he was about to board a liner in Liverpool docks at the start of an American tour they had him arrested by Sheriff's officers under the 1869 Debtors Act, and held for four hours until friends could forward on to him the sum. The Comedy Opera Company also sent a report of this to the American press to precede his arrival, in an attempt to discredit his reputation there.

The final stages of the legal battle, entitled Gilbert v. Comedy Opera Company (1879 G.220), eventually came about in March 1881, when virtually the whole theatrical world gathered to see who would literally win the famous ship. The 'stars' of the legal world were present, as well as those of the theatre. Gilbert had retained Stiff Everitt but now brought in to lead him Charles Russell, Q.C., and Fred North, Q.C. The directors had briefed Montague Cookson, Q.C., Horace Davey, Q.C., and Brunning Maddison. The main issue had been whittled down to a single proposition of fact: whether the Company's contract with Gilbert and Sullivan gave the directors external rights to produce *Pinafore*, or merely for the original run of the piece. Consequently the point turned on the definition of the term '*run of the piece*'. The evidence was mainly by affidavit, supported orally by whatever witnesses it was felt neessary to call: and a preliminary issue had to be settled when the Company, who had filed twenty affidavits in their favour, brought in yet another silk, Sir Henry Jackson, Q.C., to argue that the fifty-one affidavits filed in reply by Gilbert were not strictly confined to matters in reply and were merely intended to support the original case. This interlocutory motion was brought under the 1875 Rules of Court, Order XXXVIII r.3 (Consolidated Order XXXIII r.7) in an attempt by the directors to have Gilbert's supporting evidence thrown out. However, Vice-Chancellor Bacon would not have it because he said that until the hearing he could not tell whether the affidavits objected to were strictly in reply or not; he refused the application with costs. This early but minor victory for Gilbert was reported, much to his satisfaction, in the *Law Reports* at (1881)ChD 594, and the *Law Times*, XLIII,NS 665.

Mr Justice Fry heard the main action on 1st and 2nd March, before a gallery packed with socialites and theatrical personages; oral evidence was heard from the then household names of Dion Boucicalt, Charles Reade, H. J. Byron, E. A. Sothern, Samuel French, Howard Paul and Charles Wyndham amongst others. Faced with such an array of theatrical giants giving evidence for Gilbert, the Comedy Opera Company case all but collapsed, and the learned judge held that the rights of the Comedy Opera Company had ceased not from 31st July 1879, but actually from 24th December 1878, and that anything after that date was only on the suffrance of D'Oyly Carte, the various allegations of conspiring against whom he specifically condemned. Thus Gilbert, Sullivan and Carte won on all points and very generously agreed to forgo the considerable damages they were entitled to, which included the receipts of the ninety-one pirate performances of the Comedy Opera Company's *Pinafore*. On 5th March, the *Illustrated Sporting and Dramatic News* published a fuller report, by which time the Comedy Opera Company had passed into history:

"H.M.S. Pinafore" in Court

The trial as to the right of performing the 'Pinafore' between Messrs. Gilbert and Sullivan on the one hand, and the Directors of the Comedy Opera Company on the other, was worthy of much more extended notice than has been given to it, especially as much of the proceedings were extremely amusing. We therefore supply deficiencies, in more or less dramatic form.

After the opening statement by counsel, Mr. D'Oyly Carte's affidavit was read, and he was cross-examined by Mr. Montagu Cookson.

Mr. Cookson:	It is usual, I believe, to advertise the last nights of a successful piece before withdrawing it from the public?
Mr. Carte:	It is usually, but not invariably, done.
Mr. Cookson:	(producing a file of the Daily Telegraph): Turn to the advertisement of the Opera Comique in the Telegraph for 22nd December, 1878. (This was an advertisement to the effect that the theatre would close for repairs on the 24th December, and would re-open on 1st February, 1879).

Mr. Carte:	I here advertise the last two nights.
Mr. Cookson:	Do you consider that a run is terminated by the withdrawal of the piece for a single night?
Mr. Carte:	I do.

Mr. Bancroft's affidavit was then read, and he was cross-examined as to the professional meaning of the word 'run'.

Mr. Bancroft:	I consider that the 'run' of a piece is its uninterrupted performance at the theatre at which it is produced on days not prohibited by the Lord Chamberlain's licence, and by the same, or substantially the same company.
Mr. Cookson:	Would the closing of a theatre by an unforeseen accident, such as the illness of an important actress, break the run?
Mr. Bancroft:	Certainly not; in all properly-conducted theatres all parts are understudied.
Mr. Cookson:	But suppose the principal and the understudy were both taken ill?
Mr. Bancroft:	An actor would read the part from the manuscript.
Mr. Cookson:	Suppose the whole company were incapacitated?
Mr. Bancroft:	The prompter would go on and read the piece. (Roars of laughter). A manager who takes a piece for a run takes it at his own peril. If he cannot fulfil the conditions of his undertaking, so much the worse for him.
Mr. Cookson:	Can you imagine no circumstance which might justify him in closing his theatre without breaking the run?
Mr. Bancroft:	An earthquake might do it.
The Judge (Mr. Justice Fry)	An earthquake would certainly break the run. We are going beyond all probabilities.
Mr. Cookson:	But suppose that through absolutely unavoidable circumstances, such as a fire in the theatre, the theatre had to be closed; would that determine the run?

Mr. Bancroft:	I think we should have to come to you to ascertain that point. (Laughter).
Mr. Cookson:	You are too clever for me, Mr. Bancroft. I shall ask you nothing further.

Mr. Grossmith's affidavit was then read. It was to the effect that he was engaged for the "run" of the piece - that before the theatre closed in December, 1878, he was informed by three of the Directors, Messrs. Metzler, Bayley, and Drake, that the run and consequently the engagement, would end on 24th December - that the closure was solely owing to the fact that business at the Opera Comique always fell off after Christmas, owing to the counter-attraction of the pantomimes - that the drains were occasionally troublesome, but were always relieved by "flushing", and that he was re-engaged at an increased salary for six months from 1st February, 1879. He also defined a "run" in the terms used by Mr. Bancroft.

Cross-examined:

Mr. Cookson:	Were not the drains extremely troublesome in December 1878?
Mr. Grossmith:	Not at all. They were only troublesome in the warm weather, and they were then relieved by "flushing".
Mr. Cookson:	Was nothing said to you about the drains in December?
Mr. Grossmith:	Nothing at all. The question only arose during the hot weather when the receipts fell, and it was proposed to close the house for a term.
The Judge:	Do you connect the condition of the drains with the state of the receipts? (Laughter).
Mr. Grossmith:	I do. Whenever the receipts fell off the drains were complained of. We never heard any complaint of the drains when the house was full of money. (Laughter).
Mr. Gilbert:	Pecunia non olet. (Laughter).
Mr. Cookson:	Do you consider that the "run" ended at Christmas 1878?

Mr. Grossmith: I am quite sure that it did. The directors told me
                   that my engagement made for the "run" had
                   come to an end.

Mr. Cookson: But you went on, when the theatre re-opened,
                   with the same agreement?

Mr. Grossmith: On the contrary, I had a fresh agreement.

Mr. Cookson: Well, but it was on precisely the same terms.

Mr. Grossmith: Not at all, I demanded and received an increase
                   of two guineas per week. (Laughter).

Mr. Cookson: But you had made a great success, and had so
                   identified yourself with the piece, that the
                   directors would willingly have given you any
                   terms you liked to ask rather than annoy you
                   by a refusal?

Mr. Grossmith: On the contrary, I had the greatest difficulty in
                   inducing them to consent to this small
                   increase. (Loud laughter). I had to decline to
                   be re-engaged before they would do so. Their
                   policy was all along in favour of a
                   retrenchment.

Mr. W. S. Gilbert's affidavit was then read and he was cross-examined
on it.

Mr. Cookson: I see that you claim the right to sanction all
                   engagements and superintend all rehearsals.

Mr. Gilbert: That right is claimed by Mr. Sullivan and
                   myself. I invariably stage-manage my plays,
                   and I consider that by doing so I contribute to
                   their success.

Mr. Cookson: The Pinafore has, I believe, been played with
                   great success all over England and the United
                   States.

Mr. Gilbert: It has been played for nearly three years in the
                   English provinces with unvarying success. I
                   know nothing of its career in America except
                   by hearsay.

Mr. Cookson: At all events it has been successfully played
                   all over England - which suggests that
                   your superintendence was not essential to
                   success.

Mr. Gilbert:	I beg your pardon. Mr. Sullivan and I have carefully selected the members of all the companies that have played in England, and also superintended the rehearsals. It is principally to that fact that we attribute its extraordinary success in the provinces. We shall never allow it to be played without our superintendence.
Mr. Cookson:	What is your definition of a "run"?
Mr. Gilbert:	The consecutive performance of a play at the theatre at which it was originally produced, and by the company that originally played it.
Mr. Cookson:	Would a break of three or four nights break the run.
Mr. Gilbert:	In my opinion it would.
Mr. Cookson:	But you swear in your affidavit that you consider that a break of one or two nights would not destroy the run. Do you distinguish between "one or two" nights and "three or four"?
Mr. Gilbert:	I do. An accident might happen to the stage, immediately before the curtain rose, thus rendering it physically impossible to play the piece that night - or a whole company might be detained by the non-arrival of a train. But such disasters would certainly be remedied by the second or third night. Strictly, I think an author would be within his rights in holding that the "run" had ceased. A piece cannot "run" and stand still at the same time.
Mr. Cookson:	I observe that you do not speak positively on this point.
Mr. Gilbert:	It is rather a question for lawyers to decide.
Mr. Cookson:	But you are a lawyer?
Mr. Gilbert	No - only a barrister.

Mr. Sullivan was then shortly cross-examined as to certain parts which he had detained, and for which detention the defendants claimed damages. It was elicited that these parts were to become the property of Messrs. Gilbert and Sullivan on payment by them to Mr. Carte of half the cost of copying them, that is to say, about £10. This sum had not been paid, because it had never been demanded.

SECOND DAY

Mr. Palgrave Simpson was examined as to the definition of the word 'run'.

Mr. Simpson:	I consider that an interruption of a single day would justify an author in holding that the 'run' had ended.
Mr. Cookson:	You make no exceptions?
Mr. Simpson:	None whatever. A manager enters into a contract for a 'run' at his own risk.

Mr. Hollingshead, cross-examined as to the meaning of 'run'.

Mr. Cookson:	I observe that you say that the run must be continuous unless interrupted by "the act of God". What do you mean by this expression?
Mr. Hollingshead:	Ash Wednesday.
Mr. Cookson:	Would the break of one day interrupt the run?
Mr. Hollingshead:	I believe it would. No author, however, would be likely to hold that it did.

Mr. Irving, cross-examined as to the meaning of "run":

Mr. Irving:	I consider that a run must be continuous. A break of a single day would, strictly speaking, destroy it.
Mr. Cookson:	Take the case of the sudden illness of a principal actor.
Mr. Irving:	The understudy would play his part as a matter of course.
Mr. Cookson:	Do you consider that a piece may be said to "run" so long as there is any anxiety on the part of the public to see it?
The Learned Judge:	In that case, Mr. Cookson, Hamlet would have run from the days of Queen Elizabeth, and would be running still. (Laughter).
Mr. Cookson:	If Mr. Irving had lived in the reign of Queen Elizabeth, and had continued to live until today, I have no doubt it would. (Laughter).

Affidavits from fifty-one London and country managers to the
effect that the "run" must be continuous were then read: Affidavits
from Mr. Chatterton, Mr. Augustus Harris, Mr. Ryder, Mr. E. L.
Blanchard, and several minor actors to the effect that a manager
who had a piece for a "run" may withdraw it when he pleases
without prejudice to his right to reproduce it, having been
previously put in by the defendants. Mr. Barker, Lord Dunraven's
agent, and the stage-manager of the Opera Comique stated, in
cross-examination, that there was no necessity to close the theatre in
December, 1878, on account of the drains, but that the directors
agreed to do so as Christmas was usually a bad season for the Opera
Comique. The theatre was closed for six weeks. The drains were
repaired in less than three weeks. The remainder of the time was
occupied by re-decoration.

The affidavit of Mr. Fry, the surveyor of the Strand Board of
Works, was then read, and he was cross-examined on it by Mr.
Charles Russell, Q.C.

Then followed speeches for the defence from Mr. Cookson,
Q.C., Mr. Davy, Q.C., and Mr. Madison.

The Judge did not call on Mr. North to reply, but proceeded to
deliver judgement on all points for the plaintiffs.

Mr. North, Q.C., asked for nominal damages.

Damages to the value of one shilling were awarded.

In the 12th March issue of *Punch*, Gilbert's old rival, Frank Burnand,
brilliantly satirised the court proceedings, and naturally added a
pointed comment of his own in doing so:

A TRIAL BY JURY
(By our own Illegal Reporter)
Author and Composer of H.M.S. Pinafore v.
Opera Company Limited

This was a peculiar case. The Plaintiffs having made joint
arrangements for a pleasant "run" together, were suddenly tripped
up by the Defendants. They had not liked it and so brought the
present action. On the case being called, Mr. Justice FRY, who
took his seat on the Bench amidst several rounds of applause, which
he acknowledged with repeated bows, notified his intention of
taking the evidence on either side with proper musical
accompaniment.

Mr. C. RUSSELL, Q.C., on behalf of the Bar, thanked his Lordship in a few feeling and well-chosen words for the suggestion, which, he said, he thought would materially assist the progress of the case.

A grand piano was then brought from the Exchequer Division and, after a little good-humoured badinage in the well of the Court was finally placed on the bench by the side of the Judge.

Mr. Justice FRY:	I think if Mr. Sullivan will step up here he can give me some substantial assistance; for while I weigh out justice, he can provide me with the scales. (Laughter).
Mr. W. S. GILBERT:	You want him, My Lud, I suppose, to teach you your own Notes. (Roars of laughter).

A Juryman here rose and said that if the Plaintiff would not only mind his own business but undertake also to teach them theirs, they would be happy to sing an opening chorus.

Mr. Justice FRY:	(addressing the Foreman) - Then you propose to supply us with a musical box? Well, Gentlemen, I am quite agreeable; but I think, if you'll permit me, I may as well first tell you "How I came to be a Judge."

Mr. NORTH, Q.C., on behalf of his clients, objected. They came there prepared to tell the Bench how they came to be producers of Comic Opera.

Mr. Justice FRY:	Very well, brother North (laughter). I am not in very good voice, so am quite agreeable. By all means let Mr. Sullivan take his place at the piano and Mr. Gilbert stand on the Clerk's table and give us a verse or two.

(Prolonged applause during which Mr. Sullivan was assisted over Counsels' heads, on to the Bench, while Mr. Gilbert mounted the table amidst some vociferous banter from friends at the back of the Court.)

Mr. Gilbert then said -
    When we, good friends, discovered that "Fame"
        Spelt "impecunious party",
    We winked at each other, and said, "This game
        is a vast deal to High-Arty."
    So we turned in our minds to Ages Ago
        And to Serjeant Bouncer's fury,
    Cut Handel and Shakespeare, and stormed Soho
        With a new sort of Trial by Jury.

The Plaintiffs were about to proceed with a second verse when Mr. Russell interposed. He said he did not see the good of continuing this. They were met there this morning for the sole purpose of having a good stare at a whole host of theatrical celebrities, and for his part was most anxious to produce this thirty odd likenesses at once.

Mr. Justice FRY:	Certainly, Mr. Russell; let them all stand in a view on the Bench. I should like to have a look at them myself. Which is Mr. Bancroft?
Mr. Russell:	You shall see him, My Lud. (To the Usher). Show Mr. Bancroft to a public box. (Loud laughter).

Mr. Bancroft then entered the witness box. He said a company of walking Gentlemen could manage a run between them. He had seen it done. One of the best runs he ever had was with a Hare at the Prince of Wales's.

Cross-examined: Yes, he had known a run cut short from simply doing his duty. He did not mean absolutely his own duty - but somebody else's. A volcano in the pit of the theatre need not stop a run. All the manager would have to do would be freely to admit paper into the crater after seven, and send down the prompter with a book in a fire-escape.

Mr. Justice FRY: Excellent. Now let's look at somebody else.

Mr. John Hollingshead was then examined. He had never stopped the run of a piece in his life. On the contrary he had acted on the principle that a piece that couldn't run, and wouldn't run, ought to be made to run. He managed that very simply. He never, if he could help it, allowed a piece to try and run without legs. (Laughter).

Mr. Justice FRY: I suppose, Mr. Hollingshead, you see no
                          'arm in that? (Roars of laughter).

Mr. Arthur Sullivan was the next witness. He said he was first
led away from the paths of virtuous High-Art oratorio-writing by a
gentleman who did the libretto of Cox and Box. He would prefer
not to mention names. Regretted it exceedingly. Yes, he had not
stopped there. Meeting with his brother Plaintiff in the present
proceedings, they had gone step by step further away from the
Albert Hall. (Here the Witness was visibly agitated). He had, he
admitted, found this 'descersus Averni' remunerative. Oratorios, as
a rule, did not run for anything like five hundred nights, and so
were never very satisfactory to the composer. He should say that
the market-price of a first-class oratorio, fully scored, with the band
parts copied out would be about £4.10s. (Sensation).

Cross-examined: It was easy to stop the run of an oratorio. If you
didn't pay the band, and the chorus, and the organist, and the
principal singers, and the conductor, an oratorio would not run
long. Being asked whether, notwithstanding this, he was sorry to
have met with Mr. W. S. Gilbert, the Witness burst into tears, and
amid a scene of indescribable confusion, was carried out of Court.

After a few minutes consideration the jury returned a verdict for
the Plaintiffs.

Mr. Justice FRY: Well, Gentlemen, that will be sixpence to
                          each of you!

Upon the verdict being known, all concerned in the proceedings
joined in a break-down dance and patter-chorus, the Plaintiffs
handsomely announcing their intention of giving the Jury a cold
luncheon on the damages.

By the time the court actions finished the Comedy Opera Company
had gone into liquidation; Gilbert and Sullivan were household names,
having the successes of *Pinafore*, *Pirates* and *Patience* under their belts,
and Carte had built his own theatre with his share of the receipts; the
Savoy legend was born.

Chapter 8

'Perceptively intense and consummately utter': the Savoy contracts

Whilst the first contract between the new triumvirate was merely an expedient, owing to the dramatic collapse of the Comedy Opera Company, Carte was to discover very quickly that Gilbert and Sullivan were no mean bargainers, Sullivan surprisingly so. At this stage, probably throughout, the composer was only writing in this sphere for the money, his known aspirations being elsewhere. However, as much as his more serious works won critical acclaim, the financial rewards from his oratorios, songs and orchestral music were hardly enough to keep him moving in the social circle and at the gaming tables he frequented. The partners' respective positions were later to become reversed, but in the early days it was Carte, of course, that had to do all the cajoling.

D'Oyly Carte very nearly lost his chance: after *Trial by Jury* he had been the first to approach Gilbert and Sullivan with a proposition, before the Comedy Opera Company was ever conceived. That proposition was for a revival of *Thespis* at the Criterion Theatre for Christmas, 1875. An agreement had been reached in October that the two authors should receive two guineas per performance, with a guaranteed run of 100 performances. Sullivan stipulated, however, that the fees for fifty nights - 200 guineas - should be paid in advance. Carte was unable to raise the money and the project was shelved. To add to his problems Carte discovered that Charles Maddison Morton, who wrote the original farce *Box and Cox* (and had it set to music by Sullivan as *Cox and Box* in 1867), and who then managed the Opera Comique, approached Gilbert and Sullivan regarding the commissioning of a new work for this theatre, early in 1876. Gilbert dispatched a joint reply:

We have considered your proposal, and we are prepared to write an opera for your theatre on the following terms:

£4.4s. each per night, guaranteeing a minimum of 120 performances in town and country, within eight months of first production.

Of this, £105 to be paid to each of us in advance.

We are to select our own company.

The piece is to be set in two or three acts, as we may deem to be most suitable.

The entire control of rehearsals to be in our hands.

The selection of the subject to rest with us[1].

Carte complained bitterly to Gilbert as soon as he heard, and to his relief and good fortune Gilbert consented to put off Morton and revive or try to work out a new arrangement with Carte. However the latter was still not in sufficient funds, and Gilbert wrote to him on March 11th:

I certainly considered myself under an agreement to write a libretto for you on certain conditions. But those conditions have not been fulfilled.

Imprimis, both Sullivan and myself were to receive a sum down, before putting pen to paper. Then we were to begin on the 1st March. I wrote to you on that day to say I was ready to begin. But you left my note unanswered for a week, and then wrote to say that there was a hitch somewhere. And then it turned out that you were going to close the theatre for a few weeks and reopen perhaps with a revival comedy, perhaps with a revived opera; but in any case our little one-act 'Bouffe' was to constitute the whole substantial attraction.

Now this won't do for either Sullivan or myself. If we're to be businesslike, you must be businesslike too. Give us a fair chance, at a good theatre, and comply with our conditions precedent, and we'll work like Trojans. But we can't hold ourselves at your disposal whenever you want us.

Gilbert was discovering why some people called this young impresario Oily Carte, having been smooth-talked into a contract with no money down. The direct consequence of this, though, was the issuing of a prospectus offering investment opportunities in the new Comedy Opera Company, and the events which followed. On 4th July, the contract dated 5th June between the Comedy Opera Company Ltd, and Gilbert and Sullivan, as set out, was ratified.

That same contract obviously came to an end in a more abrupt fashion than any of the parties could have foreseen. However Carte, Sullivan and Gilbert had sufficient interests in common to form a firm basis for negotiating the contract which would administer the distribution of wealth in the gold mine they were creating: they all wanted money; and they all wanted absolute control over their respective areas of creativity - including Carte's management facility. Consequently the new partnership was based on a memorandum signed by all three towards the end of the 'original' (that is after the split productions occurred), run of *Pinafore*;

Mem: It is proposed that Sullivan and Gilbert shall enter into partnership with Carte, in the Opera Comique, from the date of the withdrawal of 'H.M.S. Pinafore'. Each partner shall contribute £1000 as trading capital. The profits of the speculation to be equally divided after all expenses have been paid. Carte's salary to be £15 per week - Sullivan's and Gilbert's fees to be four guineas per representation, each. These salaries and pay to be included in weekly expenses. The partnership to exist for the term for which Carte holds the theatre.

W.S.G.
R. D'O.C.
Arthur Sullivan

This memorandum was undated, and it may be that negotiations were conducted in or nearer the August of the break up of the Comedy Opera Company. However, Carte was still in America for the most of August and returned more concerned with the terms he had been able to get for an American tour of *H.M.S. Pinafore* by a British cast together with Gilbert and Sullivan:

... we must be prepared to open with the New Opera if necessary. I have arranged to follow [New York] in March with Chicago,

St. Louis etc. and Cincinnati is pending. I have *splendid terms* 60% in
N. York, 65 in Chicago, and 75 in St. Louis, and I hope to close at
70 for Cincinnati . . .

As far as the U.S. tour was concerned Gilbert was well-pleased with
the one-third each arrangement. However, again Sullivan questioned
the terms, and wrote to Carte on 4th October, only three days before
the proposed departure:

My dear D'Oyly,
    We agree to your proposition, subject to your giving us in
addition one sixth of your net profits ... your net profit to be
calculated over the whole tour. I think you had better close with this
and save all further bother and negotiation. I will only answer one
point in your letter. The America scheme did not originally
emanate from you, it came from *me*, in consequence of offers I had
from America to go over and conduct the 'Pinafore' whilst the rage
was still on. Ford offered me one thousand pounds to conduct it in
Philadelphia for a few nights. If I had gone over alone on my own
account, I should have probably made a large sum without any
bother. As it is, I have suggested that others share it with me.

On the return of the triumvirate from the tour, the intermediate
arrangements were producing a small fortune for the respective partners. That agreement had not covered an important area that Carte was
concerned about: the sole rights of producing the Gilbert and Sullivan
operas. In consequence of his concern the two writers agreed that the
temporary contract should be amended, and one month after *The Pirates
of Penzance* opened at the Opera Comique, it was decided that Carte
should pay a lump sum to the authors in respect of this right. Sullivan
wrote to him on 12th May, 1880, to confirm a payment to them jointly
of £2,900 for the sole rights to produce *The Sorcerer, Pinafore,* and *Pirates,*
and the sole right to license amateur performances.
    This payment was the first in a series of such lump-sum remunera-
tions for production and acting rights in the operas, sums which were
vast in their day and are still weighty by modern standards. It should
not be forgotten that Sullivan and Gilbert were also being paid large
amounts in royalties on the sale of scores, libretti and songsheets. After
Iolanthe had been written Carte negotiated the next sum: £3,500 a year
for five years, for the sole right of production of all the operas; on that

same day, 15th June 1882, he also agreed to pay a further £2,000 for the American and Canadian rights in *Iolanthe* alone. Consider, though, that these purchases of corresponding rights were well outside the mainstream of the actual partnership contract - only a side issue.

The most important contract that governed the relationship between the partners was that one specially negotiated on the completion of, and the transfer of the operas to, the new purpose-built Savoy Theatre. Carte had built the Savoy entirely from his own funds, and it was originally conceived as the home of a new British operatic revival; of course to house the Gilbert and Sullivan works but not necessarily exclusively so. In consequence of this, and the fact that Carte was paying such large sums for the exclusive performing rights, he felt it was only right to charge the partnership rent for the use of the theatre, which was accordingly assessed at £4,500 per annum, and which led to a lot of grumbling by Gilbert. The agreement, signed on 8th February 1883, was for a period of five years and embodied the original idea of an equal profit-sharing arrangement between them. Thus, the profits were to be divided into three after the rent for the Savoy and 'expenses and repairs necessary and incidental to the performance' were deducted; Carte was to produce quarterly accounts and deal with all the business management. On the question of commissions, Gilbert and Sullivan were not to write comic opera for anyone else, and Carte undertook not to produce other than for them.

In 1888 the contract was renewed, despite Gilbert's periodic complaints, as early as 1882, that Carte did not keep a sufficient degree of control of the payment and incurring of expenses. For example, he failed to see how the weekly gas bill at the Savoy in 1883 was higher than that of the Opera Comique, especially since the auditorium of the Savoy was lit throughout by electricity. Carte himself may well have been lax but he relied on his experienced wife, Helen Lenoir. It was later, as will be seen, that this aspect of the agreement was to lead to the conflict resulting in a break-up of the partnership, known as the Carpet Quarrel, 1890. However, this was probably merely the formal excuse needed to terminate what was becoming a more volatile relationship between the three men.

The resumption of the partnership for the production of *Utopia Limited*, three years later, was again on a performing rights, and not a profit-sharing, basis, in which Carte paid a lump-sum to the writers. When the last opera had finished its run 'The Savoy Theatre and Opera' became a private limited company, registered under the 1877

Companies Act, with Carte and his wife as directors and a paid-up share capital which reflected the anticipated value of the Savoy Operas' performing rights as a capital asset. In effect this meant that the Savoy was no longer to be the home for the Gilbert and Sullivan operas to the exclusion of other works, and the resident company became free to develop a repertoire of other works. After 1896 when *The Grand Duke* closed, the Savoy Operas as such were not to be professionally performed again until Helen Lenoir and Rupert D'Oyly Carte organised the revival seasons.

In 1903 there was a great deal of interest and speculation in a motion which appeared in the Chancery Division of the High Court to reduce the paid-up share capital of the Carte company; the report, and answers by way of letters, appeared in *The Times* of 27th-29th August:

Law Report: August 26th
In the High Court of Justice. Chancery Division (before Mr. Justice Walton sitting as Vacation Judge).
   Re: THE SAVOY THEATRE AND OPERAS (LIMITED AND REDUCED)
           AND RE THE COMPANIES ACT, 1867 AND 1877.

This was a petition by the Savoy Theatre and Operas (Limited and Reduced) for the approval of the Court to the reduction of the capital of the company from £75,000 to £41,250 by cancelling paid-up capital which had been lost or was unrepresented by available assets to the extent of £4.10s. per share on each of the 7,500 shares of £10 each in the capital of the company.
MR. BRAMWELL-DAVIES K.C. (Mr. Gordon Brown with him), in support of the petition, said that the creditors had no interest in the matter. The Master had certified that the certificate of debts and claims had been dispensed with and that meetings resolving upon the reduction of the capital had been duly held as required by the articles of association. The only point for the consideration of the Court was whether the loss of capital had been made out. The loss of capital was attributable to the following circumstances:- By an agreement dated August 25th, 1897 the company agreed to purchase the Savoy Theatre and the operas, and the operatic rights, scenery, properties, costumes and general stock-in-trade therein specified at a price of £165,000 payable as to £100,000 in cash and £65,000 by the allotment to Richard D'Oyly Carte (the vendor to the company) or his nominees of 6,500 shares of £10 each in the

capital of the company. At the date of the purchase the value of the Savoy Theatre was estimated at £120,000 (which was still estimated to be its value) and the value of the operas, operatic rights etc., purchased was estimated at £45,000. The company carried on business as owners and managers of the Savoy Theatre until the death of Richard D'Oyly Carte in the year 1901. He was in fact the manager of the Savoy Theatre and on his death the remaining directors of the company thought it inadvisable to attempt personally to manage the theatre and it therefore became necessary to lease the same. A lease of the theatre was accordingly granted and consequently the operas, operatic rights, scenery, properties, costumes and general stock-in-trade purchased by the company from Richard D'Oyly Carte became of no use to the company and it was therefore found necessary to dispose of the same and accordingly they were sold but only realized the sum of £7,700 and a net loss of £37,300 on capital account was therefore realized on the sale of the same. Part of the loss was counterbalanced by the excess of the company's liquid assets over its liabilities, but a realized loss on the sale of more than £33,750 on capital account still remained, as appeared from the statements of company assets and liabilities. The sum of £7,700 realized by the sale was, with other monies, applied towards the acquisition and cancelling out of part of the company's first debenture stock, which now stood at £80,000.

The company was not now carrying on any business beyond that of owning the Savoy Theatre as lessors. The directors and shareholders of the company were fully satisfied that the excess of assets of the company over its liabilities could not in any sense be regarded as equivalent to more than, at the outside, £41,000 or thereabouts, and that the deficiency referred to - namely £33,750 or upwards - must be regarded as a permanent deficiency, and that the sum of £33,750 ought to be written off the company's capital.

Mr. Justice Walton granted the petition as prayed.

Registered capital henceforth £41,250 of 7,500 shares × £5.10s.
£75,000 of 7,500 shares × £10

Gilbert immediately wrote to the editor to try and correct a misconception that he thought the report had conveyed - that the operas themselves had lessened in value:

Sir - With reference to the statement made by counsel for the Savoy
Theatre and Operas (Limited) in support of a petition for the
reduction of the company's capital on the ground (inter alia) that the
acting rights in the Savoy Operas had declined in value from
£45,000 to £7,700, I shall be glad if you will allow me to explain that
when the company was formed Mr. D'Oyly Carte's interest in the
operas had nearly eight years to run. As all rights revert to Sir
Arthur Sullivan's representative and myself in May, 1905, the
apparent depreciation in the value of this asset is, I think
considerably less than might have been expected[2].

Helen D'Oyly Carte wrote the next day, from the Savoy Hotel, to
support Gilbert and offer a further explanation of the depreciation:

Sir - Mr. Gilbert's letter in this morning's papers has, I hope,
corrected the misapprehension as to the value of the Gilbert and
Sullivan operas caused by the reports of the recent formal
application to reduce the ordinary capital of the Savoy Theatre and
Operas (Limited) - in itself a purely technical matter and made
simply for the convenience of account. May I add that the original
estimate of £45,000 included rights in other operas besides those of
Mr. Gilbert and Sir Arthur Sullivan, and also costumes, scenery
and other things of a perishable nature? Mr. Gilbert has explained
that the rights in his operas, as recently resold were only for a very
limited period; they were also, when so sold, subject to certain fees
to the author. A sum of £10,000 for working capital of the theatre
company had been contributed during the period in question. With
that and the sale price of the opera rights etc., £20,000 of first
debenture stock was paid off, so that the actual depreciation of
values over charges did not exceed £25,000; a moderate amount, I
think, over a period of years when dealing with an asset of a
temporary nature. The estimated value of these assets concerned
only the shareholders, who were all members of Mr. Carte's family,
the debenture stock being secured on the freehold of the theatre[3].

The 'Savoy contracts', despite their disputed areas which led to
sensational quarrels in court, endured over a working relationship
which lasted for twenty-five years, and ensured that three remarkably
able men in their respective fields, became remarkably wealthy
together.

Chapter 9

'Giving him the very best and getting back the very worst': the Great Carpet Quarrel

The bursting of the bubble in May 1890, did more than physically and contractually split up the world-famous partnership for three years. It gave rise to the myth, promulgated by some writers, that Gilbert and Sullivan did not get on well personally; some still think today that despite their work together, the two men hated each other in private life. If not sheer nonsense, this is very far from the truth, although it can hardly be disputed that as far as their respective artistic temperaments were concerned, they were worlds apart. Sullivan was by nature lazy and would agree to virtually anything for a quiet life, unless it happened to affect his ability to perform the role of playboy darling of London Society; Gilbert, as has been seen, was not only quite irascible; he enjoyed immensely his terrorising people with litigious threats. The whole conflict in their relationship was that they failed to recognise how much of an institution their joint work had in fact become, save in monetary terms. They both sincerely believed that their individual and more serious work was of far greater intrinsic value in artistic terms; more, they thought that the theatre and concert-going public believed that as well. Neither felt for a moment that what would be considered as their gifts to posterity, would virtually exclude everything other than 'Savoy' operettas. It naturally followed that this honest belief should progress in two directions. First, except for the financial rewards it wouldn't really matter if the partnership were broken up. Each would regard this as a pity, of course - for since they were merely writing hit musical shows (in which each thought that his own aspect was the dominant constituent), rather than creating works of art by their individuality, they must have felt that the special magic associated with the Savoy series could be reproduced with other writers, as long as each of them was there to contribute with their new respective partners. Secondly, each of them had continually to press for the place of pre-eminence for his particular creative talents, rather than ensure the harmony of the work. This could clearly be seen in their correspondence both with each other, and with Carte, throughout the 1880s. The climax to the tension came in a blaze of publicity in the summer of 1890.

On 8th February, 1888, the contract for profit-sharing set up on the completion of the Savoy was renewed. It contained what was to become a crucial clause, the interpretation of which would be questioned in the High Court:

. The said Richard D'Oyly Carte agrees to pay to them, the said W.S. Gilbert and Arthur Sullivan, one third of the net profits earned by the representatives after deducting all expenses and charges of producing the said operas and all the performances of the same including in such expense a rental of £4,000 per annum for the Savoy Theatre, and all rates, taxes, expenses of lighting, *repairs incidental to the performances and rendered necessary from time to time by ordinary wear and tear.*

During the run of *The Mikado* and before that of *Patience*, Gilbert had questioned Carte's handling of the accounts. Towards the end of 1885 he had suggested that Sullivan and he should have more say in the business management of the partnership. Carte was angered at the suggestion and threatened to withdraw; Sullivan would not press the issue, therefore it was left unresolved. Gilbert remained with the feeling that Carte's expenses were not controlled and were largely unchecked; thus the events of April 1890 came about when Carte sent to his partners a statement of the preliminary expenses for *The Gondoliers*. Gilbert very nearly had a fit, and the ensuing difficulties called the 'Carpet Quarrel' can best be told in his own words, in a letter he wrote to Sullivan on 22nd April to explain his view of what had happened when he went to question Carte and ended up by storming out of the Savoy:

I've had a difficulty with Carte.

I was appalled to learn from him that the preliminary expenses of The Gondoliers amounted to the stupendous sum of £4,500!!! This seemed so utterly unaccountable that I asked to see the details, and last night I received a resume of them.

This includes such trifles as £75 for Miss Moore's second dress, £50 for her first dress - £100 for Miss Brandram's second dress (this costly garment has now, for some occult reason, been sent on tour) - £450 for the wages of the carpenters during the time they were engaged on the scenery - Lubhart's charge of £460 for the gondola, the sailing boat, the 2 columns and the two chairs and fountain for Act 2 - £112 for timber - £120 for ironmonger - £95 for canvas - and so forth. But the most surprising item was £500 for new carpets for the front of the house. I pointed out to Carte that we (you and I) were, by our agreement, liable only for 'repairs incidental to the performances' - that new carpets could not possibly be 'repairs' - and that carpets in the lobbies and on the staircases in front could not, by any reasonable latitude of construction, be considered as 'incidental to the performances' - except in a sense that would include everything of every kind belonging to every part of the theatre. He angrily maintained that we were jointly liable for all upholstery in front (a contention that would justify him in entirely re-decorating and upholstering the theatre a month before we left the theatre for ever and charging us with two-thirds of the cost although the goods would at once become his property) - and emphatically declared that nothing would induce him to adopt any other view. I then asked him why, if you and I had to bear two-thirds of the expense, we were not consulted as to the advisability or necessity of spending so enormous a sum on goods which would at once become his property. He declined to go into the question. I then told him that if he adhered to his contention I should not commence upon a new piece unless a fresh agreement were drawn up. He replied that the only alteration he would agree to would be to put the rent of the theatre at £5000 instead of £4000 and that if I was dissatisfied with the existing state of things I had only to say so. I replied that I was dissatisfied and he said, "very well, then; you write no more for the Savoy - that's understood." - or words to that effect. I left him with the remark that it was a mistake to kick down the ladder by which he had risen - a sentiment which I hope will meet with your approval on general principles and also as singularly apposite to the case in point.

Whether for the sake of a quiet life, or whether Sullivan did not grasp what Gilbert was saying, the latter was astounded when Sullivan decided that Carte must have been in the right. Gilbert was completely unable to persuade the composer that it appeared that Carte was cheating them, and that Mrs Carte herself would tell him that Carte always fitted out the front of house before a new piece and billed the partnership. After his initial outburst Gilbert calmed down enough for a meeting to be arranged at which the three would try and draw up a new contract. However Sullivan would not sign an immediate draft and wanted to wait until a new piece was needed. Consequently Gilbert wrote to him on 5th May:

> The time for putting an end to our collaboration has at last arrived....I am writing a letter to Carte...giving him notice that he is not to produce or perform any of my libretti after Christmas 1890. In point of fact, after the withdrawal of The Gondoliers, our united work will be heard in public no more.

The preliminary account had been for the April quarter. The conflict having dragged on for the next three months, Carte would not pay out any money on the July account. As was only to be expected Gilbert wasted no further time with correspondence and had his solicitors issue a writ for his share of the profits. He consequently received a cheque for £2000, although he claimed a discrepancy involved £1000 more, and now felt certain that Carte was not to be trusted. Of course by now the actual price of the carpet in question had varied enormously: Carte told Sullivan it had been only £140, but the rumour-mongers and in one instance Gilbert himself had put the figure as high as £1400. Henry Lytton had thought it was more in line with Carte's figure, but by the middle of the summer people who knew were beginning to take sides, and Sullivan was being inexorably drawn further into the dispute.

The rumour that a split had occurred sprang up and spread very quickly. It was topical gossip and friends and associates of both parties, whether through jealousy or a desire to protect their friend's viewpoint against the other, stirred up a wide interest, in the social circles that the composer frequented, in the theatrical world generally, and also in the financial sphere of the City. Naturally enough each newspaper was vieing to officially break the story first. It was the *Star* that succeeded, with a small paragraph on its front page on 13th May that confirmed the news:

There is no longer any doubt about it. Sullivan and Gilbert have quarrelled in real earnest, and it is quite possible that they will never collaborate again. The difference began in some misunderstanding between D'Oyly Carte and Mr. Gilbert, and then it spread because Sir Arthur Sullivan refused to take up the quarrel between the author and the impresario. It is not true that Eugene Field, of Chicago, is writing the libretto of a piece for the Savoy. 'We are not thinking of it yet, and shan't for some time,' said Mr. Carte to a *Star* man on Saturday. We expect *The Gondoliers* to run for at least eighteen months more.

Gilbert brought the whole affair into the open by applying in the High Court for a receiver to be appointed to take account of the profits coming in from *The Gondoliers*. Judging by correspondence passing between them, he must have felt mortified when the proceedings were held up as Sullivan sent counsel to make an application that he should be joined to the action as a second defendant, alongside Carte. In consequence the action was prolonged by three weeks in order for Sullivan's affidavits, and Gilbert's respective replies to them, to be drawn up. Thus, the *Era* carried reports for three successive weeks: the first hearing occurred on 20th August:

In the Court of Chancery on Wednesday, before Mr. Justice Lawrence, sitting as vacation judge, the case of Gilbert v D'Oyly Carte was in the list for hearing. The dispute has reference to an agreement in respect of the Savoy Theatre, and the motion asks for an account and payment of share of the net profits of the plaintiff's operas, also for the appointment of a receiver of *The Gondoliers* takings. It was asked that the motion should stand over for a week to answer affidavits and to add Sir Arthur Sullivan as a defendant, and the application was granted.

The main part of the hearing was taken up by cross-applications; Gilbert's counsel, 'Tommy Fischer, Q.C., had to apologize for Gilbert's non-attendance and ask for the case to be put back another week, to the 27th, as Gilbert was ill at Carlsbad. The Defendants immediately applied to have the case thrown out for unfair delaying tactics, but Fischer had the day:

The Gondoliers In Court

In the Vacation court before Mr. Justice Lawrence on Wednesday last, an adjourned motion on the part of Mr. W. S. Gilbert against Mr. D'Oyly Carte in respect of an agreement and the account and payment of share of net profits of plaintiff's operas, and the appointment of a receiver of the takings of *The Gondoliers*, was down for hearing. Counsel for the plaintiff said his Lordship would remember that this case had stood over in order that the plaintiff might make an affidavit in reply. The plaintiff was at present in Carlsbad, not on pleasure, but because he was ill, to which effect he handed in a certificate from Dr. Quain of Harley-street. A draft of the affidavit had been sent to the plaintiff, which he had returned with sundry additions that he wished to have made, but which could not be made at Carlsbad because there was no English Consul or Vice-Consul there. In order to avoid trouble the plaintiff had written a letter stating that he would leave Carlsbad on Saturday, and be in London on Monday at eleven o'clock and would be prepared to swear the affidavit. He therefore asked his lordship to allow the motion to stand over till next Wednesday. The defendants counsel protested on the part of Mr. D'Oyly Carte, against the motion being allowed to stand over any further. Mr. Gilbert made the motion on totally improper grounds, and then went abroad, and left the motion to the care of his Solicitors. The affidavit made a suggestion quite unfounded with regard to Mr. D'Oyly Carte, and Mr. D'Oyly Carte felt that great injury was being done to him by the motion. Of course he could not oppose the present application, but he did protest against the cruel conduct on the part of Mr. Gilbert or his advisers in persisting in a motion of this character under these circumstances. Mr. M'Naghten on behalf of Sir Arthur Sullivan, joined in Mr. Marten's protest against the delays, and Mr. Gilbert's conduct in the whole matter. The case was allowed to stand over till Wednesday next.

During the final hearing the remarkable financial success of the partnership came to the public eye for the first time. Over the past eleven years Carte had sent to Gilbert, as his one-third share after the deduction of expenses, some £90,000. *The Gondoliers* had produced for each of them £3,000 in the first three months alone, although both Carte and Sullivan felt that the box office takings would suffer badly due to this present action. The final day's hearing was widely reported and eventually Carte's counsel made an offer of settlement that was acceptable. *The Star* of 3rd September treated the matter rather light-heartedly:

W.S. At Law
The Gilbert-Sullivan-Carte
Trio are Fighting it Out
in the Courts

When Mr. W. S. Gilbert expressed the opinion that "the law is the true embodiment of everything that is excellent", he was probably poking fun at the law. Doubtless he didn't dream then that he would before long have to seek it's uncertain aid. But recently strange differences have arisen to divide the famous Savoy triumvirate, and Mr. Gilbert's heart has said to him, "W.S." (it calls him "W.S." because it has known him from a baby and they were at school together) - "W.S., you'll have to go to law." Accordingly among the motions before Justice Lawrence sitting in the Chancery Division today was the one on behalf of Mr. Gilbert against Mr. D'Oyly Carte and Sir A. Sullivan, asking for the appointment of a receiver in respect of the librettist's alleged share in the takings arising from the performance of 'The Gondoliers.' Mr. Fischer, Q.C., appeared for Mr. Gilbert, and with him was Mr. Charles Mitchell (who ought to be

A Good Fighting Junior

well up in the upper-cutting and knocking-out styles of pleading if he wishes to be considered worthy of his name.) These counsel were instructed by Messrs. Bolton and Mote. Mr. Martin, Q.C., led for Mr. D'Oyly Carte (instructed by Mr. Stanley); and Mr. Macnaghten (who was looked after by Messrs. Lewis and Lewis) appeared for Sir Arthur Sullivan. Considering who the parties were, it would have been a pretty little piece of courtesy if the judge had opened the proceedings in the proper comic opera style laid down by the librettist -

> "A nice dilemma we have here
> That calls for all our wit".

Whereupon counsel would have responded:-

> "And at this stage it don't appear
> that we can settle it"...

The Era report of the last day's hearing, squeezed into a paragraph between a report that five members of *The Gondoliers* company had become Freemasons, and one of Edwin Cleary's company nearing Uruguay on its way to perform *Pinafore, Trial, Pirates, The Mikado* and *The Sorcerer*, among others, under licence in the Teatro Nacional at Buenos Aires, was issued on the 6th:

Mr. W. S. Gilbert, the author of the libretto of *The Gondoliers*, applied to the Vacation Judge on Wednesday for the appointment of a receiver of the takings at the Savoy Theatre. He was dissatisfied with some items in the accounts furnished to him, and wished to have the accounts since 1883 examined. The application was opposed by Mr. D'Oyly Carte and Sir A. Sullivan, on the ground that it would destroy the lucrative business at the Savoy which between April and July had yielded profits amounting to nine thousand pounds. Ultimately the plaintiff's counsel accepted an offer of an account up to July 4th, to be presented within three weeks, and an immediate payment of one thousand pounds.

Gilbert having won the day he quickly wished to make amends, if only to prove that he wasn't deriving any pleasure from this particular argument, but probably also to use his newly won stand-point at the negotiating table if he would persuade the others to become sufficiently reconciled with him to sign a new contract. He wrote to Sullivan and Helen D'Oyly Carte on 6th September, asking to let byegones be, but while Helen D'Oyly Carte was willing to meet Gilbert and act as a go-between in any reconciliation, Sullivan replied that as an act of good faith the author should first withdraw any outstanding legal proceedings that he had brought against Carte. Gilbert replied by carefully reminding Sullivan of the £1,400 error in the accounts and that he felt he had backed the wrong man, and later at his meeting with Helen D'Oyly Carte suddenly expressed the view that it would be better if the accounts since the formation of the partnership should be given for independent examination. Helen Carte appreciated that the recent proceedings had been injurious enough to her husband, catching him in the middle of negotiating the mortgage on his new Royal English Opera House. On reporting this suggestion D'Oyly informed Gilbert that he was agreeable, and told him that it would be found that bar-receipts and programme-advertisement receipts had been shared out as general profits instead of going merely to the theatre manager as his right, and that these would have to be refunded: Gilbert quickly changed his mind.

From October until January 1891 correspondence flowed freely from Gilbert to Sullivan and back: Gilbert explaining his viewpoint in the whole argument but gradually softening his tone, Sullivan stressing that he had always wanted to be a neutral and that he wanted the whole affair forgotten as quickly as possible. This was to be, and whilst the collaborators were to spend a further two years trying other partners before they wrote together again, it can at least be said that although their relationship did not finish on a wholly joyful note, it nevertheless did not finish on a completely sour one. Gilbert, always the man to get the last word in, however, wrote an extraordinary letter to Sullivan on 28th May 1891:

> As a direct result of the action I commenced against Carte a twelvemonth ago, he has admitted an unintentional overcharge of nearly £1000 in the electric lighting accounts alone. He also admits that there are other items charged in the disputed accounts which should not have been charged and he expresses his readiness to put these matters right as soon as *The Gondoliers* is withdrawn. As you will, I suppose, benefit considerably by this re-adjustment of accounts I thought it possible that you might wish to share with me the costs of the action by which it was brought about.

Given the importance of this incident in the relationship between the three men certain questions naturally arise. Was the breakdown the inevitable culmination of the growing friction between Gilbert and Sullivan? Some writers take the view that the Carpet Quarrel stands on its own as the whole reason for the dispute; the other school favours the idea of it being an excuse that the protagonists were waiting for, to release the friction that had been building up with an airing of the difficulties. Certainly by 1890 Gilbert no longer trusted Carte, viewing him as an exploiter of his and Sullivan's talents which had thus made him rich and famous. Carte could not see that - he was the controller and manipulator of talents to their best advantage, not an exploiter, and he felt his achievements were only rewarded justly. Yet from the discrepancies uncovered or admitted it was true that even if he were not cheating Gilbert and Sullivan, there was a certain laxity in keeping the accounts. Whilst Carte should not be portrayed as the villain of the piece, as he popularly is, it must be borne in mind that the Carpet Quarrel was between Gilbert and Carte. It was with total reluctance that Sullivan had to become involved to protect an investment of more importance to him than the Savoy operas: for Gilbert was singularly unlucky in that he let his temper get the better of him just when both Carte and Sullivan were nearing the fulfilment of their combined ambition, the dream of English grand opera and a new home for it. Carte was building the English Opera House for grand opera on the revenue of the new school of English comic opera that had been his creation. Sullivan was writing *Ivanhoe* for Carte, at the request of the Queen herself. Neither was prepared to give up their dream, or their financial investment, if that meant turning their attention to another of Gilbert's squabbles, even should that result in a split-up of the great triumvirate, the significance of which they just could not see. Gilbert had brought the issue to the forefront when Sullivan needed Carte, Carte needed Sullivan, and neither needed Gilbert. If the carpet was then merely an excuse, the tragic split was inevitable at some stage before the opening of *Ivanhoe*, which Sullivan and Carte saw as the progression to a higher plane, and Gilbert could not. We can only speculate on what would have happened had both Carte and Sullivan been content with the Savoy and comic opera. Would it be too much to say that 'carpets' may then never have been heard of?

Henrietta Hodson—Mrs. Henry Labouchere. *(photo: Jeremy Zeid after an original by H. N. King)*

Richard D'Oyly *(photo: Jeremy Zeid after an original)*

Page of the First-Night programme of *Trial by Jury*, 25th March 1875.

The original Learned Judge, Sullivan's brother Fred; after the original cabinet photograph he presented to Gilbert, in August 1875. *(artist: Marianne Fountain)*

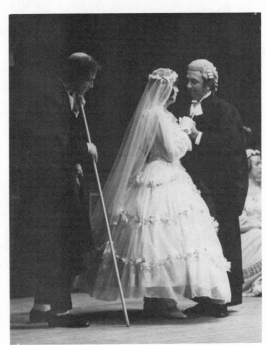

ohn Broad as the Usher, with Marjorie Williams as the Plain-ff, Angelina, and Michael Ray-er as her Counsel. *(photos: ourtesy of the D'Oyly Carte Opera rust)*

From a recent D'Oyly Carte production of *Trial by Jury:* Jon Ellison as the Learned Judge.

PART III

'Yet everybody says I'm such a disagreeable man!'

Chapter 10

'Grand Llama or Sacred Elephant': The battle with The 'Era'

The last major suit that Gilbert brought was as spectacular and imaginative as any of the Savoy Opera plots; in the closing months of 1897 it became the heated topic of conversation throughout the ranks of the theatrical profession, the newspapers, certain sections of the Bar and the country at large. Limbering up to do battle in a libel action against the *Era* weekly theatre newspaper were, on his behalf, Lawson Walton, Q.C., with the rising new star Marshall Hall as junior, and opposing Edward Carson, Q.C., then at the peak of his career[1].

Having written seventy-five plays in thirty years the dramatist ostensibly considered himself well content to rest on his laurels at his beautiful country home at Grim's Dyke, near Harrow Weald. He carefully followed through the productions of all works that bore his name, and when a recent work, *The Fortune Hunter*, was refused by certain London theatres (and did very poorly, having opened at the Theatre Royal, Birmingham, on 27th September 1897,) he resolved to travel to the show's next venue, Edinburgh, to catch a performance and offer the producer, an actress named May Fortescue, his assistance. On the evening of his arrival he had consented, after pressure from a friend, to give an exclusive interview to the *Edinburgh Evening Dispatch*, and a staff reporter named Isaac Donald duly appeared. To the great good fortune of that reporter Gilbert was in a foul temper - his play had received terrible notices; he could not obtain sleeper accommodation on his train north; he disliked his hotel - the interview comprised a blistering, scathing and clearly unthinking attack on his professional colleagues, writers, actors and critics alike. The *Dispatch* printed his remarks in full on 5th October, created a sensation and scooped the country. Among his freely given opinions, followed up in most British newspapers the next day, Gilbert had said:

The fact is managers cannot judge a play when they see it in manuscript. If Pinero writes a play and sends it to Sir Henry Irving it is accepted, not because it is a good play but because it is Pinero. If a stranger who may be a clever dramatist sends Sir Henry or Mr. Tree or anybody else a play, it is not accepted, however good it may be, because they can't judge...

We ought to leave the French stage alone. They have good actors and atrociously bad plays . . . Their actors, of course, can so speak and deliver speeches as to chain the attention of the audience, while ours, why, we have no actor who can make a thirty-line speech interesting! Whoever heard in this country "All the world's a stage" disclaimed by a Jaques who did not in every line make it plain he had learned it off by heart. There is always the same monotony of delivery. Every living actor - Sir Henry Irving, Beerbohm Tree, Alexander, excellent though they may be otherwise - have that dull monotony of delivery. They keep to one note throughout the sentence and finish a semi-tone higher or a semi-tone lower as the case may be!

The direction of dramatic taste lies today in musical comedy - bad musical comedy, in which half-a-dozen irresponsible comedians are turned loose upon the stage to do exactly as they please.

The theatre is as strong as ever it was. At this moment, certainly, there are perhaps fewer original plays before the public than one would desire to see... The press is largely responsible for the fact that there are so many adaptations on the English stage... because they seem to draw no distinction between the production of an original play and the translation of a French one... I blame the press for considering them seriously as original work. Why, I hear Sydney Grundy put on the same level as Arthur Pinero, while the fact is that Mr. Grundy is only a translator. He is a creditable translator, but to put him on the same level as Mr. Pinero is a monstrous injustice. Remember I do not wish, in saying this, to deny Mr. Grundy in any sense.

I think Pinero a giant, but he finds his name bracketed with hacks.
There is a tendency to look upon the author of a bad or an
unsuccessful play, not as a poor devil who has tried his best, but as a
man who has committed an outrage against nature. The critics attack
him as if he were a Scoundrel of the worst type, and they go on at it
week after week. I don't feel myself disposed to put myself forward as a
cock-shy to these gentlemen.

Gilbert probably realised little of what he had said until he saw a copy
of the interview a few days later. Being very conscious of the law of
defamation he quickly wrote to Irving's secretary and Tree, Alexander
and Grundy personally to explain that he had been misreported, that his
words had been taken completely out of context, and that he would sue
the *Dispatch*. It was the following week's edition of the *Era*, however, that
really brought him down to earth; it is not difficult to imagine the
righteous indignation of the critic being attacked, and its irony, as
Gilbert read the particularly biting editorial:

Mr. Gilbert's abnormal self-esteem has with advancing years
developed into a malady. In his own estimation he is a kind of Grand
Llama or Sacred Elephant of dramatic literature. The mildest
criticism on his work, the most gentle disapproval of one of his plays, is
a crime of lese-majeste for which, if it were in his power, he would
punish the culprit severely. It is a significant fact that one of the first
things Mr. Gilbert did when he retired, as it was trustfully believed,
from the business was to become a J.P. It is most evident that did we
live under a more despotic dispensation he would commit all the
London critics for contempt of court....Mr. Gilbert's career has been a
succession of combats with the object, alas! unattained, of vindicating
the Gilbert theory of the universe against sceptics and revels...his real
kindliness and good-nature have simply been obscured by the
abnormal protuberance of his bump of self-esteem. That this–what's
his name–Grundy should have written successful original works,
while he, the Great Gilbert, has met with failure after failure in
modern drama, is preposterous and not to be borne.

Very little time was lost in the issuing and serving of a writ for libel
against the *Era* with a claim for £1,000 in damages being made. The case
came on for hearing in the Queen's Bench Division of the High Court
before Mr. Justice Day on 1st April 1898. Surprisingly, Gilbert had

received offers of support both from Grundy and Tree, the latter even agreeing to testify that Gilbert's standing and reputation as a dramatist entitled him to speak with authority as a critic. Irving, Tree and Alexander were present for the court hearing which, as expected, quickly turned into a scene not out of place at the Savoy Theatre itself.

Marshall Hall had no easy task in leading Gilbert through his evidence-in-chief: the author and plaintiff seemed determined to stray from his proof of evidence and conduct as much of his case on his own as possible.

Hall: You have read what was said in the article about your bump of self-esteem. Do you regard that as written in joke or seriously?

W.S.G.:   I can hardly take it seriously, because I cannot suppose that anyone thinks I wish to reconstruct the universe. I am perfectly satisfied with Cosmos as it is. (Laughter.)

Hall: Is it true to say that you have had successive combats with anybody to vindicate your theory of the universe?

W.S.G.:   Oh no! I have no theory of the universe, and I am not a combative man. (Laughter.)

Hall: Then with regard to the inability of any English actor to make a thirty-line speech interesting, was that a statement by you?

W.S.G.:   It was not. I was asked whether I intended to write any more blank verse plays, and I replied that I did not. I was then asked if I thought that the taste for modern blank verse had entirely died out, and I said no - that what I objected to was the present fashion of delivering blank verse, which allowed the metrical, the iambic structure to dominate the verse, caused the audience to lose the thread of the discourse, and obliged them to give up the speech for a bad job and wait for the next speech in the hope that they would find better luck with it. (Laughter.) That statement was only intended to apply to blank verse. It would be most untrue to apply it to the great proportion of actors in regard to ordinary prose. It was not at all personal and referred solely to the principle upon which blank verse is spoken.

Hall: You did not intend these remarks as an insult to Sir Henry Irving, Mr. Tree, or Mr. Alexander?

W.S.G.:   No, certainly not. It was merely my comment upon the
          state of the blank verse stage.
Hall: As a matter of fact, did you mention their names at all?
W.S.G.:   They were suggested to me by the interviewer, who said
          "Do your remarks apply to Irving, Tree and
          Alexander?" and I said, "Yes, all living actors who deal
          with blank verse."

Carson rose to cross-examine; three years earlier he had had his first
opportunity of questioning a great literary genius - Oscar Wilde.
Gilbert was openly hostile to the eminent advocate because of his
treatment of Wilde on that occasion, despite the dramatist's own brutal
satire of the man in *Patience*.

Carson: You don't like reading hostile criticism?
W.S.G.:   Not at all. I have a horror of reading criticism at all, either
          good or bad, though I prefer the latter. I know how
          good I am, but I do not know how bad I am.
          (Laughter.)
Carson: (having read the notices of the *Fortune Hunter*):
          You would admit that that is a formidable list of hostile
          criticism?
W.S.G.:   Distinctly I am prepared to admit that the play is a very
          bad play. (Laughter.) A play that fails is for all practical
          purposes a bad play.
Carson: Did you observe from the public press that a short time
          afterwards Sir Henry Irving, at a dinner of the
          Sheffield Press Club, spoke good-humouredly but
          warmly about the criticism upon himself?
W.S.G.:   I do not admit that he spoke good-humouredly but
          warmly. I noted that he spoke most angrily and most
          spitefully concerning me. He described me as a
          librettist who soared to write original comedy.
Carson: You were not angry with Sir Henry Irving?
W.S.G.:   I was most angry at that coming from a gentleman whom
          I have never given occasion for such an utterance.
Carson: Do you think that Sir Henry Irving spoke angrily?
W.S.G.:   I am sure he did.
Carson: And spitefully?

W.S.G.: Most spitefully. I cannot conceive why he did so. I have never had an angry word with him, and I cannot conceive why he should be so spiteful.

Carson: Did you read what he said?

W.S.G.: I read a report of it. I do not know whether it is accurate or not.

Carson: You say, sir, that you consider Sir Henry Irving was angry at what appeared to be your opinion expressed to the interviewer. Did you ever write to the paper to contradict it or withdraw any single sentence of the offensive statement put forward about English actors?

W.S.G.: No. I wrote to Sir Henry's secretary, and as I see him in court he may have the letter about him.

Carson: Don't you think it would have been only fair to have written and publicly withdrawn them in the press?

W.S.G.: The matter was in my Solicitor's hands and this action had begun. I had also written to Tree and Alexander telling them that I had been misreported and that my remarks were only meant to apply to the delivery of blank verse.

Carson: Would you give the court your opinion as to the direction of current dramatic taste?

W.S.G.: In the direction of musical comedy; bad musical comedy, in which half-a-dozen irresponsible comedians are turned loose upon the stage to do as they please.

Carson: Will you mention one of them?

W.S.G.: Oh, there are plenty of them!

Carson: I wish you would mention one.

W.S.G.: Well, take the pantomime at the Drury Lane Theatre, with the great Dan Leno. (Loud laughter.)

Carson: But that only goes on for a short time in the year.

W.S.G.: It goes on for a long time in the evening. (Laughter.)

Carson: Do you really describe a pantomime as a bad musical comedy?

W.S.G.: No, but I would describe a bad musical comedy as a pantomime. (Great laughter.)

Carson: That is very clever but I would like to know what you mean by bad musical comedies. Give me the name of one.

W.S.G.: There are fifty of them.

Carson: Give me one.

W.S.G.:   I would say such a piece as *The Circus Girl*.

Carson: Would you call it a bad musical comedy?

W.S.G.:   I would call it bad. I believe the manager calls it a musical comedy. (Laughter.)

Carson: Have they half-a-dozen irresponsible low comedians turned loose in *The Circus Girl?*

W.S.G.:   I don't know how many there are. (Laughter.) Then there are musical comedies that have been played at the Gaiety. I do not know their names but there is 'The Shop Girl' and there is 'The Bar Girl' I think. (Loud laughter.)

Carson: You mean the actors in these are irresponsible low comedians?

W.S.G.:   Not all of them. Certain of them are as in the plays produced by Mr. Arthur Roberts at the Lyric where he says and does what he pleases.

Carson: He is an irresponsible comedian?

W.S.G.:   Certainly. Most irresponsible. (Loud laughter.) And most amusing. (Laughter.)

Carson: Are these words which you wrote: (reads from *Rosencrantz and Guildenstern*)

The acts were five- though by five acts too long,
I wrote an act by way of epilogue,
An act by which the penalty of death
Was meted out to all who sneered at it.
The play was not good, but the punishment,
of those who laughed at it was capital.

W.S.G.:   Those were the words of Claudius of Denmark not of myself. I wrote them but I do not hold myself responsible for anything King Claudius says. (Laughter.)

Carson: I leave it to the jury whether you did not repeat King Claudius' words in the box a moment ago. You say that as the critics do not discriminate between original plays and translations, and that consequently there are fewer original plays on the stage?

W.S.G.:   When at school I translated the Greek dramatists but never claimed for myself the authorship of their plays. I have always given Sophocles the credit for his share of the work in them. (Laughter.) I once translated a French play, sitting up all night to do it, and I got £3000 out of it.

Carson: That was better than the Bar?

W.S.G.:   It is better than my experience of it. (Laughter.)

Carson: There is a passage here in which you are described as Gilbert the Great, to which you take exception?

W.S.G.:   Yes, I do not feel I deserve the compliment. (Laughter.)

Carson: Would you say that you were quick-tempered?

W.S.G.:   Certainly not.

Carson: Well, are you mildly touchy and not a little quarrelsome?

W.S.G.:   No.

Carson: Is it right that your temper has affected your personal and business interests to such an extent that you ended your partnership with Sir Arthur Sullivan and D'Oyly Carte?

W.S.G.:   I have never had any quarrel with Sir Arthur who remains a firm friend to me.

Carson: Did you quarrel with Mr. Clement Scott?

W.S.G.:   I wrote to him nine years ago complaining of a criticism.

Carson: You said, "I am determined not to expose myself again to your insulting gibes"?

W.S.G.:   Yes, no doubt I wrote that.

Carson: You were cool and calm?

W.S.G.:   Yes, calm and deliberate. I don't know my temperature at the time. (Prolonged laughter.)

Carson: Did you bring an action against Mr. Horace Sedger, with whom you had a quarrel over the production of *The Mountebanks?*

W.S.G.:   I did not quarrel with Mr. Sedger.

Carson: You were friendly with him afterwards?

W.S.G.:   I was not friendly with him before. (Laughter.)

Carson: Did you fall out with Mr. John Hare at the Garrick?

W.S.G.:   I am not on terms with John Hare just now because he chose to quarrel with me over the manner in which I referred to his action in transferring the lease of the Garrick Theatre, which belongs to me, to a syndicate formed to exhibit a music-hall dwarf.

Carson: It was all his fault?

W.S.G.:   There was no fault on either side. (Laughter.)

Carson: What damages do you expect for being called a Grand Llama?

W.S.G.:   I am not seeking heavy damages. I am bringing the action on the article as a whole.

Carson, however, had the opportunity of commenting on Gilbert's character during his closing speech for the defence, without being hampered by torrents of laughter every few minutes as a result of the flashing duel of wits and word-play. Powerless to reply, Gilbert left the courtroom in a temper; and when Sir Charles Day summed up the case for the jury he told them quite wrongly since it had no bearing on the case before them:

The plaintiff, while objecting to criticism, had not been sparing in his own criticism of others.

The jury retired for over three hours, only to return to the court to state that it was impossible for them to reach an agreed vertict[3]. The judge discharged them, dismissed the action and ordered each side to return its own costs. Gilbert, thoroughly disgruntled with the outcome, showed his feelings in two letters which closed the episode: he complained to Helen D'Oyly Carte:

The judge summed up like a drunken monkey. He is in the last stages of senile decay and knew absolutely nothing whatsoever about the case. It is a frightful scandal that such men should be allowed to sit in judgment[4].

The second letter was written to Beerbohm Tree's wife, Maud, thanking her for her husband's support, and was of much the same tone:

I was charged with having made an unworthy and malicious attack upon a body of men, many of whom I hold in high regard, and it was (as it seemed to me) incumbent upon me to refute the charge. The only way of doing this was to bring an action. The case would have been mine but for the judge who was simply a monument of senile incapacity. To the very last he hadn't the faintest notion as to what the trial was about. My case was comparatively trivial, but it is fearful to think that grave issues are at the mercy of an utterly incompetent old doll. Lawson Walton conducted my case with admirable dignity and restraint - Carson conducted his in the spirit of a low-class police court attorney. But I believe he did me no harm. I was particularly impressed by your husband's kindness in trying to make peace . . .[5]

Gilbert had occasion to meet Carson twice more in his lifetime, and on both occasions Gilbert showed his bitterness; at two small dinner parties, one given by his friend and actor, Sir Squire Bancroft, he turned his back on and refused to speak to the advocate.

Chapter 11

'By this Ingenious law': His Excellency, *Wilde* and *Workman*

Sadly the strain and recriminations of the past were never far from the surface in the two last working relationships between Gilbert and Sullivan. Whilst Gilbert was writing *Utopia Limited* and beyond the end of 1892, he was still sending letters to Sullivan questioning points that the latter had raised in his affidavits, attacking Carte and reminding him of his infidelity. Sullivan weathered the storm but in many cases was simply too ill to argue. However, now acting independently of each other and without a business manager, they became very much aware of the need to protect their financial interests, especially in the light of what Gilbert had understood to have happened, and Sullivan was beginning to discover. The author cannot be said to have been slow in protecting his interests in the past, and was now even more vigilant. The composer had been unfortunate in money matters: a reckless gambler anyway, his stockbroker had gone into liquidation on the day of the opening of *Iolanthe* and he had lost £6,000. His grand opera *Ivanhoe* had been a dream fulfilled, but was not a financial triumph, nor could it have been expected to be.

Gilbert was back to his litigious tricks by 1894 when he had a brush with journalist Anna de Brémont and spent a considerable amount of money in solicitors' and private detectives' fees in trying to prove that her

131

title of Comtesse was fraudulent. When it was discovered that this was true, and that the lady had at least as many vices as virtues, an action against Gilbert for damages for defamation was squashed flat. Gilbert instructed his solicitors not to apply for his costs and wrote to a friend of his genuine sorrow 'to see the poor woman vivisected in the witness-box'.

This incident had occurred whilst Gilbert was preparing *His Excellency* for the Lyric Theatre with Osmond Carr. This show was to provoke many quarrels between Gilbert and Rutland Barrington, George Edwardes and even George Grossmith. However before it was even produced *His Excellency* became the subject of a legal tussle which brought Gilbert's name to the Law Reports for a second time. The premiere was due on 27th October, yet on the Wednesday before, Gilbert discovered that his closely guarded plot had been leaked to the press, and *The Star* newspaper had disclosed it. He was, as can be expected, furious and on the following motion day in the Chancery Division, Friday 26th, he dispatched a silk, Byrne, with Lewis Coward to try and obtain an interim injunction to stop the newspaper printing any further advance information, whilst he tried to find the culprit responsible for what he considered to be an enormous breach of confidence. Mr. Justice Chitty granted the order required, even though there were literally only a few hours remaining that mattered. Nevertheless they mattered to Gilbert.

Chancery Division   1894
Chitty J.   October 26th

Gilbert v. *The Star* Newspaper Company (Limited)

Copyright - Stage Play - Publication of plot by newspaper - Injunction

This was an ex parte motion on behalf of the plaintiff, Mr. W. S.
Gilbert, for an interim injunction to restrain the defendants, the
proprietors of *The Star* newspaper, from further publishing a
number of the newspaper issued on the evening of October 23 last
with an article or any similar article giving the plot of a comic opera
styled 'His Excellency', of the libretto of which the plaintiff was the
author and proprietor. It appeared that 'His Excellency' had been in
course of rehearsal for about six weeks, and had been advertised to
be publicly performed at the Lyric Theatre on Saturday, October
27th, 1894. The plaintiff stated that the plot of the opera was
original, and had never been produced in public, and that it was a
distinct breach of confidence on the part of any actor or employee at
a theatre, to whose knowledge the plot and details of a new piece

must or would probably come in the course of his employment, to disclose such plot or details concerning such new piece, and it was further stated that the existence of such an obligation on the part of actors, etc., against disclosure was well known to actors, etc., and every engagement with them was made upon the footing that such custom, which was believed to be universal, would be observed. The article complained of was headed "His Excellency. The Gilbert-Carr Opera due on Saturday. An outline of the plot of the play which every theatre-goer and music lover will be discussing next week." The article commenced as follows:-

> "In view of the widespread interest awakened by the promised production of Mr. W. S. Gilbert's new comic opera with Dr. Osmond Carr's music which will take place on Saturday evening at the Lyric Theatre, *The Star* pocket hypnotist has been at work amongst the critics. Fortunately he came across one more susceptible than others to the wheedling influence, by virtue of which he is now able to set out in anticipation of a fair summary of impressions which would not in the ordinary way be experienced until the last evening of the week."

This introduction was followed by a full column, which gave the plot of the play with a summary of some of the play's points and incidents which, as the plaintiff stated, he intended should be a surprise to the audience on the occasion of its public performance. The plaintiff stated that he had neither directly nor indirectly authorized any of the actors or employees or any other person whomsoever to convey to *The Star* or any other newspaper any information relative to the opera and that the publication of the article was calculated to do the plaintiff considerable injury; that the information apparently obtained by the writer of the article could only have been obtained by a gross breach of confidence on the part of some actor or employee in violation of his implied contract with his employer; and that it was essential that the incident and plot of a new play should not be disclosed before the first performance, as these might be telegraphed to the United States with the view of producing there some similar work in anticipation of the production of such plays by the author's assignees.

Mr. Byrne, Q.C., and Mr. Lewis Coward appeared for the plaintiff in support of the motion.

Mr. Justice CHITTY said that the ground upon which the application for an injunction was made was that there had been a disclosure and publication of the work of an author before it had been published by him or by his authority, and the principle enunciated in the case of 'Prince Albert v Strange' (1. Mar. and C.25) was relied on in support of the relief sought for. It was also part of the ground of the application that the information upon which the article in question was founded had been obtained by means of a breach of confidence on the part of some person or persons who, according to the evidence, were bound to silence and not at liberty to disclose what had taken place at the rehearsals. He was only dealing with an ex parte case, but the introductory observations at the commencement of the article showed that the information would have been obtained in the way suggested by the plaintiff, and improperly obtained. Mr. Gilbert swore that he had given no authority to any person to give the information, and to avoid any objection on the ground that the contract on the part of the employee at the theatre was not with Mr. Gilbert but with the manager of the theatre, the latter must be joined as plaintiff, and an affidavit be made by him showing that he had not given authority. No doubt the injury which the plaintiff complained of would to a large extent already have been done, but that was no ground why the Court should decline to stop, although only for a few hours, that which, speaking on the evidence before it, appeared to be unjustifiable. It therefore, subject to the manager being joined as plaintiff and making the requisite affidavit, granted the injunction asked for. The injunction would be confined to the article complained of, and would not be in a form which would prevent *The Star* itself giving an account of the opera when and after it was performed.

The manager was accordingly joined as plaintiff and Mr. Byrne subsequently stated that the requisite affidavit had been made.

The quarrels with Grossmith and Barrington during the rehearsals of this show were relatively of minor importance, and were concerned with 'ad-libbing' during the performance. Gilbert kept a stern control over his cast, almost as much to protect his words from them as to drill them into his single-minded concept of the usage of his script. When two of the absolute stars of his troupe indulged in their 'interpolated badinage' the author was as tough with them as if they had been chorus extras. Both actors were principal comedians and both felt indignant that in the furthering of their craft Gilbert treated them as schoolboys. However they both knew him well enough to expect nothing better, and were deluding themselves when they considered that he would respect their achievements and status in the acting world.

The third dispute during the run of *His Excellency* was one that Gilbert had with the then manager of the Lyric, and Carte's most successful protegé, George Edwardes, later of Gaiety and Daly's fame. He had purchased from Gilbert the sole acting rights of the piece in London and the provinces, America and the colonies, for £5,000 in December 1894. Eight months later Edwardes tried to send a production outside the area of the agreement and Gilbert immediately accused the manager of trying to usurp his translation rights. The author by his correspondence and threats of not attending the rehearsals of touring companies, swiftly put Edwardes into a position where he had to back down and issue the kind of apology that Gilbert revelled in.

In the meantime Sullivan's health had been rapidly deteriorating, so much so that it became a supreme effort for him to attend the premiere of the last 'Savoy Opera', *The Grand Duke* in 1896. The Savoy era, indeed the Victorian era, was drawing to an inevitable close, and as Percy Young in his biography of Sullivan intimates[1], the composer was feeling the effect: England as a whole was yet to feel the euphoria of Victoria's Diamond Jubilee celebrations, and the spirit of fin de siècle. Equally the eighties and their attitudes and values had changed; and the most controversial and well-known case of the nineties, involving two of Sullivan's friends and many compatriots, whilst it could have at a stretch formed the basis of a satirical plot in the eighties, was all too serious a matter now:

Oscar Wilde, the butt of Gilbert's satire in *Patience*, had become one of the most successful dramatists of the day. He had two long-running shows currently in production at the Haymarket and Westminster Theatres. He had close personal relationships with many male friends including one with Lord Alfred Douglas, son of the eighth Marquess of Queensbury, a man well known in sporting and especially boxing circles. The Marquess was a coarse, brutal man who accused Wilde of being a homosexual and corrupting his son. He sent a letter to Wilde's club stating his belief and provoked the dramatist into having no option other than to sue him for libel. The nobleman put up a defence of justification to the charge: for this had become a matter of criminal libel by virtue of the unfortunate consequences of s.11 of the Criminal Law Amendment Act 1887 which made acts of procuration of, indecency with, or intercourse between males whether eligible to consent or not, and whether in the privacy of their own homes or not, illegal. Consequently the Marquess was being tried for something which, should a jury consider it justified, would inevitably mean that Wilde could be tried for a breach of the section. Sullivan discovered that whilst he was friendly with and sympathetic to the plaintiff, his good friend and solicitor Charles Russell was also instructed by the Marquess. He retained the great Edward Carson, Q.C., and Wilde engaged Sir Edward Clarke. The great cause célèbre was held in the precincts of the Old Bailey and the three trials, in which the Marquess was acquitted by a jury of libelling Wilde, where subsequently a second jury remained undecided as to whether Wilde had committed a s.11 offence, and where finally Wilde was convicted and sentenced to a term of imprisonment, dragged on from 3rd April 1895 to 31st May. The great legal brains which became involved were: on the bench Mr Justice Henn, Mr Justice Charles and Mr Justice Wills, and to assist them from the Bar, Sir Francis Lockwood, the Solicitor-General, Charles Gill, William Matthews, Horace Avory and Travers Humphreys. Sullivan, not one to get involved in decisions as to which party to support, was also perterbed by the fact that here was a changing society, one that he felt was doing little more than hounding the eccentrics that had entertained it so freely only a decade earlier, and he gave up trying to reason and fled to Paris.

Gilbert's last legal battle was against C. H. Workman in the year prior to the author's death. Workman was the principal comedian of the D'Oyly Carte company in the 1906-9 revival series, taking all the Grossmith parts. Workman had formed a syndicate in 1909 entitled the Comic Opera (Syndicate) Limited, much on the same lines as, and very reminiscent of, the old Comedy Opera Company, to promote and sponsor a joint work to be written by Gilbert and Edward German of *Merrie England* fame. Gilbert produced *Fallen Fairies* for Workman but on stringent terms, one of which was that his adopted daughter, actress Nancy McIntosh, should play the female lead. This was to be in accordance with his usual demand that the authors of a piece should have complete control over the casting of its first production. Gilbert's financial terms were on a scale in accordance with the position he had attained in his profession and he dictated them to Workman:

The terms 15% on the gross receipts are extremely low and cannot be reduced in any way. My 10% is the fee that I have always received during the last 35 years, except when I was on sharing terms at the Savoy. It is what I received for 'The Mountebanks', 'His Excellency', 'Utopia Limited' (with a guaranteed minimum of £6,000 on certain conditions),'The Grand Duke' etc. In the case of the first two pieces the percentage was turned into a payment of £5,000 with contingencies. In those cases Cellier and Dr. Osmond Carr received 5% on gross receipts. On all these pieces I have received 10%
    . . .Please let me know your decision at once as another manager is coming on Friday to hear the piece and music unless I stop him. The cost of the production might have been anything about £2,500 but as a matter of fact it should not exceed £600[2].

The premiere passed off successfully, but less than a week later Workman informed Gilbert that Miss McIntosh would have to be replaced as he was under considerable pressure from his Syndicate backers to drop her from the lead. Gilbert was livid and threatened Workman that unless Nancy kept her place he would withdraw the show, writing on 27th December:

This is to give you notice that I intend to apply today to a Judge in Chambers for an ex parte injunction restraining you from playing 'Fallen Fairies' this evening except with Miss McIntosh or her accredited understudy Miss Venning in the part of Selene. I give you this notice that you may be in a position to face the contingency.

He forced a showdown dragging in his composer, German, as well, and to his consternation found that yet another partner of his did not wish to become involved. Nevertheless he went ahead on 13th January and sent a telegram to Workman, 'I forbid you to introduce into Fallen Fairies a song that has not been authorized by me - Gilbert.' His application for an injunction the following day was reported:

Times Law Reports   January 19th, 1910.
High Court of Justice
Chancery Division   Mr. Justice Neville
                    Gilbert v Workman: Injunction discharged

At the sitting of the Court today (18th) this case was mentioned. It
was an action by Sir William Gilbert to restrain Mr. Charles
Workman and the Comic Opera (Syndicate) Limited from
introducing or allowing to be introduced into the performance of
the Opera entitled 'Fallen Fairies or The Wicked World' now being
performed at the Savoy Theatre, a song that begins with the words
"Oh, love that rulest in our land." On Friday last, the 14th inst. on
the ex parte application of the plaintiff, an interim injunction was
granted until next Friday restraining the performance of that song.
Mr. S. Earle who appeared for the defendants now applied that the
injunction might be discharged and the action stayed as the
following arrangements had been made:-

'The defendants by their counsel admitting that they were not
entitled to introduce the song "Oh, love that rulest in our land"
without the permission of the plaintiff and expressing their regret
for having done so and acknowledge the plaintiff's courtesy and
consideration in allowing the song to be sung. And the defendants
undertaking to insert the following into all the house bills, at the
head of the list of characters throughout the run of the piece - That
the song "Oh, love that rulest in our land", will be sung in Act 2 by
the courtesy and consideration of Sir William Gilbert."

And the defendants undertaking to make no public reference, direct
or otherwise, to the fact that the song had been made the subject of
an injunction, without at the same time mentioning or inserting the
above notice in such public reference. And the defendants
undertaking to pay the plaintiff's costs as between Solicitor and
Client to be taxed in case the parties differ. Let the order of the 14th
January be discharged and all further proceedings stayed except so
far as may be necessary to give effect to this order.'

Mr. C. Gurdon, who appeared for the plaintiff, consented.
Mr. Justice Neville: You may take the order by consent.

The result was that the show was withdrawn after a mere six and a half weeks. Gilbert refused to let Workman carry out his original intention of reviving *Ruddigore* afterwards. Yet when revival rights in the Savoy Operas were put on the open market in June 1910, Workman put in a bid using Arthur Sullivan's nephew, Herbert, as an intermediary. Gilbert gave his offer short shrift: 'It is enough to say that no consideration of any kind would induce me to have dealings with a man of your stamp'[3].

Gilbert's last purposeful encounter with the law was in writing a dramatic sketch entitled *The Hooligan*, based on the sensational Crippen trial which so fascinated him. Through the auspicises of his good friend Sir Charles Matthews, the then Chief Magistrate, he attended the five days of Crippen's committal proceedings at Bow Street, although he was abroad for the trial at the Old Bailey. When he returned, a little time after the murderer's execution, he visited Pentonville prison where he saw the condemned man's cell and gibbet, by courtesy of Basil Thomson. He finished the one-act piece in January, 1911, and it was successfully played at the Coliseum from 27th February, running at various London and provincial theatres for two years. It was his last play, a swan-song in which he showed that his genius for realism was still strong. The message was clear and brutally simple in its Dickensian - or rather Gilbertian - attack on a social evil, with comedy but no laughter: the master dramatist had finished his works not so much on a deadly serious note but with a great indication that his audience, if they wanted truth as well as comedy, should look at the words they were laughing at.

Chapter 12

'Here we live and reign alone': On the bench

After long years of caricaturing both the bench and the Bar, Gilbert was suddenly put in the acutely embarrassing position of being offered a local lay magistracy. In 1891 he had taken a large mock-Tudor house at Harrow Weald to escape the bustle of the city. Set in 110 acres of woodland, Grim's Dyke became the country seat of the dramatist playing the role of squire. For perhaps the first time he found his neighbours, the owners of the nearby Blackwell estate and Bentley Priory, to be relatively tolerant, which was just as well since he imported a menagerie of pets that roamed the grounds freely. In 1893 he was approached by the High Sheriff of the county to join the local bench; that dignitary knew of Gilbert's background, as anyone would in the 1890s, and also knew of Gilbert's legal training, although he would probably have been the first to agree with the dramatist that for a lay magistrate that is indeed more of a drawback than an advantage. Later the same year he took up the time-honoured office of Justice of the Peace for the division of Gore Middlesex, and set about a concerned and conscientious effort to apply his precepts of justice to the cases that were brought before him.

His decisions soon created a reputation for himself, in quite a new sphere. Gilbert's sentencing was generally regarded as severe, although it became clear that he meted out only punishment which was just. More than that, it soon became apparent that, for the time, he had the rare distinction of being one of the few magistrates that would not bend over backwards to believe the word of the police automatically. In this he often became at odds with fellow members of his bench, and conflicts inevitably grew. He was particularly galled when his opinions were overruled two-to-one, in the three-member bench system. The consequence of such a conflict was for him to often take the extraordinary step of paying the prisoner's fine and costs personally, and especially so on behalf of debtors who, under archaic legislation, were still confined to prison until they could pay off their creditors.

The great man began his service at the Petty Sessions at Edgware, where his fellow magistrates became considerably in awe of him, and later, in 1910, began to alternate between these and the Harrow Sessions sitting at the Wealdstone courthouse. Reminiscences and records of Gilbert as a magistrate are both more numerous and more accurate than those of Gilbert at the Bar; naturally enough, since his fame was internationally recognised only after he had left the precincts of the law. This is why many thought it ironical and humorous that he should again become part of the system he so scathingly attacked. Thus, a good example of this difference of opinion that quite often arose with his fellow magistrates can be seen in a letter he wrote to the chairman of the bench, Irwin Cox, on 27th May 1909:

As I told you in court on Tuesday, I wholly disagree with the sentence that you passed on the man who was charged with assault, with threats, of a solicitor who had engaged against him in a previous case . . . . I am sorry that I did not dissociate myself from your judgement at the time - but, in future, when I happen to be sitting with you, I must ask you to give full value to any arguments I may use that may be in opposition to your judgement, as I shall certainly take the course of publicly disclaiming concurrence with your decision.

Two of Gilbert's jibes as a judicial humourist - exactly in the same vein as his 'nisi prius nuisance' - are very well-known. A solicitor before him recorded his comments in a case where a wife was complaining that her husband beat her, and that he had an abscess on his back: Gilbert mused that it was 'not a case of abscess making the heart grow fonder'. He also reprimanded an attempted suicide that should he try again the defendant might well end up beyond his jurisdiction.

Hesketh Pearson records[1] a more serious aspect of Gilbert's attempt to make his fellow magistrates feel the same sense of public responsibility as he himself. It arose out of the playwright's concern for more perjury actions to be brought against witnesses who lied blatantly:

A betting case was brought against the licensee of a public house, and as the verdict of the bench was sure to be followed by an action for perjury against the defendant one of the justices disagreed with the rest solely because he could not be bothered to go on with the case. Gilbert wrote a stern note to this easy-going fellow, concluding: 'It would be better that we should not sit together in the second court when that association can be avoided.' The case went to the Public Prosecutor, Sir Charles Mathews, who informed Gilbert privately that the magistrate concerned had been seen talking to the defendant during the lunch interval. Gilbert's annoyance with his associate did not affect his honesty and he denied the accusation, saying that the magistrate had lunched with his fellow-justiciaries. He then reported what had happened at his interview with Mathews to the accused magistrate. Mathews discovered what he had done and gravely reprimanded him. Admitting his error, which he said was due to his desire that the magistrate should not think he was acting inimically, Gilbert demanded the withdrawal of the reflection on his honour and good faith implied by the Public Prosecutor's statement that he had acted deliberately and intentionally. Sir Charles at once withdrew the reflection.

Gilbert's especial concern was with motoring offences, with which he dealt exceedingly severely, and employed the maximum penalty available to him whenever he felt it necessary. The reason he felt this way was twofold: first he was a keen motorist himself, starting with an American steam-powered car in 1902, and then acquiring a Cadillac, a Darracq, a Napier and a Rolls-Royce. Secondly, and of a very exceptional incentive, was the fact that on 25th February 1899, at the top of Grove Hill[2], near Harrow School, slap bang in the middle of the jurisdictional division of Gore and less than a mile from Grim's Dyke, was recorded a motor accident involving the first fatality ever known on the roads of Great Britain and Ireland. It was this occurrence that led to the enforcement of speed limits in the Harrow area on a scale unheard of in the rest of the kingdom. That motorists soon began to travel miles out of their way to avoid Gilbert's 'territory' is fact not folklore, and avoiding what was inevitably his wrath was no joke. He personally checked the justice and efficiency of police speeding 'traps' and if he felt that a defendant's driving was positively careless and inconsiderate, and not merely a subconscious infraction of the twenty miles per hour limit, he fined very heavily. In one famous instance he bitingly rebuked a rich young man who claimed that he was above the speeding laws. Gilbert fined him £5 for reckless driving and deflated the man's vanity by adding "had you been a gentleman, I should have fined you ten".

The grand old man of the theatre had found a new home, in which he enormously enjoyed, and worked hard at making a positive contribution to the administration of justice. He dealt fairly and firmly, and as far as he felt able within the bounds of the system, with a kindly regard for justice as he saw it. The practical application of new ways to avoid things he had criticised in his writing appealed to him greatly, but he found himself confronted by the staid approach that he could not hope to overcome. However his influence in the county was considerable, and he became appointed Deputy-Lieutenant of Middlesex in 1908. Gilbert remained active in his magisterial role until his tragic death on 29th May 1911 when, trying to rescue a young friend (Ruby Preece) who became in difficulties while swimming in Gilbert's lake at Grim's Dyke, he died of heart failure in the water. Many knew of his kindness and consideration whilst on the bench, as in looking after his theatre companies, and his duties that kept him very occupied gave him great pleasure in what were to be his final days.

Chapter 13

'Not in blank verse and three hundred years old': A note on censorship

In 1751 theatres and music halls were specifically mentioned in an act of Parliament designed to regulate 'disorderly houses'; and as late as 1843, people associated with the theatre were still regarded as rogues and vagabonds by the law. In that latter year the Theatres Act extended and redefined the powers of the Lord Chamberlain with regard to the licensing and censorship of public presentations:

> s14.   The Lord Chamberlain may forbid any Play.] -And be it enacted, that it shall be lawful for the Lord Chamberlain for the Time being, whenever he shall be of the opinion that it is fitting for the Preservation of Good Manners, Decorum, or of the public Peace so to do, to forbid the acting or presenting any Stage Play, or any Act, Scene, or Part thereof, or any Prologue or Epilogue, or any Part thereof, anywhere in Great Britain, or in such Theatres as he shall specify, and either absolutely or for such Time as he shall think fit.

This power was also extended to lay Justices of the Peace under the conditions envisaged in the traditional Riot Act. Initially the Lord Chamberlain's office was empowered by the 1843 Act to make

144

regulations concerning all aspects of theatrical management, from fire control and crowd safety, later transferred to the London County Council, to what could actually be presented on stage:

Regulations As To Theatres

13. A copy of every new piece, or alterations of old pieces intended to be produced, to be forwarded for Licence to the Examiner of Plays seven clear days before such intended production. No alteration of the text when licensed for representation to be permitted without sanction.

14. Copies of all Play Bills to be sent to the Lord Chamberlain's Office every Monday, and whenever a change of performance is announced.

15. Notice of the change of title of a piece to be given to the Examiner of Plays.

16. The name and private address of the actual and responsible manager to be printed in legible type at the head of each bill.

17. Admission to be given at all times to authorised officers of the Lord Chamberlain's Department, and of the Police.

18. No profanity or impropriety of language to be permitted on the stage.

19. No indecency of dress, dance or gesture to be permitted on the stage.

20. No offensive personalities or representations of living persons to be permitted on the stage, nor anything calculated to produce riot or a breach of the peace.

21. No exhibition of wild beasts or dangerous performances to be permitted on the stage. No women or children to be hung from the flies, nor fixed in positions from which they cannot release themselves.

22. No masquerade or public ball to be permitted in the Theatre.

23. No encouragement to be given to improper characters to assemble, or to ply their calling in the Theatre.

Theatre Licences are granted for one year, from the 29th September. Licences are granted also for shorter periods, but all Licences cease on the day above-mentioned.

BY ORDER OF THE LORD CHAMBERLAIN
ST. JAMES'S PALACE.

These rules were still in force, in one form or another, at British theatres until 1968[1].

Gilbert as a writer grew up with these restrictions, and as unpopular as they were with him and his fellow dramatists, they became quickly institutionalised, and something to be attacked with humour or good-natured grumbling rather than serious radical opposition. Gilbert was probably affected less than other writers, his work being conservative and even prudish. He had little need of vulgarity in order to raise a laugh, and reminiscences back-stage at the Savoy show that he was always opposed to anything that might possibly be considered an impropriety. It is Gilbert as the author speaking through Archibald Grosvenor in *Patience* when he says, "I believe I am right in saying that there is not one word in that decalet which is calculated to bring the blush of shame to the cheek of modesty...it is purity itself". Gilbert was his own, and his company's, censor.

The effect of these rules, however, was to be seen in the burlesques of the period and Gilbert's friend Hollingshead had more than a few problems with the Chamberlain's men, down the road at the Gaiety. After his many battles with on the one hand the Examiner of Plays and on the other an era of scathing critics, he wrote:

'as a manager, I had nothing to do with the taste or even the morality of any drama produced under my management. The Government had kindly relieved me from this responsibility by appointing a reader and licensor of plays and accepting a fee for this watch-dog work. When I had paid my one, two, or three guineas to the Lord Chamberlain's office I left him to justify the amusement he had officially sanctioned and I had provided for my public'[2].

In one area however, Gilbert's writing style was severely restricted. For in as much as he did not have to rely on vulgarity, in all his plays, from the early burlesques and through the period of the Savoy Operas, a hard-hitting and sometimes bitter satire was punched home to the audience, attacking nearly all the cherished Victorian institutions. It was in Gilbert's satire, and especially in his political satire, that he fell foul of the Lord Chamberlain and Regulation 20. After the incident of *The Wicked World* and 'the *Era*' quarrel, Gilbert determined to salvage what he could from that piece, and using his pseudonym of F. Latour Tomline he worked in collaboration with Gilbert à Becket to produce a burlesque of the same plot as a political satire, for Marie Litton at the

Court Theatre. As *The Happy Land* it opened on 3rd March 1873, and due to public interest in the attention paid to it by the Chamberlain's men, and indeed the Prime Minister himself, it ran for two hundred performances. On stage was to be seen a close portrayal of three leading Liberal politicians and members of the Government: Gladstone, Ayrton and Lowe[3]. The Lord Chamberlain barred its performance until the representation of the politicians was suitably altered so that they became less recognisable. In response to this the same costumes were retained and the collars of their coats turned up, whilst their hat brims were pulled down, which gave 'Gladstone' the air of a Guy Fawkes conspirator. Gilbert was to admit years later that it was a piece of youthful folly, but at the time he was flattered by the real Gladstone attending and enjoying the play: it was clear that the author had cleverly capitalised on the Chamberlain's censorship being imposed, but the reluctance of the authorities to close down the show altogether must have proved to Gilbert that his satire was relatively immune from prosecution. Established, wealthy and successful, he showed even less restraint in the Savoy operas and, in later life, in his portrayals of well-known men of the day; notable examples being Fred Sullivan in *Trial by Jury* being made up as the Judge to resemble Sir Alexander Cockburn, the then Lord Chief Justice; George Grossmith in the *Pirates of Penzance* having Major General Stanley appear to be Sir Garnet Wolseley; and again in *Patience*, where Reginald Bunthorne was clearly made up as James MacNeill Whistler[4].

Gilbert continually pokes fun at the institution of censorship and it is very difficult to tell whether there is a genuine tinge of bitterness, or merely good humour. In *Rosencrantz and Guildenstern* (1891) the two title players are searching for the manuscript of King Claudius' banned play:

Ophelia:	In his capacity as Lord Chamberlain (All bow reverentially at mention of this functionary) he has one copy. I this night, when all the Court is drowned in sleep, will creep with stealthy foot into his den and there abstract the precious manuscript!
Guildenstern:	...Your father may detect you.
Ophelia:	Oh, dear no.

My father spends his long official days
In reading all the rubbishing new plays
From ten to four at work he may be found:
And then - my father sleeps exceeding sound!

Two years later, in *Utopia Limited*, the Chamberlain is one of the 'Flowers of Progress' of British life bringing their ways to the tropical island:

Zara: This is a Lord High Chamberlain,
       Of purity the gauge -
       He'll cleanse our Court from moral stain
       And purify our Stage.

and later, the Flowers of Progress having got to work, the Utopian islanders consider the changes -

King: The Chamberlain our native stage has purged, beyond a question
         Of 'risky' situation and indelicate suggestion;
         No piece is tolerated if it's costumed indiscreetly,
Flowers: In short this happy country has been Anglicized completely!
Phantis: ... our Burlesque Theatre is absolutely
         ruined! ...Are you aware that the Lord Chamberlain,
         who has his own views as to the best means of
         elevating the national drama, has declined to license
         any play that is not in blank verse and three hundred
         years old - as in England?

As if in reply, but also to prove that the Theatre Act regulations were not merely formalities, Gilbert was given an unpleasant surprise when for the 1906-9 revival series Helen D'Oyly Carte applied to the Lord Chamberlain's office for an annual licence to perform *The Mikado;* the application was refused on the grounds of a proposed visit by a member of the Japanese Imperial household, Prince Fushimi, in August 1907, and that it might cause offence. In early May the subject was discussed on the floor of the House of Commons and even the Prime Minister was drawn into the argument. It had started on the 2nd with a question to the Foreign Secretary:

MR. VINCENT KENNEDY (Cavan.W.): I beg to ask the Secretary of State for Foreign Affairs if he will say whether the views of the Japanese were consulted in withdrawing the licence for The Mikado; on whose advice did the Lord Chamberlain act; and will he state what were the considerations that prompted his action in this matter; whether the responsibility for the decision rests solely with the Lord Chamberlain; and will he generally reconsider the whole question as affecting the case of this play with a view to withdrawing the prohibition and limiting, by legislation or otherwise, the power of the Lord Chamberlain?

SIR EDWARD GREY: I understand that the Lord Chamberlain acted on his own responsibility solely. But, with regard to the best part of the Question, I may say that if my advice had been asked or given it would have been entirely in accord with the action which the Lord Chamberlain has taken, for reasons which I would have thought would have been obvious at this moment. I am not, therefore, prepared to reconsider the Question, even if it were in my province to do so.

MR. VINCENT KENNEDY: Who is responsible in this House for the actions of the Lord Chamberlain?

SIR EDWARD GREY asked for notice.

On the following day another attempt was made to raise a discussion on the issue, and with a body it was hoped of more influence, the Senior Service:

MR. TREVELYAN (Yorkshire W. R. Elland): I beg to ask the Secretary to the Admiralty whether naval bands have been forbidden to play any selections from 'The Mikado'; and, if so, will he explain the reason for this prohibition.

THE SECRETARY TO THE ADMIRALTY (MR. EDMUND ROBERTSON, Dundee): The licence for the play was withdrawn by the Lord Chamberlain, who asked that instructions should be given to all naval and marine bands to exclude from their musical programmes any music from 'The Mikado' during the visit of His Imperial Highness Prince Fushimi of Japan to this country.

VISCOUNT TURNOUR (Sussex Horsham): Can the Right Hon. Gentleman state more fully the grounds on which the Admiralty came to this extraordinary decision?

MR. EDMUND ROBERTSON: I have stated fully the grounds.

MR. GEORGE FABER (York): May I ask whether there is any buffoonery in the music?

MAJOR ANSTRUTHER-GRAY (St. Andrews, Burghs): Will the Government reconsider their decision?

Finally on 6th March the Prime Minister was questioned on the matter:

MR. VINCENT KENNEDY (Cavan W.): I beg to ask the Prime Minister if he will state whether any Minister of the Crown is responsible to the House of Commons for the action or inaction of the Lord Chamberlain.

THE PRIME MINISTER and FIRST LORD OF THE TREASURY (SIR HENRY CAMPBELL-BANNERMAN, Stirling Burghs): The Home Secretary has been in the habit of answering the Parliamentary Questions on behalf of the Lord Chamberlain, and of seeing that he is furnished with the best legal advice; but it would require legislation to make him Parliamentarily responsible for the Lord Chamberlain.

The *Pall Mall Gazette* had, in common with all social magazines and newspapers, been closely following events, and took up the cause in its editorial of 1st May 1907:

We shall await with real interest the Prime Minister's reply to the question Mr. Vincent Kennedy will put to him tomorrow with respect to the play of 'Hamlet'. He will be asked whether his attention has been drawn to the fact that in the play the King of Denmark is portrayed as a murderer; whether, in view of the fact that Denmark is a friendly Power, he will request the Lord Chamberlain to prohibit the further production of this play; or whether he intends to introduce legislation to define and limit the powers of the Lord Chamberlain. Really, this withdrawal of 'The Mikado' licence, after twenty years of inoffensive fooling, seems to argue a lack of sense of humour somewhere, and does set people asking how many classical English plays may have to disappear unvenerably at the capricious hest of an excessive diplomatic delicacy. It is a great nonsense for the play has been produced in Japan itself; but it is more than nonsense - it is quite an alarming grievance. Since the art of government began it was known to be specially dangerous to interfere with people's amusements; but a democracy with classic ones constitutes what the Americans call a new proposition.

Generally, the newspapers jumped at the story and the curious action taken by the Chamberlain, (especially since the opera had been played for twenty years, and had been translated into Japanese itself) affected not only Gilbert and the Savoy Company, but also various amateur groups throughout the country. A group performing at the Lyceum, Sheffield, deliberately flaunted the censor's instructions, and performances at Cripplegate in London and at Middlesbrough were actually closed. It was not until 28th April 1908, that the D'Oyly Carte Company was allowed an unhindered revival; although unconfirmed reports had it that when the Japanese royal party landed from the warship carrying them, a naval band on the ship's foredeck was playing selections from ...*The Mikado*!

The final word on stage censorship was Gilbert's himself. He appeared, on 19th August 1909, before the Parliamentary Joint Select Committee on Stage Plays (Censorship) to give evidence as an expert witness, as one of the leaders of his profession:

> Sir William S. Gilbert is called in and Examined.
> Chairman: Your long experience as a dramatic author would lead you to form some conclusions with regard to the censorship?
>   - Yes. I am very strongly of opinion that there should be a Censor, but I am still more strongly of opinion that the responsibility of vetoing a play should not rest exclusively on the shoulders of that Censor but that there should be an appeal from him to a body consisting of an arbiter appointed by the author, another arbiter appointed by the Lord Chamberlain, and a third arbiter appointed by those two. These are the views that I had the honour of submitting to the Home Secretary some eighteen months ago, or thereabouts, in accordance with the resolution arrived at by a body of about a dozen dramatic authors who were all more or less of that opinion. Some were of the opinion that there should be no Censor, but that if there was a Censor, that would be the most convenient and legitimate way in which his functions should be controlled.
>   But I gather from you that some leading dramatic authors are of the opinion that there should be a Censor?
>   - Some of them on that occasion were of that opinion eighteen months ago.
>   So that you are not single in that opinion?
>   - I believe not.

Why do you think that a censorship of some kind is desirable?

- Because I think that the stage of a theatre is not the proper pulpit from which to disseminate doctrines of possibly anarchism, or socialism, and of agnosticism; and it is not the proper platform upon which to discuss questions of adultery and free love, before a mixed audience, composed of persons of all ages and both sexes, of all ways of thinking, of all ways of life and various degrees of education.

And you consider that control after the production of a play would not be adequate?

- I do not think it would. It appears to me that the first night's audience has as great a claim to be protected from outrage as the audiences that follow.

Do you consider that censorship as at present constituted inflicts any injury upon the English drama?

- I am not in a position to say, because I know nothing about the plays that have been censored. I only know about those that have been passed.

You have not read any of the censored plays?

- I have not read any of the plays that are talked about - "Monna Vanna", "Press Cuttings", and so forth. I know nothing about them.

Are you quite of opinion that if the censorship were remodelled in the way that you suggest no injury would be done to the English drama?

- I am very far from saying that but I think it would be a very important protection to the author from any act of injustice or want of judgement on the part of the Censor, and it would relieve the Censor of a weight of intolerable responsibility of ruining the hopes of professional authors through an opinion when he himself may possibly admit to be fallacious.

Should you say that such an action should be open, not only in the case of a play that had not yet been performed, but which the Examiner of Plays subsequently intended to stop the performance of, owing to the special circumstances of the moment?

- I think it should apply to both cases.

I have in my mind your own case and the stoppage of your play "The Mikado" recently. Do you consider that an appeal should have lain in that case?

- I consider that it was an unwarrantable and illegal act altogether. I also think that it was an act of depredation to take a play, which was worth £10,000 to me, and without any communication with me to prohibit its performance.

You would not wish to be a casus belli?

- I should certainly have made myself out so but the play for the moment happened to be in the hands of Mrs. D'Oyly Carte.

I mean a casus belli between the two Powers concerned?

- I do not think the Powers were concerned at all. The music of "The Mikado" was being played on the Japanese ships in the Medway during the prohibition of the play - a sort of musical commentary on the absurdity of the prohibition.

With reference to this tribunal of appeal that you suggest, by whom do you think that the expense of reference to that tribunal should be borne?

- I think that in the event of an appeal being rejected it should fall upon the author. I think in the event of an appeal being successful it should fall upon the Lord Chamberlain's Office. I think in the event of their being, so to speak, contributing negligence on both sides, the costs should be apportioned as the majority of referees should direct.

The procedure you think should be that of the courts of law?

- Precisely.

Do you think that music-halls should be allowed to produce any dramatic performances they like?

- I think that all dramatic performances should be licensed by the Censor.

Would you extend that to songs?

- No; I do not think it would be possible for the Censor to exercise control over every item and every turn, as they call it, in the music-halls.

Do you think it would be possible for an Act of Parliament to draw the line between dramatic entertainment and the other entertainments given at the music-halls?

- I believe it held that an Act of Parliament can do anything and perhaps it can do that, but I am not prepared to say that it would be a judicious thing.

I understand you to say that it would be desirable to have a censorship over dramatic performances in music-halls, but not over songs in music-halls?

- I think it is desirable for a censorship over songs if it could be achieved but I do not see what machinery could be applied for that purpose.

Therefore you have to draw a distinction between those things which are to be held dramatic performances and those things which are to be held to be songs. For example when persons sing a song it may or may not be a dramatic performance, according to the way in which it is done?

- Yes; if a story which instances some dramatic action were suggested by a song I should say that it would be such as would be analogous to the dramatic performances that are now permitted in the music-halls under certain conditions.

Do you think it is possible to draw a distinction between these two classes of cases to say, roughly, what is a dramatic entertainment and what is not?

- I do not know that I could suggest any means by which a test could be applied. It seems to me that all performances that require licence for a theatre should require a licence for a music-hall.

You are aware, of course, of the controversy that is proceeding between the theatre managers and the music-hall managers as to production of sketches?

- Yes.

Lord Newton: Would you mind telling me exactly what did occur in the case of "The Mikado"? As far as I know I was informed that the Lord Chamberlain or Censor - it was the Lord Chamberlain in point of fact - had forbidden the production of "The Mikado" on the ground that it might give offence to our Japanese allies?

- I was not communicated with the Lord Chamberlain; he did not refer to me at all; he simply took my property and placed an embargo upon it.

You did not have any correspondence with him?

- Not before he stopped the performance; I did afterwards. Lord Althorp sent for me, and I had an interview with him at St. James's Palace.

It appears to me that it was a case in which the Lord Chamberlain interfered, and not the Censor?

- It was the Lord Chamberlain.

The Censor had nothing to do with it?

- No.

It was an autocratic action on the part of the Lord Chamberlain?

- So I understand from him - at the representation of a member of the Japanese Embassy.

Therefore it would be very unfair to blame the Censor for the action which was taken?

- Absolutely. I looked upon it as entirely the action of the Lord Chamberlain.

Is that the only occasion on which you have had any difficulty with the Lord Chamberlain or the Censor?

- No. Many years ago I had a difficulty with the Lord Chamberlain over a piece called "The Happy Land". That piece, I should explain, was not written by me, it was informed by me; that is to say, I drew up the scenario for a private performance to take place at the old Prince of Wales's Theatre on an Ash Wednesday, a day when theatres at that time were closed. Before this could take place I read the scenario to Miss Litton, the manageress of the Court Theatre, who was delighted with it and asked me to allow her to have it. I said that that was impossible as it was written for a special private performance. That special private performance did not come off, owing to a death, and I then said to Miss Litton, "Here is the scenario, take it and use it if you can, but do not describe me as the author of it." It was written by Gilbert à Beckett; and she produced it at the Court Theatre.

If I remember aright, it ran for some time before any alteration was insisted upon?

- For about a week.

Then it was the Censor of the Lord Chamberlain who came down?

- I believe it was the Lord Chamberlain, but he did not communicate with me; he communicated with the manageress, Miss Litton.

That had nothing to do with foreign politics; it was a question of domestic politics?

- Yes; and perhaps I may be allowed to say that my maturer judgement teaches me that the Lord Chamberlain's interference was absolutely justified.

To turn to another point, you probably know as much as anybody else, if not more, about the theatre-going public. Should you say that the theatre-going public was dissatisfied with the Censor as an institution?

- I do not think that the theatre-going public consider the Censor at all.

You do not know that they were aware of his existence?

- No.

And had it not been for the appointment of this Committee many people might never have heard of his existence?

- Probably not[5].

THIS IS HOW GILBERT AND SULLIVAN TREATED THE DIRECTORS.

"How Gilbert and Sullivan treated the Directors". One of the many satirical caricatures that appeared after the riot at the Opera Comique.

John Hollingshead, the great innovator, from an original cartoon.

Sir Arthur Sullivan at 44. *(photo: Jeremy Zeid after the original by Ellis & Walle*

"Sir Arthur Sullivan and Mr. W. S. Gilbert have quarrelled and they never speak as they pass by." *Midland Weekly News*, 24th May 1890.

Mr. Justice Day. *Punch*, 26th October 1889.

Edward Carson, Q. C. *(artist: Marianne Fountain after the original by Spy)*

PART IV

'An affidavit from a thunderstorm, or a few words on oath from a heavy shower'

Chapter 14

'At the very heart of the fog': the Dickens influence

No social writer working after the first half of the nineteenth century could fail to have been affected by the most popular author ever to use the English language for his craft, Charles Dickens. Gilbert was; and profoundly so. He was born in the same year as the first publication of *The Posthumous Papers of The Pickwick Club*, in 1836, and there can be little doubt that he was spoon-fed on Dickens' works as he grew older. Whilst Dickens was writing from the late 1830s until the early 1850s setting his period works mainly in the 1820s Gilbert savoured the taste of what the great author was trying to do, and later might be thought to have adopted a social message of his own, in spite of the fact that the society that Dickens was concerned with, and more especially the social evils that concerned him, were fifty years away from Gilbert's own day. Nevertheless Dickens was Gilbert's earliest professional hero, and one of the Savoyard's earliest works was a dramatisation of *Great Expectations* and even his last stage work, *The Hooligan*, though original, could well have been the setting of a Dickens short story.

Dickens shared with Gilbert an experience of the law at first hand, early on in his life. Both were familiar with the precincts of the Inns of Court, although unlike Gilbert, Dickens also knew of the inside both of the Fleet and Marshalsea prisons in which his father had been incarcerated for debt. At 15 he had started work clerking for Edward Blackmore's firm of attorneys at 1 Raymond's Building, Gray's Inn. Within three years he had decided to take up law reporting and was attending Lord Chancellor Lyndhurst's court, the Doctors' Commons, and the Chief Magistrates court at Bow Street, at a time when the 'Runners' were being transformed into Peel's newly envisaged 'police' force. Looking back, Gilbert greatly admired Dickens' success as a private litigant when, in 1844, he had successfully protected himself from five pirate versions of his *Christmas Carol*, although that success was not repeated in a later action to protect his interest in *Martin Chuzzlewit*.

Both Gilbert and Sullivan were friendly with the writer's son, Henry Fielding Dickens, a silk, and certainly Sullivan as a young man knew the father also. Dickens numbered many lawyers among his friends - men who were influential and at the top of their profession - including Lords Denman and Campbell, Mr Justice Talfourd[1], and Sullivan's good friend, Lord Chief Justice Cockburn. Just as Gilbert would have known Dickens' friends, he shared the writer's great love for the places that Dickens chose for his characters to work and live: Traddles lived in Gray's Inn; Tom Pinch used to meet his sister in Fountain Court; Sir John Chester had rooms in Paper Buildings; Pip lived in Garden Court; Lightwood and Wrayburn were among Dickens' firms of attorneys in Middle Temple Lane; the murder in *Hunted Down* was enacted at the end house in King's Bench Walk; Grewgious, Picket and Gargery were associated with Staple Inn and Barnard's Inn; and Serjeant Snubbin had his chambers at Old Square, Lincoln's Inn. Indeed the greater part of *Pickwick* was written whilst Dickens lived at a house in Furnival's Inn.

The legal satire in Dickens' work appealed to Gilbert as a trained lawyer, and as a budding author himself; the thumbnail plots and characters thatDickens created became a model for the kind of finished product Gilbert wanted to achieve. This is the starting point for the similarities that have become so apparent in their work. Both men, working either in or closely by the atmosphere of legal thinking pervading the Temple, were critical of the deficiencies in the legal system of their day. Both lived through a period of great upheaval in the law which fundamentally changed procedure and the court systems, criminal penalties and legal personnel, though not the conditions of penal institutions. Dickens saw this in the 1830s; Gilbert in the 1870s. Much was done to remedy the situation that the authors had pointedly complained about, yet Gilbert persisted in sniping at the system as if conditions were no better than in Dickens' time. A good illustration of this is the treatment by both authors of the Court of Chancery to which each regularly turned his attention with particular emphasis, and which institution may be taken to have epitomised for them the ills of the law.

In August 1853, that is two years before Gilbert entered the Inner Temple, Dickens wrote his most blistering attack on the Chancery Court in *Bleak House*, in one of his most famous passages:

> The raw afternoon is rawest, and the dense fog is densest, and the muddy streets are muddiest, near that leaden-headed old obstruction, appropriate ornament for the threshold of a leaden-headed old corporation: Temple Bar. And hard by Temple Bar, in Lincoln's Inn Hall, at the very heart of the fog, sits the Lord High Chancellor in his High Court of Chancery.
>
> On such an afternoon, if ever, the Lord High Chancellor ought to be sitting here - as here he is - with a foggy glory round his head, softly fenced in with crimson cloth and curtains, addressed by a large advocate with great whiskers, a little voice, and an interminable brief, and outwardly directing his contemplation to the lantern in the roof, where he can see nothing but fog. On such an afternoon, some scores of members of the High Court of Chancery bar ought to be - as here they are - mistily engaged in one of the ten thousand stages of an endless cause, tripping one another up on slippery precedents, groping knee-deep in technicalities, running their goat-hair and horse-hair warded heads against walls of words, and making a pretense of equity with serious faces, as players might. On such an afternoon, the various solicitors in the cause, some two or three of whom have inherited it from their fathers who made a fortune from it, ought to be - as are they not? - ranged in a line, in a long matted well (but you may look in vain for Truth at the bottom of it), between the registrar's red table and the silk gowns, with bills, cross-bills, answers, rejoinders, injunctions, affidavits, issues, references to masters, masters' reports mountains of costly nonsense piled before them[5]

At the time when this work was set, the Chancellorship of Lord Lyndhurst, in or about 1827, the Chancery Court was in a particularly bad state[3], and this passage well reflects the evils of delay and expense - namely legal foggery. In term time it sat at Westminster Hall, but out of term it sat in the old hall of Lincoln's Inn which it continued to do throughout the period in which Gilbert was practising at the Bar, and even a few years after the Savoy was built. The Judiciary and Parliament both regarded the state of affairs then as appalling, yet little was to be done until *Bleak House* was published. The abuses were due to the archaic nature of its procedure and machinery - both of which were medieval. Dickens claimed that he was not exaggerating and wrote in his introduction:

> Everything set forth in these pages concerning the Court of Chancery is substantially true. At the present moment there is a suit before the court which was commenced nearly twenty years ago; in which thirty to forty counsel have been known to appear at one time; in which costs incurred amount to £70,000; which is a friendly suit, and which is no nearer to its termination than when it was begun.

Consequently he presents his readers with:

> the greatest of Chancery suits known, in itself a monument of Chancery practice, in which every difficulty, every contingency, every masterly fiction, every form of procedure known in that court is represented over and over again and a cause that could not exist outside this free and great country: Jarndyce v Jarndyce.

Gilbert developed a fascination for the Chancery Court, though he never practised there. His attention was drawn to the concept of wards of Chancery which was a residue of the medieval jurisdiction of the Crown as guardian of the interests, and more particularly the estates of young people until they reached the age of majority. Wardship is a very popular theme with Gilbert, and is introduced as early as *The Pirates of Penzance:*

> Mabel: 'Hold, monsters! 'Ere your pirate caravanserai
> Proceed, against our will, to wed us all,
> Just bear in mind that we are Wards in Chancery,
> And father is a Major-General!

And the plot of *Iolanthe* revolves around proceedings concerning both that court, and one of Gilbert's most colourful and best-loved characters, the Lord Chancellor. Grossmith took great delight in making-up as the then Chancellor, Lord Selbourne; yet while it is fair to consider such similarities as there are between Dickens and Gilbert writing about the law, it is important to draw a distinction between Selbourne's court and that of Lord Lyndhurst. Certainly with such positive and modern-thinking men as George Jessel on the bench, the court system was by then moving forward rather than stagnating. By 1882, Gilbert was writing jokes at the expense of the Lord Chancellor merely in good humour, and not to point out in any exaggerated way what he might have thought was a contemporary social evil. A great advance had been made even since his call to the Bar less than twenty years before. Thus Strephon's complaint, and the Lord Chancellor's well-known aria, are no more than an example of Gilbert's delightful and good-natured silliness:

Strephon: To all my tearful prayers (the Lord Chancellor) answers me, "a shepherd lad is no fit helpmate for a Ward in Chancery". I stood in court, and there I sang him songs of Arcadee with flageolet accompaniment - in vain. At first he seemed amused, so did the Bar, but very quickly wearying of my songs, bade me get out.
A servile usher...led me, still singing, into Chancery Lane!'

Lord Chancellor: The law is the true embodiment of everything that's excellent,
It has no kind of fault or flaw,
And I, my Lords, embody the law.
The constitutional guardian I,
Of pretty young Wards in Chancery,
All very agreeable girls - and none
Are over the age of twenty-one...

But though the compliment implied
Inflates me with legitimate pride,
It nevertheless can't be denied
That it has its inconvenient side.
For I'm not so old, and not so plain,
And I'm quite prepared to marry again,
But there'd be the deuce to pay in the Lords,
If I fell in love with one of my Wards!

> And everyone who'd marry a Ward
> Must come to me for my accord,
> And in my court I sit all day,
> Giving agreeable girls away - ...'

The similarity with Dickens was immediately obvious to the critics if not to the public. A comparison between the cross-examination of Sam Weller by Serjeant Buzfuz in the cause of Bardell v Pickwick from the *Pickwick Papers,* and the Lord Chancellor examining Strephon, can suffice:

Weller: Quite enough to get, Sir, as the soldier said ven they ordered him three hundred and fifty lashes.

Mr. Justice Stareleigh:[4] You must not tell us what the soldier, or any other man, said, Sir, it's not evidence.

....

Lord Chancellor:[5]   At present there is no evidence before the court that chorused Nature has interested herself in the matter.

Strephon: No evidence! You have my word for it, I tell you she bade me take my love,

Lord Chancellor: Ah! But, my good sir, you musn't tell us what she told you - it's not evidence. Now, an affidavit from a thunderstorm, or a few words on oath from a heavy shower, would meet with all the attention they deserve.

Goldberg states that *Punch*, in its 9th December 1882, review of *Iolanthe* had accused Gilbert of plagiarising Dickens. This took the form of a back-handed compliment:

The first-night audience roared with laughter at the Lord Chancellor informing Strephon that the latter must not tell him "what Nature had said, as it was not evidence", just as if they had never heard of Sam Weller being rebuked by Mr. Justice Stareleigh, when the former spiced his evidence with "as the soldier said."

Following its usual pattern of snide remarks against Gilbert's talent and originality, Burnand's magazine also claimed that the song 'Said I to myself said I' was a traditional folk song, and:

In the Second Act the patter-song, descriptive of a nightmare, seems to have been suggested by Planche's well-known, "I'm in such a flutter I scarcely can utter."

Punch was, of course, not the only one to spot similarities and Gilbert's friend Rowland-Brown wrote in *Cornhill* magazine about the dramatist's peculiar fondness for Dickens, and points out a passage from *A Tale of Two Cities* in which 'Mr. Stryver's self-examination of himself before an imaginary court on the subject of his offer of marriage to Lucie Manette foreshadows unmistakably the remarkable performance of the Lord Chancellor in *Iolanthe*.'

Those familiar with *Pickwick* and the action of Bardell v Pickwick will recognize immediately the model upon which Gilbert based his plot in *Trial By Jury*[6]. However, actions for breach of promise were as common in Gilbert's day as they were in Dickens', and could be read about daily in the newspapers or be seen posted on the lists at the High Court, City Court, Quarter Sessions and even the Old Bailey. Both writers were working before the new Royal Courts of Justice opened in 1884, and both were aware that the different courts and offices were scattered over London. The Court of Chancery, and the Master of the Rolls Court, were upon either side of Chancery Lane. The Masters' offices of the King's Bench were in the Temple; those of the Common Pleas at Serjeant's Inn; and those of the Exchequer were at Stone Buildings, Lincoln's Inn; whilst all three of these full courts sat at Westminster Hall. Dickens set Bardell v Pickwick in the Court of Common Pleas, where the highest branch of the legal profession, the Serjeants-at-law, then had an exclusive right of audience. Gilbert's text shows the action of Angelina against Edwin to be in the Court of Exchequer, next door, where ordinary mortal barristers could perform. Writers analysing both have complained of procedural inaccuracies, but neither piece was produced by its author in a serious vein. The works had comedy in common, rather than a shared existence of serious social criticism, and whilst Gilbert's relies more on farce, both are uniquely 'theatrical' gems. Yet both within the running plot and the dialogue it is a wonder that *Punch's* critic failed to point out that demand for heavy damages for poor Angelina could have been directly taken from Serjeant Buzfuz's magnificent climax to his opening speech to the jury:

'But Pickwick, gentlemen, Pickwick, the ruthless destroyer of this domestic oasis in the desert of Goswell Street - Pickwick, who has choked up the well and thrown ashes on the sward - Pickwick, who comes before you today with his heartless tomato sauce and warming-pans - Pickwick still rears his head with unblushing effrontery, and gauges without a sign on the ruin he has made. Damages, gentlemen, - heavy damages - is the only punishment with which you can visit him; the only recompense you can award to my client. And for those damages she now appeals to an enlightened, a high-minded, a right-feeling, a conscientious, a dispassionate, a sympathising, a contemplative jury of her civilised countrymen.'

With this beautiful peroration, Mr. Serjeant Buzfuz sat down, and Mr. Justice Stareleigh woke up.

The Central Criminal Court was another favourite of both Gilbert and Dickens. On the bailey site stood Newgate Prison next to the court, and Dickins had Fagin tried there and locked away next door to await his execution. Dickens' two most poignant descriptions of the Old Bailey occur in *Great Expectations*[7]:

I saw the great black dome of St. Paul's bulging at me from behind a grim stone building which a bystander said was Newgate Prison. Following the wall of the jail, I found the roadway covered with straw to deaden the noise of passing vehicles; and from this, and from the quantity of people standing about, smelling strongly of spirits and beer, I inferred that the trials were on.

While I looked about me here, an exceedingly dirty and partially drunk minister of justice asked me if I would like to step in and hear a trial or so; informing me that he could give me a front place for half-a-crown, whence I should command a full view of the Lord Chief Justice in his wig and robes - mentioning that awful personage like a waxwork, and presently offering him at the reduced price of eighteenpence. As I declined the proposal on the plea of an appointment, he was so good as to take me into the yard and show me where the gallows was kept, and also where people were publicly whipped, and then he showed me the Debtors' Door, out of which culprits came to be hanged; heightening the interest of that dreadful portal by giving me to understand that "four on 'em" would come out at that door the day after to-morrow at eight in the morning to be killed in a row.

and in *A Tale of Two Cities*, which is set thirty years earlier[8]:

> They hanged at Tyburn, in those days, so the street outside
> Newgate had not obtained one infamous notoriety that has since
> attached to it. But, the gaol was a vile place, in which most kinds of
> debauchery and villainy were practised, and where dire diseases
> were bred, that came into court with the prisoners, and sometimes
> rushed straight from the dock at my Lord Chief Justice himself, and
> pulled him off the bench. It had more than once happened, that the
> Judge in the black cap pronounced his own doom as certainly as the
> prisoner's, and even died before him. For the rest, the Old Bailey
> was famous as a kind of deadly inn-yard, from which pale travellers
> set out continually, in carts and coaches, on a violent passage into
> the other world.

Gilbert referred to the court, but not the prison, and used a variety of
expressions, Old Bailey, Ancient Bailey, or even, as in *Pirates:*

> Chorus: 'No pirate band shall take its stand
> At the Central Criminal Court[9].

Westminster Hall attracted the favour of Gilbert in his writing, and he
knew exactly what it was like to brieflessly dance like a 'semi-
despondent fury' there. Dickens did not leave a picture of the main
courts - Common Pleas, King's Bench and Exchequer - that were
situated in the corners inside the great hall of St. Stephen. He wrote of
the Chancery courts outside the hall itself but nearby; these were
rehoused in a building together in 1828, and comprised the Bail Court,
the Lord Chancellor's and Vice-Chancellor's Court, and the Master of
the Rolls' Court, to all of which Gilbert was a stranger, except as a
private litigant later on in life.

Gilbert was as influenced by current affairs, topical scandal and
legal suits as any writer or dramatist, and just like Dickens or even
Shakespeare, many of his throw-away references are magnificent contemporary satire - as must seem obvious enough. A good example is
what appears to be an obscure reference in *H.M.S. Pinafore*, which
turns out to be an integral part of the plot:

> Little Buttercup: When I was young and charming
> I practised baby-farming.

This was a reference to the practice of placing young children in foster homes due to the absence, or even the whim, of parents, and was subject to considerable abuses of which Gilbert was well aware. In the *Law Times* of 17th March 1875, it was reported that sitting at Exeter Quarter Sessions, Mr Justice Lush had said:

> Baby-farming has of late prevailed to such an extent that it has been necessary to vigorously suppress or efficiently regulate it.

This followed an attempt to enforce the registration of 'baby-farmers' with local authorities under the Infant Life Protection Act, 1872[10].

In 1884, when *Princess Ida* was produced, the income-tax rate for Britain was five pence in the pound. King Gama refers to this humourless subject:

> A charitable action I can skilfully dissect
> And interested motives I'm delighted to detect,
> I know everybody's income and what everybody earns,
> And I carefully compare it with the income-tax returns.

The librettist was quick to score popular approval when, less than two years later, Gladstone raised it by 40 per cent to sevenpence[11], he wrote in *Ruddigore* where Sir Ruthven, on pain of death, must commit a daily crime and says that on Tuesday he made a false income-tax return. He is rebuked with, 'that's nothing; everybody does that, it's expected of you'.

Thus satirist, social commentator or merely commercial comic, the Savoy's librettist pulls no punches in criticising the institutions and procedure of the law. The influence of Dickens is very clear, yet it is fair to say that Gilbert went on making capital out of jokes at the expense of the legal system long after most of the worst conditions existing in Dickens' day had been improved by a series of reforms. In this he is effectively a bridge between Dickens' sentimentality and Shaw's sociology, as *Goldberg* had suggested[12], but it could not be said that Gilbert expressed in this way the underlying liberal or socialist principles that motivated the other two. Consequently his humour should probably best be taken at face value, and in looking at his literary relationship with Dickens, he uses the novelist's works as a model for plot, character and dialogue, but thankfully nothing more.

Chapter 15

'Oh, Captain Shaw!': Characters, plots, connotations and contemporary satire

The essence of Gilbert's humour was satire on a very large scale. Within an extraordinarily complex matrix of word play, stereotype character-isation, plots with ludicrous solutions, and an important thematic presence, he succeeded in ridiculing on many different levels the insti-tutions loved and respected by the society in which he lived. It is all the more delightful to the modern-day reader of his texts that his comedy was absolutely galling to several members of the aristocracy, the judici-ary, the armed forces and Parliament. How harmless his satire was, or was intended to be at the time, is extremely difficult to judge. His characters were 'Dickensian' cut-outs; that is caricatures depending only on one virtue or vice each in order to attract the attention of and produce the desired effect in the audience, generally laughter. For example, as if the simple everyday vanity of Alexis in *The Sorcerer* is not enough to put over Gilbert's comment on this particular human trait, the audience is treated to the balloon-like super-vanity of Grosvenor in *Patience* or dear old Pooh Bah in *The Mikado* (though each fulfils a different function). Sometimes, however, the more biting satire of the author has almost a reverse effect: his scandalous treatment of middle-aged spinsters generally results in sympathy, and not the scorn he is thought to have desired. His plots, though highly institutionalised,

169

show a technical proficiency which was revolutionary in the stagecraft of his day. It is well known that Gilbert spent many hours aboard H.M.S. *Victory* at Portsmouth for the *Pinafore* quarterdeck set; and equally his sketches of the Tower for *Yeomen* and of Clerkenwell Sessions House for *Trial* underline his appreciation of the need for a real and technical detail to contrast his absurdities with recognisable everyday places. Considering that he is generally thought to have written in the idiom of a 'topsy-turveydom world', the only two sets that are based on fantasy in the Savoy operas are those for *Princess Ida* and Act I of *Utopia Limited*.

Gilbert's ready familiarity with many different walks of life helped this process of creating a juxtaposition between absurdity and reality. His concern for exploiting human weaknesses such as snobbery and prejudice is self-evident in such characters as Sir Joseph Porter and Captain Corcoran, concerning their relationship with the enlisted tars, Marco and Giuseppe's idea of republicanism and Alexis' condescension; and of course not to be forgotten is that most dreadful of Gilbert's chauvinist heroes Colonel Fairfax in *Yeomen*. The inevitable conclusion to be drawn is that the dramatist had a specific policy in creating his characters. Educated in the finest Victorian chauvinist traditions it is fairly easy to see where his treatment of women comes from. Similarly he hated the concept of social acceptability which drew very strict barriers between classes and sexes, and his attack was chiefly aimed at the institutions that raised and maintained such divisions in society. He made little distinction between satirising the old and established targets, namely the law, the monarchy and peerage, the armed forces and the clergy, and the new fads and fashions which he considered either as false or dangerous, namely aestheticism, radical social reform such as women's education, or radical political reform, for example republicanism. The Savoy Operas were thus a curious mixture of comments on the dominant values of society, but written so skilfully that whilst the contemporary satire they contained may be lost on the audience or reader of today, they have not lost the humour that made them so successful. Or perhaps our institutions have not changed that greatly in a century?

Bearing in mind the extensive width of subject matter under which Gilbert himself brought actions for defamation, and the problems that he faced at the hands of the censor, it is difficult to believe that the Savoy Operas escaped totally unscathed from the vast celebration of social bodies and personages that were given notorious treatment in them. The cases are generally so well-known, and would have been even more so at the time, that it is a wonder that Gilbert and Sullivan did not become a famous partnership of defence to successive libel actions. The most renowned incidents were the association of Sir Joseph Porter from *H.M.S. Pinafore* and Bunthorne from *Patience*. As will be seen, however, it was not Gilbert alone who moulded the identity of a particular character, and for someone as rigidly in control of his acting company he surprisingly allowed the comedians to change the popular association of his characters. The practical joke of the jurymen dressed as the counsel in the Tichborne case gave the principals the idea of modelling their character's appearance on well-known men of the day. Since Gilbert had deliberately produced Gladstone, Ayrton and Lowe in *The Wicked World* he shouldn't mind as long as the Censor was happy. Consequently Grossmith, Passmore and Lytton all developed a particular role's make-up and characteristics in an individual way. Despite protestations to the contrary by Gilbert, Grossmith's 'Sir Joseph Porter' really did look like the relevant cabinet minister, W. H. Smith, and incidentally what fewer people realise is, so did the 'Pirate King'. Alexander Cockburn on visiting *Trial* found himself looking at Fred Sullivan's 'Judge' looking remarkably like himself. Lytton, in his conscientiously researched parts, developed a 'King Gama' based on Henry Irving's Richard III and a 'Jack Point' based on Touchstone from *As You Like It*.

As far as his collaboration with Sullivan was concerned, the first public figure of renown to be portrayed was as early as Act I of *Thespis* when Gilbert created the Chairman of the Board of Directors of the North South East West Diddlesex Junction Railway Company, a gentleman whose characteristics were by some strange chance amazingly similar to those of the then Duke of Sutherland, coal-owner and real-life director of the London North Western Railway:

> I once knew a chap who discharged a function
> On the North South East West Diddlesex Junction,
> He was conspicuous exceeding,
> For his affable ways and easy breeding.
> Although a Chairman of Directors,
> He was hand in glove with the ticket inspectors,
> He tipped the guards with bran-new fivers,
> And sang little songs to the engine drivers.

Sutherland was at the time well-known for riding on the footplates of his own engines. The association which has been lost to modern-day audiences would have been immediate then; so much so that the duke's obituary notice in *The Times* of 24th September 1892 makes an attribution.

From this early start Gilbert moved four years later to the perfect satire of *Trial*, which revels in the detail of the author's 'home ground'. His satire of legal beings, offices and procedure appears with regularity throughout the Savoy series. Although subsequently changed for fear of repetition, Gilbert's 1881 plot-book shows that his original intentions for the story of *Iolanthe* were that the fairies should fall in love en masse with barristers of the Northern Circuit, the piece to also be set in a courtroom, with the Fairy Queen to marry the Home Secretary.

In *The Sorcerer*, the pet hates that W.S.G. burlesques are the clergy, epitomised in the country parson of Dr Daly, and the snobbery of the country petty bourgeoisie, shown by, amongst others, Alexis:

> I have spoken on the subject at Mechanics' Institutes, and the mechanics were unanimous in favour of my views. I have preached in workhouses, beershops, and lunatic asylums, and I have been received with enthusiasm. I have addressed navvies on the advantages that would accrue to them if they married wealthy ladies of rank, and not a navvy dissented.

In the reviews of the piece Sullivan was taken to task by the critics for his association with the satire of the piece:

> From one so experienced as Mr. Gilbert some amusing book ought to be expected. Cynical and sarcastic, of course, but with some reasonable ground for those qualities of thought and expression. In 'The Sorcerer' such qualities exist, but it is doubtful whether they are fitted for association with music...Let vice be the subject of sarcasm, but let virtue, even though it be negative, remain unscathed by the corroding fluid of cynicism. Mr. Gilbert sees fit to make the earnest, hard-working and serious clergy merely the subject of his sneering caricature.

His light-hearted treatment of ministers of religion was neither appreciated nor understood. Lewis Carroll wrote of Gilbert's seeming craze 'for making bishops and clergymen contemptible'.

Despite Gilbert's protestations of innocence, the most often associated character that he created was Sir Joseph Porter, K.C.B., with Disraeli's real Lord of the Admiralty, W. H. Smith, the popular bookseller[1]. The coincidence of neither being seamen was really too obvious to be missed by the audience, and in spite of Gilbert writing to Sullivan that Smith wouldn't be suspected because his own Admiral was a 'Radical of the most pronounced type', it is unlikely that he really believed that. In Hesketh Pearson's biography *W. S. Gilbert - His Life and Strife*, the author suggests that the letter was merely intended to 'allay any possible suspicion on the part of Sullivan' whose friendships in high quarters might have made him nervous of satire at the expense of a cabinet minister', and this is probably right. There is no evidence to suggest that Smith took the joke badly, although he was probably acutely embarrassed when Disraeli himself began to refer to his Minister of State as *Pinafore* Smith. In that same letter to Sullivan, Gilbert throws light on another popular interpretation: that of the Admiral's song 'When I was a lad' in Act I of *H.M.S. Pinafore*. It is thought to be based on a legal career with the 'office boy in an attorney's firm' starting in a solicitor's office and working his way through clerkship and articles to the 'pass examination at the Institute', that being the Law Society. Gilbert, however, tells Sullivan that the First Lord's song is:

> tracing his career as office-boy in cotton broker's office, clerk, traveller, junior-partner, and First Lord of Britain's Navy.

Gilbert's technical detail for *Pinafore*, and for the navy in general, is of an extremely high standard, matched by Sullivan's love for nautical music to be seen in the intricacy of the hornpipe in *Ruddigore*. On 13th April 1878, Gilbert went down to Portsmouth with Sullivan and Lord Charles Beresford, a close friend of the Prince of Wales. There he sketched the *Victory* and the *St. Vincent* and also boarded the *Thunderer* and *Invincible*. One of his more private hobbies was sailing, and he obtained a master mariner's certificate and constructed his own yacht. He had many naval friends, and in an era when the British Navy was the supreme military force on the entire globe he kept well up to date in naval trends and detail, reflected so typically well in *Pinafore* and introduced in *Ruddigore* and *Utopia Limited*.

Less well-known is the association between the 'Modern' Major General Stanley in the *Pirates of Penzance* and his real life counterpart Viscount Sir Garnet Wolseley[2], the greatest military hero of the day.

It was common knowledge that Wolseley had an extraordinarily versatile mind but that his ideas of military tactics were dated. Hence Gilbert makes him sing:

> 'For my military knowledge, though I'm plucky and
> adventury,
> Has only been brought down to the beginning of the century.'

In as much as everyone in the theatre would instantly recognise this popular hero appearing in *Pirates*, the words probably constitute a libel, and a case to which Gilbert would not have had an easy answer: the slang phrase of the era was 'All Sir Garnet', meaning 'all's correct', coming into fashion after his victories over the Ashanti, at Red River and in the Crimean War. Indeed the *Dictionary of National Biography* states that George Grossmith made himself up as Wolseley to sing the Modern Major-General. When Lytton came to take the part to the provinces, and later to take it over in London, he modelled it on another great soldier and hero of the Indian Mutiny, Field Marshal Lord Roberts[3], who again was easy to caricature within the part, but again whose displeasure at the connotation in the song must surely have been aroused. The measure of success by which Gilbert's most brilliant contemporary satire, *Patience*, can be judged was its popular acclaim in America where, broadly speaking, audiences were totally unfamiliar with the subject of the satire - the English craze of aestheticism in the late 1870s and 1880s. Gilbert had intended the plot to revolve around country clergy by using as a basis his 'Bab' ballad entitled *The Rival Curates*, but he must have been mindful of the adverse criticism he had received over Dr Daly in *The Sorcerer*. Other pressures - and the fact that currently society was dominated by the amazingly fanciful new fashion in every sphere of art, literature, and even modes of speech and thought - presented a target too irresistible to the dramatist's sense of the absurd. Aestheticism, created by Oscar Wilde and other apostles of the Pre-Raphaelite movement, had taken England by storm and Gilbert took his chance to use the theme just as other satirists and writers were turning their attention to it. Du Maurier's characters and F. C. Burnand's *The Colonel* were moderately successful, but as usual to be overshadowed by the child of the great triumvirate, whose *Patience* was the first of their works, albeit transferred, to play at the purpose-built Savoy. The two curates had become two rival aesthetic poets, and at the height of this fad the audience well remembered the leading case of

November 1878, the trial for defamation of Whistler v Ruskin, showing the irony of the aesthete artist suing the aesthete critic[4]. Consequently, whilst the writers maintained that they were attacking the imitators, the sham aesthetes who became 'affected' to indulge in the fashion, the two leading parts of Bunthorne and Grosvenor caricatured the mannerisms and individual details of the more well-known leaders of the movement. Whistler's eyeglass and hairstyle, Walter Crane's velvet coat and Oscar Wilde's knee breeches and mannerisms were all exhaustively featured. Elements of Morris, Ruskin, Pater, Rossetti and Swinburne could also be detected. Naturally the text flows with references to the aesthetes' models and great heroes, Botticelli, Fra Angelico, the early English ideal and of course, things Japanese, the invention of Whistler. Gilbert's characters cheerfully admit that their ideals are false and that their movement is a superficial nonsense; it is probably true to say that except in high-art circles, the laughter at *Patience* helped a great deal to kill off the more ridiculous side to the fashion.

The close association of *Patience* with Oscar Wilde came about for a number of reasons. More than any other he could be seen to be Bunthorne. He was in exact detail:

> A most intense young man,
> A soulful-eyed young man,
> An ultra-poetical, super aesthetical,
> Out-of-the-way young man!

More important, his business manager who arranged his lecture tours and poetry recitals was, by coincidence, Richard D'Oyly Carte, with whose agency he had registered on coming down from Oxford. So contemporary was Gilbert's satire, Carte realised that *Patience* would not be understood in the United States. In sending Wilde on a cleverly timed lecture tour to America in advance of the new Opera, Carte managed to create a great deal of interest in both. The tour was an immense success both for his client and his stake in the triumvirate's production, yet even when Wilde was 'playing' the same town as *Patience*, no relation between the two was advertised. Opening at Chickering Hall, New York City, on 9th January 1882, Wilde spent one of his most pleasant years, touring the United States, before the scandal which caused his eventual tragic downfall a few years later.

Apart from his conventional satire in character and plot, Gilbert delighted in indulging in light-hearted practical jokes. The finest example occurred on the opening night of *Iolanthe*, 25th November 1882, although many writers conclude that it must have been accidental. Among the glittering array of royalty, peers, socialites and the well-known first-nighters, sat the very popular head of the London Fire Brigade, formed by him after the disastrous Tooley Street fire of 1861, Captain Eyre Massey Shaw, in the very centre of the stalls. To his discomfort, and in front of many friends in the stalls, circles and boxes, he heard Alice Barnett, a veritably Wagnerian Fairy Queen, sing out to him 'with arms outstretched across the footlights':

> On fire that glows
>   with heat intense,
> I turn the hose
>   Of common sense,
> And out it goes,
>   At small expense.
>
> We must maintain
>   Our Fairy law;
> That is the main
>   On which to draw -
> In that we gain
>   A Captain Shaw!
>
> Oh, Captain Shaw,
> Type of true love kept under!
> Could they Brigade
> With cold cascade
> Quench my great love? - I wonder.

Some critics thought that Gilbert was playing with fire in introducing so broad an attack on the House of Lords and its political capabilities. This was probably inevitable. The topicality of reforming that ancient House is still current today, although critics would not assess an attack by way of satire as being in bad taste per se. The technical detail in the peers' costumes is and was superb, the originals being supplied by Ede, who remain as court robemakers today. In fact Gilbert's eye for detail was so good that the Prince of Wales in surveying the state regalia on stage discovered an order being worn by a peer that only he personally was entitled to. The management quickly removed the offending star.

Again the satire on the law in the person of the Lord Chancellor creeps into the plot, of which more must be said. To be content with the satire of *Iolanthe*, a new analysis recently appeared in which the Lord Chancellor is thought to be a thinly veiled Gladstone, and the Fairy Queen, Victoria herself[5]. It is extraordinarily difficult to conceive of Gilbert being so disrespectful towards the Queen, although his feelings on the monarchy come out more broadly in *The Gondoliers*. Certainly it seems clear that if that connotation could even have been vaguely thought of at the time the Lord Chamberlain's Office would have reacted immediately with censorship.

The high point of Gilbert's satire comes in the second Act of *Utopia Limited* where he constructs his very controversial Royal Drawing Room. While King Paramount asks the Lord Chamberlain to make sure that everything is in accordance with the practice of the Court of St. James, and receives the assurance that it is in practice with St. James Hall (a well-known music-hall, the home of the Christy Minstrel Company), clearly the immaculate detail of the costumes, Court etiquette and *mise en scène* indicated to the Royal Household that the author knew exactly what he was talking about. So closely did Gilbert draw on the practice at Windsor, the Prince of Wales on seeing the piece realised that whereas the opera's King Paramount offered refreshments to his visitors, Victoria did not; immediately afterwards he asked for the introduction of tea and biscuits at his mother's Drawing Rooms.

The satire on contemporary life in the Savoy Operas remains a source of humour to audiences, and source material to historians of that era which held such curiously classical values; yet the laughter emanating from any theatre where a Savoy opera is performed today is indicative not so much of Gilbert's intentions with regard to any particular satirical message, but on the tremendous polish and finish of the pieces. The humour of satire is universal, but especially so in the Savoy series, as it continues long after the object of the jape has disappeared, and also in parts of the world where it could never have been recognised anyway. It is also a tribute to the fact that Gilbert's characters, with their human failings and curiously Victorian virtues, still live and work among us today.

Chapter 16

'Of Everything that's excellent': Aspects of law in the Savoy Operas

As the curtain for the premiere of *The Grand Duke* arose on Saturday, 7th March, 1896, among the socially prestigious 'first-nighters' was a small band of lawyers, faithful followers of the Savoy series since its inception. Unlike the Lord Chief Justice twenty years before, they could not see how Gilbert's masterly use of legal buffoonery in his characters, and the logic of his absurd plots, could possibly be calculated to bring their great profession into contempt. On that night the final Savoy plot had a distinctly legal flavour, to be hugely enjoyed by the former Solicitor General, Sir Francis Lockwood, Baron Shand, member of the Judicial Committee of the Privy Council, and Frederick Inderwick, Q.C.

Gilbert's comments on the legal profession of his day were as wide as they were scathing. As has been said, he followed the lead taken by Dickens in attacking the abuses of the process of law on many different levels: whilst there is more humour than truth in Ko-Ko's memorandum of victims:

> And that Nisi Prius nuisance, who just now is rather rife,
> The Judicial humourist - I've got him on the list!

there is clearly more truth than humour, then as now, in the Lord
Chancellor's reminiscence of when he went to the Bar, as did Gilbert
himself:

> Ere I go into court I will read my brief through,
>   (Said I to myself - said I)
> And I'll never take work I'm unable to do,
>   (Said I to myself - said I)
> My learned profession I'll never disgrace
> By taking a fee with a grin on my face,
> When I haven't been there to attend to the case,
>   (Said I to myself - said I!)

Within the series of the Savoy Operas nearly every rank among the
legal professions is covered, from the Lord Chancellor in *Iolanthe* and
the Learned Judge in *Trial by Jury* to Sir Bailey Barre, Q.C., in *Utopia*,
Counsel for the Plaintiff in *Trial*, and the humbler Bunthorne's Solicitor of *Patience*, the Associate and Usher of *Trial*, and the various
public notaries in *The Sorcerer*, Annibale from *The Gondoliers* and Dr
Tannhauser in *The Grand Duke*. Not to be forgotten, of course, is
Pooh-Bah who has rolled all the judicial offices of Titipu into one, save
for the post of Lord High Executioner.

What the author's attitude was towards his former colleagues is
difficult to assess. He uses his legal characters to pinpoint particular
weaknesses in the system, but they are also designed to reflect the
pomposity, albeit good-natured, and humbug natural to them, that in
real life he came to detest. His most concise picture of what a lawyer
was to him is given by Princess Zara in *Utopia Limited*, where she
introduces her 'eminent Q.C.', especially sent from England to reform
the Utopian legal system:

Zara: 'A complicated gentleman allow me to present,
          Of all the arts and faculties the terse embodiment,
          He's a great Arithmetician who can demonstrate with
              ease
          That two and two are three, or five, or anything you
              please;
          An eminent Logician who can make it clear to you

That black is white - when looked at from the proper
point of view;
A marvellous philologist who'll undertake to show
That 'yes' is but another and a neater form of 'no'...

Sir Bailey: All preconceived ideas on any subject I can scout,
And demonstrate beyond all possibility of doubt,
That whether you're an honest man or whether
you're a thief
Depends on whose Solicitor has given me my brief.'

For Gilbert's favourite characters, Sullivan has created some of the
most famous and well-known arias concerned with the law - the Judge's
song from *Trial by Jury*, the Admiral's song from *H.M.S. Pinafore* and
the Lord Chancellor's three arias in *Iolanthe*. Indeed the Lord Chancellor stands next to Gilbert's greatest achievement in characterisation, the
formidable Pooh-Bah whose 'particularly haughty and exclusive person
of pre-Adamite ancestral descent', in point of fact who can trace his
ancestry back 'to a protoplasmal primordial atomic globule', is of a
delightfully legal flavour: his consequentially degrading duty to serve as
all the great officers of State under Ko-Ko produces one of the finest
scenes in the annals of the Savoy:

Ko-Ko: Pooh-Bah, it seems that the festivities in connection
with my approaching marriage must last a week. I
should like to do it handsomely, and I want to consult
you as to the amount I ought to spend upon them.
Pooh-Bah: Certainly. In which of my capacities? As First Lord of
the Treasury, Lord Chamberlain, Attorney-General,
Chancellor of the Exchequer, Privy Purse, or Private
Secretary?
Ko-Ko: Suppose we say as Private Secretary.
Pooh-Bah: Speaking as your Private Secretary, I should say that, as
the city will have to pay for it, don't stint yourself, do
it well.
Ko-Ko: Exactly - as the city will have to pay for it. That is your
advice.
Pooh-Bah: As Private Secretary. Of course you will understand
that, as Chancellor of the Exchequer, I am bound to
see that due economy is observed.

Ko-Ko: Oh! But you said just now 'Don't stint yourself, do it well.'

Pooh-Bah: As Private Secretary.

Ko-Ko   And now you say that due economy must be observed.

Pooh-Bah: As Chancellor of the Exchequer.

Ko-Ko: I see. Come over here, where the Chancellor can't hear us.

                          [They cross the stage]

           Now, as my Solicitor, how do you advise me to deal with this difficulty?

Pooh-Bah: Oh, as your Solicitor, I should have no hesitation is saying 'Chance it -.'

Ko-Ko: Thank you. [Shaking his hand] I will.

Pooh-Bah: If it were not that, as Lord Chief Justice, I am bound to see that the law isn't violated.

Ko-Ko: I see. Come over here where the Chief Justice can't hear us. [They cross the stage] Now, then, as First Lord of the Treasury?

Pooh-Bah: Of course, as First Lord of the Treasury, I could propose a special vote that would cover all expenses, if it were not that, as Leader of the Opposition, it would be my duty to resist it, tooth and nail, or, as Paymaster-General, I could so cook the accounts that, as Lord High Auditor, I should never discover the fraud. But then, as Archbishop of Titipu, it would be my duty to denounce my dishonesty and give myself into my own custody as First Commissioner of Police.

Ko-Ko: That's extremely awkward.

Pooh-Bah: I don't say that all these distinguished people couldn't be squared; but it is right to tell you that they wouldn't be sufficiently degraded in their own estimation unless they were insulted with a very considerable bribe.

In general terms each of the legal characters of the Savoy has a particular regard for the law as an institution. The Lord Chancellor and the Learned Judge owe their respective positions to their conscientious hard work and social advancement, but the former is very clear that:

> The law is the true embodiment
> Of everything that's excellent.
> It has no kind of fault or flaw,
> And I, my Lords, embody the Law.

whilst the latter maintains his position in an even more autocratic manner, aided by Sullivan's magnificent Handelian anthem for his entrance:

> 'For now I'm a Judge! . . .
> Though all my law be fudge,
> Yet I'll never, never budge,
> But I'll live and die a Judge!'

despite the fact that his Ludship cheerfully admits that his position was 'managed by a job', and as if to underline the fact that his law is fudge, Gilbert makes that plain in the judgment:

> All the legal furies seize you!
> No proposal seems to please you,
> I can't sit up here all day,
> I must shortly get away.
> Barristers, and you, attorneys,
> Set out on your homeward journeys;
> Gentle, simple-minded Usher,
> Get you, if you like, to Russher!
> Put your briefs upon the shelf,
> I will marry her myself!'

The dialogue abounds with legal terms and phrases - 'it is a legal fiction, and legal fictions are solemn things!' - 'Just bear in mind that we are Wards in Chancery' - 'We know the complicated laws, a Parliamentary draughtsman draws, cannot be briefly stated.' However a number of legal themes that thread their way through the Operas can be followed, reflecting Gilbert's special interest in aspects of law and its reform. He seems to have been overtly concerned with penology, and was often accused of blood-thirstiness; he expressed strong opinions on the new Company Law; he seemed to impose his legal training in the form of abstruse logic on all of the more fanciful plots of the Savoy; and finally he showed exactly his ideas and desires for the 'topsy-turvey' world he is credited with creating in his work, within a legal framework.

The author's concern with contemporary methods of criminal punishment can be found in a number of his works, and gives reign to a peculiarly sanguine trait in Gilbert that more than one person has commented upon. Sir Arthur Quiller-Crouch in his book *Studies in Literature* commented:

> Gilbert had a baddish streak or two in him; and one in particular which was not only baddish but so thoroughly caddish that no critic can ignore or, in my belief, extenuate it. The man, to summarize, was essentially cruel, and delighted in cruelty.

Gilbert's look at penology started mildly enough: in the *Pirates of Penzance* the Sergeant of Police declares earnestly:

> It is most distressing to us to be the agents whereby our erring fellow creatures are deprived of that liberty which is so dear to us all - but we should have thought of that before we joined the Force.

and similarly the comic paradox where those characters who should be hard and brutal - the Pirate King, the Lord High Executioner, the bad Baronets of Ruddigore - apparently wouldn't dream of hurting anyone. Trouble came with what was destined to become the most popular of the Savoy Operas, and one of the most popular and brilliant satires ever written; few who today fill the houses for revivals of *The Mikado* think of the play as it was generally seen in 1885. It would no doubt come to them as a surprise to read a typical contemporary review - and a view popularly held - by Beatty Kingston, drama critic of the *Theatre* magazine:

> Decapitation, disembowelment, immersion in boiling oil or molten lead are the eventualities on which [the audience's] attentions are fixed with gruesome persistence!

The plot does indeed revolve around the various ways in which the Mikado would exercise the punishment of his new law - that flirting in public should be a capital offence:

Pish Tush: 'Our great Mikado, virtuous man,
            When he, to rule our land began, ...
            ...Decreed in words succinct,

That all who flirted, leered or winked
(Unless connubially linked)
Should forthwith be beheaded.

Yum Yum ...The laws against flirting are excessively severe ...
To flirt is capital.

Nanki Poo: It is capital.

Yum Yum: And we must obey the law.

Nanki Poo: Deuce take the law!

Yum Yum: I wish it would, but it won't.

Gilbert has worse in store for Yum Yum and Nanki-Poo:

Ko-Ko: I've just ascertained that, by the Mikado's law, when a
married man is beheaded his wife is buried alive...
It's a most unpleasant death.

Nanki Poo: But whom did you get that from?

Ko-Ko: Oh, from Pooh-Bah. He's my Solicitor.

Yum Yum: But he may be mistaken!

Ko-Ko: So I thought; so I consulted the Attorney-General,
The Lord Chief Justice, the Master of the Rolls, the
Judge Ordinary, and the Lord Chancellor. They're
all of the same opinion. Never knew such unanimity
on a point of law in my life!

Nanki Poo: But stop a bit! This law has never been put in force.

Ko-Ko: Not yet. You see, flirting is the only crime punishable
with decapitation, and married men never flirt.

Nanki Poo: Of course they don't. I quite forgot that!'

Explanations as to these very Draconian measures, and the way they
are to be administered are forthcoming however:

Pooh Bah: Our logical Mikado, seeing no moral difference
between the dignified judge who condemns a
criminal to die, and the industrious mechanic who
carried out the sentence, has rolled the two offices
into one, and now every judge is his own
executioner!

It is the Mikado's, and thus Gilbert's scheme of things that essentially the concept of penology should be to make the punishment fit the crime, the epitome of which being the Mikado's own aria, 'My object all sublime.' Who but Gilbert could have written in comic sanguinity:

Ko-Ko: I can't execute myself ... because in the first place self-decapitation is an extremely difficult, not to say dangerous, thing to attempt, and, in the second, it's suicide - and suicide is a capital offence.

Mikado: I know the punishment is something humorous, but lingering, with either boiling oil or melted lead in it ... unfortunately the fool of an Act[1] says 'compassing the death of the Heir Apparent.'.. There's not a single word about a mistake...or not knowing...or having no notion..., or not being there... there should be of course... but there isn't.

Gilbert's various punishments include the rehabilitative commuting of Iolanthe's sentence of death to one of penal servitude for life and never seeing her husband again. Don Alhambra has no qualms in announcing that the poor old nurse of the infant son of the late King of Barataria is awaiting his interview in the Torture Chamber. Finally in *Utopia Limited* it can be seen that over ten years Gilbert's views failed to change:

Lady Sophy: Well, you are a Despot - have you taken steps to slay this scribbler?

King Paramount: Well, no - I have not gone so far as that. After all it's the poor devil's living, you know.

Lady Sophy: ...If this man lies, there is no recognized punishment that is sufficiently terrible for him.

King Paramount: That's precisely it. I - I am waiting until a punishment is discovered that will fit the enormity of the case. I am in constant communication with the Mikado of Japan, who is the leading authority on such points; and moreover, I have the ground plans and sectional elevations of several capital punishments in my desk at this moment.

It might be thought that here is an exaggeration of Gilbert's intentions. It is true to say that many thought Gilbert to be as concerned with reform of the Victorian penal institutions as was Dickens, although equally many considered him a good deal too bloodthirsty - his cruelty stands out in his works as something serving little purpose other than its own sake.

Gilbert's knowledge of the new Company Law[2] which had emerged in England in the 1850s and 1860s was mainly gleaned from his own experiences. He had seen Sullivan lose all his stocks and shares; he and Sullivan had suffered alike when the Comedy Opera Company could not find the money for the costs awarded against it in the major action; and after the Carpet Quarrel he had dealings with Carte and the Savoy then registered as a limited liability company. The dramatist had a great mistrust of the concept of limited liability, which was a very new idea both in legal and commercial terms, and this became increasingly obvious in his later works. A definite theme of comments on Company Law is seen to emerge, much as the law on that subject was evolving at the time. As early as 1871 Gilbert wrote of the 'Diddlesex Junction' railway company in *Thespis* in keeping with the railway boom of the 1840s and 1850s. It was during the period of his own legal training that the two most important pieces of legislation concerning companies arrived on the scene - the Joint Stock Companies Act, 1856[3], and the consolidating statute of the same name, six years later in 1862[4]. These two acts introduced and institutionalised the concept of limited liability, the symbol of modern Company Law, and an idea for which Gilbert's particular suspicion was liberally dispersed throughout his text. A warning of things to come is in the famous 'Nightmare Song' in *Iolanthe* where the author gives some vent to his feelings:

> Lord Chancellor: ...and he's telling the tars all the particulars
> of a company he's interested in,
> It's a scheme of devices to get, at low prices, all
> goods
> from cough mixture to cables ...
> ...the shares are a penny and ever so many are
> taken
> by Rothschild and Baring.

The librettist excelled himself in the skill with which he created the amazing 'Duke of Plaza Toro, Limited' in *The Gondoliers*, and the state of *Utopia Limited* in the opera of that name. In *The Gondoliers*, in order to create a worthy dowry for their daughter Casilda, the Duke and Duchess register themselves under the 1862 Companies Act as a limited company, for the considerable emoluments to be gained in the then common practice of selling aristocratic endorsements of worthless products and securities, or references to people needing social or occupational introductions. Gilbert bashes this practice is one of his most brilliant songs[5], 'Small titles and orders, for Mayors and Recorders':

Duke of Plaza Toro: I sit by selection upon the direction
of several companies bubble[6],
As soon as they're floated I'm freely bank-
noted,
- I'm pretty well paid for my trouble.

The Duke has previously announced his plans to his daughter that:

a Company ..... is in the process of formation to work me; an influential directorate has been secured, and I myself shall join the Board after allotment.

His daughter is worried that her father might in the future have to undergo liquidation, but the Duchess retorts:

If your father should stop it will, of course, be necessary to wind him up.

Utopia Limited is a work of sheer genius: the entire society of a tropical island, from autocratic ruler down to private citizens, organises itself as a limited liability company under the 1862 Act, by the skills of the Company Promoter, Mr Goldbury, who explains to King Paramount exactly what the idea entails - according to Gilbert:

Some seven men form an Association,
(If possible all peers and baronets)
They start off with a public declaration,
To what extent they mean to pay their debts.
That's called their 'capital': If they are wary
They will not quote it at a sum immense.
The figure's immaterial - it may vary,
From eighteen million down to eighteen pence.

> (I should put it rather low; the good sense of doing so
> Will be evident at once to any debtor.
> When it's left for you to say, the amount you mean to pay,
> Why, the lower you can put it at, the better).

The hostility of the author is self-evident, and it would seem that Gilbert might at some stage even have lost money through such a trading venture; this is not known, however, but the song continues:

> They then proceed to trade with all who'll trust 'em,
> Irrespective, quite, of their capital,
> (It's shady but it's sanctified by custom)
> Bank[7], Railway[8], Loan or Panama Canal[9].

The crux of the matter is in the last verse: the criticism of the system is quite straightforward. The author is attacking incorporation, public corporate financing, and the concept of new limited liability, because he views as non-existent at that time the high degree of responsibility and moral culpability needed in company management - as far as Goldbury is concerned he is merely promoting a 'device for raising funds from the public for doubtful schemes with a minimal risk of accountability':

> If you come to grief, and creditors are craving,
> (For nothing that is planned by mortal head
> Is certain in this Vale of Sorrow - saving
> That one's liability is limited) -
> Do you suppose that signifies perdition?

> If so you're but a monetary dunce -
> You merely file a Winding-Up Petition,
> And start another company at once!

> Though a Rothschild you may be in your own capacity,
> As a company you've come to utter sorrow,
> But the liquidators say, "Never mind - you needn't pay,"
> So you start another company tomorrow.'

It is little wonder that King Paramount looks dubious, but replies:

Well, at first it strikes us as dishonest, but if it's good enough for
virtuous England, the first commercial country in the world, then
it's good enough for us,

and he logically inquires:

And do I understand that Great Britain, upon this joint-stock
principle is governed?'

Goldbury is forced to concede:

We haven't come to that exactly, but we're tending rapidly in that
direction.

Gilbert absolutely exhausts the subject: perhaps he did not know
how to edge off, and throughout the rest of the opera the quips and
puns resound: the Utopians, as the audience, find that the Goldbury
principle can be overdone: he has in fact 'applied the limited liability
to individuals, and every man, woman and child is now a company
limited with liability restricted to the amount of his declared capital'.
The finale of Act I contains another of Sullivan's skits on Handel's
anthems:

> All hail, astonishing fact!
> All hail, invention new -
> The Joint Stock Company's Act
> of Parliament Sixty-Two!

Contemporary reviews seem to have been amazingly oblivious to
the ideas that Gilbert was hurling forth. George Bernard Shaw,
reviewing as a music critic for the *London Saturday Review*, seems to
have missed the point completely and has been taken in by the surface
plot as Gilbert's message. Clearly contemporary business scandals
were on Gilbert's mind, and probably the more specific roots of his
attack. The librettist was under considerable disillusionment as to
contemporary business ethics and commercial morality, and beneath
the surface humour there is to be found a balanced argument for a
close scrutiny of the Companies Acts, with repeal suggested. It
appears that Gilbert was extremely concerned with the fact that the
legal liability of companies of the day did not reflect the duty they

owed to their investors. The relevance of his concern is something which could equally be felt today in an age of multi-tiered, multi-national corporations, and consequently shows the immense far-sightedness of the legal mind.

Gilbert's fanciful logic abundantly flows in his extraordinarily tangled plots where by the close of the action he has to bring in an equally absurd deus ex machina in the form of an idea to bring the opera to a summary, and convenient, close. The best example is the way in which he ends *Ruddigore*; it is probably also the one that audiences find most difficult to follow:

> Sir Ruthven: I can't stop to apologize - an idea has just occurred to me. A Baronet of Ruddigore can only die through refusing to commit his daily crime.
> Roderick: No doubt.
> Sir Ruthven: Therefore, to refuse to commit a daily crime is tantamount to suicide!
> Roderick: It would seem so.
> Sir Ruthven: But suicide is, itself, a crime[10] - and so, by your own showing, you ought never to have died at all!
> Roderick: I see - I understand! Then I'm practically alive!

In the original text an extra passage is in the finale, which probably accounts for the fact that modern audiences have difficulty in following the current ending of the plot:

> Roderick: We are all practically alive!
> Sir Ruthven: Every man jack of you!
> Roderick: My brother ancestors! Down from your frames! You believe yourselves to be dead - you may take it from me that you're not, and an application to the Supreme Court is all that is necessary to prove that you ought never to have died at all!

Gilbert used exactly the same line of thinking only a year previously in the Mikado:

> Ko-Ko: When your Majesty says let a thing be done, it's as good as done, - practically it is done - because your Majesty's word is law. Your Majesty says kill a

gentleman... consequently that man is as good as
dead - practically he is dead - and if he is dead,
why not say so?

Why should I kill you when making an affidavit
that you've been executed will do just as well?

However, it is for the Lord Chancellor that Gilbert reserves his
logical lines, with a natural legal flavour:

The feelings of a Lord Chancellor who is in love with a Ward of
Court are not to be envied. What is his position? Can he give his
own consent to his own marriage with his own Ward? Can he marry
his own Ward without his own consent? And if he marries his own
Ward without his own consent, can he commit himself for contempt
of his own Court? And if he commits himself for contempt of his
own Court, can he appear before himself by counsel, to move for an
arrest of his own judgement? Ah, my Lords, it is indeed painful to
have to sit on a Woolsack which is stuffed with thorns such as these!

. . . [In entertaining the motion] I pointed out to myself that I was
no stranger to myself; that, in point of fact, I had personally been
acquainted with myself for a number of years. This had its effect. I
admitted that I had watched my professional advancement with
considerable interest, and I handsomely added that I yielded to
no-one in admiration for my private and professional virtues. This
was a great point gained.

and his dialogue as well as soliloquy is filled with Gilbert's ridiculous
points which must be considered as serious:

Chancellor:	Now, Sir, what excuse have you to offer for having disobeyed an order of the Court?
Strephon:	My Lord, I know no Courts of Chancery; I go by Nature's Acts of Parliament . . . Sir, you are England's Lord High Chancellor, but are you Chancellor of birds and trees, King of the winds and Prince of thunderclouds?
Chancellor:	No! It's a nice point. I don't know that I ever met it before.

Fairy Queen:　The law is clear - every fairy dies who do marry a
　　　　　　　mortal!

Chancellor:　Allow me, as an old Equity draughtsman, to make a
　　　　　　suggestion; the subtelties of the legal mind are
　　　　　　equal to the emergency...

　　　　　　　Let it stand that every fairy dies who don't
　　　　　　marry a mortal!

As every satirist, Gilbert seeks to put something in place of that
which he is attacking, and in the various Savoy Operas he does so
effectively and on different planes: his 'Utopian' system provides
delightful dialogue and verse:

Lord Mountararat:　His Lordship is constitutionally as blythe as a
　　　　　　　　bird. He trills upon the bench like a thing of
　　　　　　　　song and gladness. His series of judgements
　　　　　　　　in F sharp minor, given andante in six-eight
　　　　　　　　time, are amongst the most remarkable
　　　　　　　　effects ever produced in a Court of
　　　　　　　　Chancery. He is, perhaps, the only living
　　　　　　　　instance of a judge whose decrees have had
　　　　　　　　the honour of a double encore. How can we
　　　　　　　　bring ourselves to do that which would
　　　　　　　　deprive the Court of Chancery of one of its
　　　　　　　　most attractive features.

The Usher:　　　　Now, jurymen, hear my advice,
　　　　　　　　All vulgar kinds of prejudice
　　　　　　　　I pray you set aside
　　　　　　　　With stern judicial frame of mind
　　　　　　　　From bias free of every kind
　　　　　　　　This trial must be tried.
　　　　　　　　Oh listen to the Plaintiff's case,
　　　　　　　　Observe the features of her face -
　　　　　　　　The broken-hearted bride ...
　　　　　　　　Condole with her distress of mind.
　　　　　　　　And when amid the Plaintiff's shrieks
　　　　　　　　The ruffianly Defendant speaks
　　　　　　　　Upon the other side.
　　　　　　　　What he may say you needn't mind!

Gilbert pulled out all the stops for his brilliant guying of peculiarly British institutions in *Utopia Limited:*

Scaphio:	Are you aware that Sir Bailey Barre has introduced a law of libel by which all editors of scurrilous newspapers are publicly flogged - as in England?
	Your County Councillor has passed such drastic Sanitary laws that all the doctors dwindle, starve, and die! The laws, remodelled by Sir Bailey Barre, have quite extinguished crime and litigation: The lawyers starve, and all the jails are let as model lodgings for the working-classes!
King Paramount:	Society has quite foresaken all her wicked courses,
	Which empties our police courts, and abolishes divorces,
	Divorce is nearly obsolete in England.
	No tolerance we show to undeserving rank and splendour,
	For the higher his position is the greater the offender.
Captain Fitzbattleaxe:	In England, when two gentlemen are in love with the same lady, and until it is settled which gentleman is to blow out the brains of the other, it is provided, by the Rival Admirers' Clauses Consolidation Act, that the lady shall be entrusted to an officer of the Household Cavalry as stake-holder, who is bound to hand her over to the survivor (on the Tontine principle) in a good condition of substantial and decorative repair.
Scaphio:	Reasonable wear and tear and damages by fire excepted?

Captain
Fitzbattleaxe: Exactly.
Phantis: Well, that seems very reasonable.

Gilbert makes exhaustive use of his legal training in the Operas, yet as in so much of his social criticism his message rings as true today. He lived through an age of great reform of the law and seems to have been a proponent of even more that the Victorian reformers felt able to unleash, and this became increasingly apparent as his works progressed.

Part V

'A regular terrible story'

Chapter 17

'To gain a brief advantage you've contrived' : Domestic copyright issues

The underlying principle upon which all copyright law is based is that a man should be protected in the enjoyment of the fruits of his own labour, and consequently authors and investigators should rightly have a monopoly in the publication of their work. In Britain, unlike the United States, this idea was as prevalent in Gilbert's time as it is now. By the 1880s it was usual for a dramatic author to be able to claim copyright protection for his work and royalties for his efforts from well-established Common Law and statutory rules. Cases had been decided over a hundred years earlier and the governing statute of the day was the Copyright Act, 1842[1], which extended the period of copyright to the duration of the author's life and seven years afterwards, or a period of forty-two years, whichever was longer. This act also gave musical pieces the same protection as books, and remained the most important guideline to this area of law until 1911.

Copyright had first been protected as early (or late) as 1710[2] by the Statute of Anne. The preamble declared that the mischief to be cured was that:

> Printers, booksellers and other persons have of late frequently taken the liberty of printing, reprinting and publishing, or causing to be

printed, reprinted or published books and other writings without
the consent of the authors or proprietors of such books and writings,
to their very great detriment and too often to the ruin of them and
their families.

However even with the later protection afforded by the 1842 Act
the maximum penalty that could be imposed for a breach of dramatic
copyright was 40 shillings per public performance. Abuses led to the
passing of two further statutes, the Copyright (Musical Composition)
Acts of 1882 and 1888. In 1892 the case of Lee v. Gibbings[3] gave the
author another remedy against pirates - the law of libel. In that case
the plaintiff complained that in an unauthorised copy of his work,
omissions from the work, which was of a serious and scholarly nature,
were so important as to be injurious to his reputation as an author and
scholar; this argument was upheld. This interesting decision moved
away from the recommendations of the latest Royal Commission on
Copyright, which reported its findings, generally in accordance with a
policy of no change, in 1878.

In the 1860s and 1870s it was common practice for dramatists to
adapt existing works for the stage. Whether these adaptations were
being written to spoof or burlesque the originals, or to emanate their
qualities in novel form, they were generally considered to be original
in themselves and were given protection from piracy where such
adaptations were authorised. Gilbert adapted both English novels and
French and Italian opera for the British stage. A good example of the
former is his early work, *A Sensation Novel*, in 1871, and the special
relationship he had with Sullivan in imitating the styles of Offenbach,
Halévy and Donizetti shows the latter.

Gilbert succeeded, in 1884, in cleverly adapting Tennyson's poem
The Princess, from which came *Princess Ida* which ran for over 240
performances; some fourteen years earlier the author had used the
poem as the basis for a farce which ran quite successfully at the
Olympic Theatre. There is no record of Gilbert's parodies having
given offence to Tennyson or having been in breach of his copyright.
However the theme was popular, yet when Hollingshead tried to
produce a show burlesquing *The Princess* in 1875 he received a
surprising letter from Tennyson's solicitors enquiring what compensation he intended to make for potential breaches of copyright. The
manager of the Gaiety was particularly annoyed because he was one of
the most well-known supporters of a campaign to give dramatic

authors performing rights at the time. He sharply replied that the copyright law did not extend to dramatic versions of printed books, but dropped his ideas for the play.

The Savoy triumvirate's problems at home began with the split with the Comedy Opera Company directors over *H.M.S. Pinafore*. Until then the astute Carte had created a system for licensing copyright productions by amateur groups, a system which lasted until the expiration of the Savoy copyrights, and also sent touring companies into the provinces to prevent unauthorised productions of Gilbert and Sullivan. After the fracas on the evening of 31st July 1879, applications to stop the Comedy Opera Company mounting its rival *H.M.S. Pinafore* failed, and Gilbert and Sullivan saw their royalties being threatened. Two days later they issued a signed notice from the Opera Comique:

> In face of the fact that our Opera, H.M.S. PINAFORE, is being played at another London Theatre, we, as the author and composer respectively of the above-mentioned Opera, feel it to be due to ourselves and to the Company of the Opera Comique to state that the performances at the Opera Comique are conducted by the artists, operatic, dramatic and orchestral, who were selected by us for the purposes of the representation, and whose exertions have contributed so largely to the exceptional success of the Opera; that the Opera, as performed at the Opera Comique, is, and always has been, personally superintended and sanctioned by us in every detail; that we have superintended the rehearsals and sanctioned the engagements of no other London Company whatever; and that the Opera, as represented at the Opera Comique, is played with our entire concurrence and approval[4].

The effect of this notice was to act as a joint advertisement for the rival productions, although quite soon afterwards, popular preference for the original was clearly expressed. During the litigation that followed until 1881, no argument arose as to copyright of the piece: legal questions centred on the rights to perform and produce the piece on the stage, as there could be no dispute that the score and libretto rights remained vested in the respective authors.

Carte continued to give warnings against unauthorised copying, and in the 1881 provincial tour preview programme he issued the following:

CAUTION
'Patience', 'The Pirates of Penzance', 'H.M.S. Pinafore', 'The Sorcerer'.

The Sole Right of Performances of these Operas in the Provinces having been ceded to me by Messrs. W. S. Gilbert and Arthur Sullivan, I hereby give notice that I shall take immediate legal proceedings against any person performing the said Operas, or any portion thereof, in Public, without permission.

No Songs or Concerted Pieces from either Opera can be introduced into Pantomimes, Burlesques or any other Entertainments, either with the original or any other Words.

I will also give a reward to any person furnishing me with such information as may enable me to recover damages for any unauthorised performances.

The above does not refer to performances of the Dance Music, Instrumental Arrangements, and Selections for Orchestra or Military Band, or to single detached pieces sung at concerts.

Whilst D'Oyly Carte, having purchased the performing rights, was busy acting in the interests of all three to protect their copyright, Gilbert had to use his own vigilance to protect his personal copyright in his independent works. A good example occurred in October 1885, when he prevented an amateur adaptation of his *Pygmalion and Galatea*; however the critic of the *Entr'Acte* magazine took him to task for exercising his rights:

Canterbury - On the night of our visit to the Canterbury (Tuesday) the entertainment entitled 'Life in Art' was not forthcoming. At a former part of the day Mr. W. S. Gilbert had recorded a protest against this bagatelle in a law-court, as bearing too close a resemblance to 'Pygmalion and Galatea'. This proceeding resulted in the temporary withdrawal of the entertainment until this alleged infringement of copyright had been adjudicated upon.

I am really surprised that Mr. W.S. Gilbert should take action against Messrs. Crowder and Payne for permitting in an entertainment at the Canterbury by two or three performers, such entertainment being considered by Mr. Gilbert to be a colourful imitation of his 'Pygmalion and Galatea.' That two or three people on a music hall stage could in ten or twelve minutes give anything like a colourful imitation of one of the most charming works of the sort ever written, a play which takes a couple of hours and about eight good actors to do it anything like justice at the theatre, seems to be palpably straining a point; at the same time it is an indirect way of paying a compliment to the performers responsible for this alleged piracy.

I have seen this little sketch given on several occasions and if I had suspected Mr. Gilbert was being injured by it I should have said so without the slightest hesitation: for, I hold it to be only right that the brain-work of an author should be protected from the plundering onslaughts of those pirates whose genius as robbers is considerably ahead of their talent as inventors. I trust, as this case is still unsettled, that I may not be considered presumptuous if I hope that Mr. Gilbert will retire from it, and that we may hear no more about it[5].

The difficulties that authors faced in protecting their works were largely solved by the Copyright Act of 1911 which reformed that law considerably. However, as little or great as such problems were, they seemed minuscule when compared with the attempts of British authors to secure their rights in the face of blatant American thievery across the Atlantic; and the struggle of Gilbert and Sullivan for their just dues were destined to be of epic proportions.

Chapter 18

'With base deceit' : American piracy

Almost alone amongst the nations of the 'civilised' world, the United States maintained a position with regard to international copyright which was as anomalous as it was blatantly objectionable, right until the end of the nineteenth century. American business entrepreneurs pirated the Savoy Operas until as late as 1891 when at last the first piece of Federal international copyright legislation appeared on the statute books of Congress.

The peculiar attitude of successive American governments through-out the second half of the last century could probably be explained as official U.S. isolationist policy being carried a little too far; certainly as, during the same period, American authors could maintain inter-national protection for their own works in most European countries, including Britain. The British position was, then, that an alien friend, temporarily residing in the British Empire or Dominions, and con-sequently owing a temporary alliegance to the Crown, was entitled to copyright in any work published whilst so residing, no matter how short his period of residence[1]. Generally speaking British court decisions favoured the American authors. As early as 1838 the case of Bently v. Foster[2] held that an American could obtain British copyright by publishing in Britain one day before publication in the United States. In the same year, however, an American court ruled in the case of Captain Marryat that even twelve months residence was insufficient for the protection of copyright in the novels of foreign nationals unless the authors were prepared to change their nationality[3].

The history of copyright in the United States begins almost with the birth of that nation. The Continental Congress of May 1783[4], declared that for a fourteen-year period of copyright from the date of first publication the author had to be a 'citizen, inhabitant, resident or subject of the United States', in order to gain protection. Dramatic copyright, including exclusive performing rights, was not introduced until August 1856. As late as 1870 foreign dramatists were specifically excluded[5]. At least by the 1880s the American government was beginning to make clearer the reasons for its xenophobic attitude: the question was one of prohibiting monopoly because of a general need for cheap books. Therefore the U.S. was willing to confer on alien authors a royalty compensation but would not sanction any type of monopoly agreement. A good example is Macaulay's *History of England*: by the time 10,000 bound copies had been sold at 16 shillings each in London over 100,000 pirated copies had been sold at 1 shilling each in America. The force of American arguments was so strong that even Gladstone had to agree to copyright by royalty and not monopoly.

In 1886 Britain, along with eighteen other nations, signed the articles of agreement as parties to the Berne International Copyright Convention. The principle adopted by these nations was that 'authors within the jurisdiction of one of the countries of this Union, or their heirs, shall enjoy in the others' countries the rights which the respective laws of these countries now accord, or shall subsequently accord, to their own countrymen[6]'. The United States declined to enter into the agreement of the Berne Convention, which was to govern the law relating to international copyright for some decades.

Pressure was now being brought to bear on Congress by various groups in America. In the 1886-7 session two bills were introduced into the Senate by the American Copyright League for International Copyright Law. Admittedly both failed; however one did get as far as scrutiny by the Senate Committee on Patents[7], and was presented to the House as the Hawley Bill, based on the terms of the Berne Convention; both paved the way for the piece of legislation that was eventually, and perhaps inevitably, to arrive on the statute books, five years later. Again it was organised pressure groups that forced the Chace-Breckinridge-Adams-Simonds-Platt Copyright Act of 1891. This gave authors, whether resident or not, a statutory protection of twenty-eight years, with an additional fourteen if the author were still alive at the expiration of the first term. All editions of the work to be copyrighted had to be entirely manufactured in the United States. For non-residents this protection could only be given if there existed a reciprocal arrangement with that author's national government. Finally, the work had to be published in America not later than the first date of publication elsewhere. At last Gilbert and Sullivan had a legitimate remedy against American pirate productions of their work.

In December 1871, when the libretto for *Thespis* was printed, there appeared on the copyrighted title page a paragraph entitled 'Caution to American Pirates'. This paragraph, and others like it, had no legal standing, a fact which unfortunately American theatre managers knew only too well. It shows, however, that the problem of sham American forgeries was one known to the partners from the time of their earliest collaboration. Gilbert and Sullivan were faced with the fact that the publication of their operas made the works public property in the United States. There, anyone could produce from a published libretto. Thus, on 15th November 1875 the first unauthorised version of *Trial by Jury* took place at the Eagle Theatre, New York City, though the costumes, set and probably the detail of the lyrics would have been scarcely recognisable to its British parent. It was with the arrival of *H.M.S. Pinafore* on the shores of the American continent that the full magnitude of Gilbert and Sullivan's loss, in terms of tens of thousands of dollars, was to be realised.

With hindsight it could be argued that whether piratical or not, it was purely American interest in the opera that made it so successful internationally and at home. Certainly the authors did not think so at the time and were most resentful that whilst their piece was extraordinarily popular, American law prevented them from earning a brass farthing from its success. They claim also to have been particularly concerned as much with the mutilation of their work as with the loss of revenue. Indeed from the very first unlicensed production in America, omissions and additions to be found in *Pinafore* would have made Gilbert apoplectic and Sullivan uncharacteristically angry. That first performance came on 28th November 1878, at Montgomery Field's Boston Museum Theatre, and the part of Ralph Rackstraw was played by a female, Rose Temple. Little Buttercup was played by a man; in the craze that swept the country not only in theatres, but on advertisement hoardings and trade cards, there appeared Germanic *Pinafores*, burlesques interpolating all manner of stage-business and music added by courtesy of Mozart, Handel, and Wagner. By Christmas 1878, there were eight pirate productions in New York and six in Philadelphia alone; early in 1879 London newspapers announced that over a hundred companies were simultaneously playing unauthorised versions. Accordingly Carte was dispatched to discover exactly what the situation was, and eventually, a year and a half after the show had first opened in London, Gilbert and Sullivan arrived in New York with their own company to show America what the original *H.M.S. Pinafore* was really about. The success of that production and its subsequent tour encouraged the authors to consider what should be done about their next opera in relation to the pirates. Only one American manager, John Ford, paid Gilbert a royalty on *Pinafore*, and consequently he was granted the rights for his Fifth Avenue Theatre, New York, for the first production of *The Pirates of Penzance*. Sullivan spoke of his American experience:

> Of course Gilbert and myself had been kept informed of the unique business which 'Pinafore' was doing in America, and our visit was prompted by the notion that, as the authors of the piece, we ought to profit by it. Meanwhile, we did not trust to the 'Pinafore' opera to do us any material monetary good in America; we determined to produce our next opera in the States first and in Great Britain afterwards. The Americans acknowledged that the author had a right in his unpublished work in the same way that he could lay claim to his own personal apparel or any other form of property, and only lost his prerogative after his composition had been published. So all we could do was to follow the course I have indicated and produce our piece in America first and get our own company well under weigh before others could bring out their imitations. With this object in view we took with us the half-completed opera of the *'Pirates of Penzance'*. I had only composed the second act, without the orchestration, in England. Soon after my arrival in America I wrote the first act, and scored the whole opera. We produced it at the Fifth Avenue Theatre on New Year's Eve - December 31, 1879.
>
> Of course at that time there was no copyright between the two countries, and so we were compelled to retain possession of the whole work in manuscript. To have stolen that from us would have made the thief amenable under common law, but if we had published it, and had proceeded against any thief who had made use of the opera we should have had to take action against him under Statute Law, and should have failed. The moment any portion of

the opera appeared in print it was open to any one in the States to publish, produce, or do what he liked with it. Apart, however, from the absence of international copyright, the law concerning artistic questions was very involved and uncertain, and in a very unsatisfactory state altogether. Keeping the music in libretto and manuscript did not settle the difficulty, as it was held by some judges that theatrical representation was tantamount to publication, so that any member of the audience who managed to take down the libretto in shorthand, for instance, and succeeded in memorising the music was quite at liberty to produce his own version of it. This made matters exciting for us, although the excitement was far from being a pleasant one. We kept a sharp look-out, and if anyone in the theatre was observed taking notes or anything of the kind the note-taker was promptly turned out.

Yes, it very often happened, and many other dodges were practised. It is impossible to memorise orchestration, and consequently some of the members of my orchestra were bribed to hand over the band parts. Incidents of this sort became of constant recurrence. I remember that I was dining one night with Mr. Sam Barlow, the George Lewis of New York, when my copyist came from the theatre to see me, positively livid with excitement. He had made the discovery that one of the members of the orchestra had been offered the bribe of one hundred dollars if he would supply the first violin part of the opera.

However, notwithstanding the absence of copyright law, we did very well in America, as is evidenced by the fact that Stetson offered us £5,000 down for the right to play the piece for a short time in Boston, an offer which we declined, preferring to send our own company, and taking the risk of making what we could out of it. We sent out a great number of companies on the road to different towns in the States. Some of the tours showed a slight loss, and others a considerable profit, and, taking it all round, we did excellently well, more especially when one remembers that our attempt to retain possession of our own property involved us in a guerilla warfare. On the other hand, before producing anything in America, it was necessary, in order to comply with English copyright law, to have a bogus performance in this country. This was always carried out in some out-of-the-way village, and arranged with great secrecy.

Apart from the activity of the piratical people of those days, I was most hospitably treated everywhere, and I liked the American people immensely[8].

Despite the fact that immense care was taken with regard to security, and that not one of the members of the orchestra succumbed to the temptations being offered them, and most important that the score and libretto were not published in America until ten months after the work's premiere, the memory pirates still managed to make notes of the performance and recreate a sufficient amount of dialogue and music for a production to be mounted. Thus in Boston there appeared a medley entitled *Recollections of the Pirates of Penzance*. Carte lost no time in retaining an eminent lawyer, Alexander Browne, to fight this and other cases should they arise. In this first case he succeeded in pursuading Judge Lowell of the Massachusetts Circuit Court of the justice of his case. However later the same year an action was brought against another adaptation, not Gilbert and Sullivan but Edward Solomon's *Billee Taylor*, being pirated in Baltimore, Maryland. There Judge Morris considered but declined to follow his brother Judge Lowell's decision, and Carte lost out. However in comparison with *Pinafore*, unauthorised versions became a rarity and trade advertisements and other commercial objects were successfully stopped.

Gilbert, Sullivan, and Carte now tried to devise a way to overcome their difficulties, and by *Princess Ida* in 1884 they felt that they had found a way. Sullivan takes up the account:

With the subsequent operas, 'Patience', 'Iolanthe', and so on, we tried all sorts of expedients to preserve our own rights in our own work. For example, it had been laid down in the Massachusetts circuit - the most important legal circuit in the States - and in accordance with a very unfortunate precedent in the British law of the time that the pianoforte arrangement of a work should be regarded as a separate copyright and a separate property. It was a ridiculous and an indefensible notion, but, unfortunately, it had been so decided in an important case - Boosey v Cramer - on this side of the water.

However, we decided to act on the American judgement to which I have referred, and induced an American citizen to come over here from the States to make the pianoforte arrangements of the score here, and by means of a sort of silly fiction, I allowed him to use the vocal parts of my opera as being part of his pianoforte arrangement of the score. He then copyrighted, in his own name, the pianoforte arrangement of my work, and it became his property, with the private understanding that he subsequently handed it to

me for a small monetary consideration. This was a very round-
about way of doing business, but we thought that by this means the
pianoforte and vocal parts, being legally the property of an
American citizen, we should be able to hold on to it. Nevertheless,
the copyright in question was promptly infringed, and when an
injunction was sought, the judges in the same circuit
(Massachusetts) gave a verdict against us, thus stultifying their own
previous decision. It seemed to be their opinion that a free and
independent American citizen ought not to be robbed of his rights
of robbing somebody else.

We tried similar expedients with two or three of the subsequent
operas, but although the companies we sent out had a great vogue in
America, the methods adopted for preservation of copyright did not
really pay, mainly owing to the trouble and expense of the law-suits
in which we became involved in the effort to protect our rights.

All we could do, as I have indicated, was to send out our
companies before the operas were published, and to refrain from
publishing in Great Britain until after the operas had been produced
in America. As soon as the work was in print, any action that we
might take came under Statute Law, but as long as it remained in
manuscript the action came under Common Law, and any one
attempting to deprive us of the manuscript was no less amenable to
the law than any other thief, who, for example, might try to get
hold of one's purse or one's handkerchief[9].

The idea of copyrighting a piano transcription of the operas
belonged to the triumvirate's American lawyers, Joseph Choate, later
to become the United States Ambassador to the Court of St. James',
and Alexander Browne. They first devised it for *Princess Ida*, but the
fact that no difficulties arose merely indicates that *Ida* was not a
commercial success across the Atlantic. A Bostonian pianist and
arranger, George Lowell Tracy, completed a piano version of the
score and this copyright scheme seemed to work well. However in
1885 *The Mikado* reached American shores and the problem arose on a
scale even larger than that of *Pinafore*. Carte brought a test case of
breach of copyright on the Tracy arrangement against a firm of Boston
music-sellers who had produced pirate songsheets. The pirates
watched the outcome anxiously, as did Gilbert and Sullivan themselves. The case came before Judge Nelson in the Massachusetts
Circuit Court in February 1886, and was reported in the *Federal*

Reporter. Carte was represented by another well-known attorney, Causten Browne, and the judgment was delayed for nearly four months and eventually given on 21st June:

Judge NELSON: This case was heard in February last, but the decision has been delayed to enable the parties to complete certain proofs which were found to be necessary for its proper determination, and it is only recently that it has been in a condition to be finally disposed of. The suit is a bill in equity for an injunction to restrain the infringement by the defendants in the plaintiff's copyright in an arrangement or adaptation for the pianoforte of the orchestral score of an opera called 'The Mikado, or The Town Of Titipu'. It appeared that William S. Gilbert and Sir Arthur Sullivan, both British subjects resident in London, were the authors and composers of a comic opera entitled 'The Mikado, or The Town of Titipu', the words of the opera being the work of Gilbert, and the musical parts being composed by Sullivan. It was admitted that the orchestral score of the opera has always remained in manuscript, or in print only for the use of the performers, and has never been published, either in this country or in England. The piano-forte arrangement for which the plaintiff holds a copyright was composed by George Lowell Tracy, a professional composer and arranger of music, residing in Boston, and a citizen of the United States. The work of composition was performed by Tracy, in London, under an agreement made by him with Gilbert and Sullivan, and with the plaintiff, who is the representative of their interests in this country, the latter also being a British subject resident in London, that a copyright of the piano-forte arrangement, when completed, should be taken out in this country by Tracy and transferred to the plaintiff. For his part of the work Tracy was paid a salary. After the completion of the work, with the consent of Tracy and the plaintiff, a copyright was taken out here in the name of Alexander P. Browne, a resident of Boston, and a citizen of the United States, acting as the attorney for all the parties, and was afterwards, with Tracy's approval assigned by Browne to the plaintiff. The original orchestral score, as composed by Sullivan was, of course, designed to be played by numerous performers, and on a great number and variety of musical instruments, ranging in compass from the highest to the lowest; and Tracy's work consisted in reducing, condensing, and reconstructing a score composed for a

full orchestra of wind and stringed instruments, and producing
from it a score that could be played by a single performer on an
instrument of the limited capacity of the piano-forte. The Tracy
arrangement was intended to be played as an accompaniment to the
vocal score, and in that respect to take the place of the orchestral
score, as played when the opera was given on the stage.

That an arrangement for the piano-forte of the orchestral score of an
opera, such as Tracy had produced, is an original musical
composition, within the meaning of the copyright law, is well
settled. In executing such a work the ideas of the composer of the
opera cannot be wholly reproduced, and other ideas, more or less
resembling them, or wholly new, have to be substituted and
added... An arrangement of this character would undoubtedly be
piracy of the original opera, unless the arranger has in some way
acquired the right to make such use of the original; but if he has
acquired that right, the arrangement is substantially a new and
distinct composition, and as such is entitled to the protection of the
court: Wood v Boosey L.R. 2Q.B. 340;...

Tracy's work was done with the consent of the original composers
of the opera, and in their interest. There is nothing in our copyright
law to prevent one of our own citizens from taking out a copyright
of an original work composed by him, even though the work of
composition was performed at the procurement and in the
employment of an alien; or from assigning his copyright to an alien
under an agreement made either before or after the composing of
the work. A non-resident foreigner is not within our copyright law,
but he may take and hold by assignment a copyright granted to one
of our own citizens. The proprietor as well as the author is entitled
to enter the work for copyright. The consent of Tracy was
sufficient to constitute Brown the proprietor for the purpose,
without a formal assignment. The effect of the transaction was the
same as if Tracy had made the entry in his own name and then
assigned to Carte.

The defendants insist that the method of proceeding by which
the copyright was procured, and afterwards vested in the plaintiff, a
non-resident foreigner, was a mere evasion of our copyright act, and
as such is not entitled to the protection of the court. But I am unable
to perceive how it can properly be called an evasion, if by that is
meant a proceeding by which the letter or spirit of the law is
directly or indirectly violated. The thing copyrighted was an

original work, by an American composer, and therefore the lawful subject of copyright. All the steps taken to secure the copyright, and vest it in the plaintiff, were authorized by our statute. Undoubtedly the plan adopted displayed great ingenuity, and the effect is to vest in these foreign authors valuable American rights in their work; but there is nothing of evasion or violation of law. The plaintiff is therefore entitled to the protection of the court against infringers, if his copyright is otherwise valid...

On the eleventh March, 1885, Browne, as proprietor, filed with librarian of Congress a title in these words; "Piano-forte Arrangement of the Comic Opera, The Mikado, or The Town Of Titipu, by W. S. Gilbert and Sir Arthur Sullivan. By George L. Tracy." On the twentieth April, 1885, the publishers delivered at the office of the librarian two copies of the printed book... which contained... the vocal score of the original opera to which the arrangement was an accompaniment.

The published title indicates with perfect certainty that the musical work contained in it is an arrangement for the piano-forte, composed by Tracy, of Gilbert and Sullivan's opera entitled "The Mikado, or The Town of Titipu," which is copyrighted. The only value of the arrangement was in its connection with the vocal score, and they must necessarily be published together, and some slight addition to the title of the book will be allowable on that account.

The defendants, who are music dealers in Boston, were selling, when this bill was filed, a book of their own publication, entitled "Vocal Gems from the Mikado or The Town of Titipu," which contains the songs and vocal score of the opera, and a piano-forte accompaniment composed by George E. Jackson, of Boston. On this part of the case it is only necessary to remark that it was clearly proved at the hearing, by the testimony of musical experts of the highest authority, that Jackson's accompaniment is nothing but an ill-disguised imitation of the Tracy arrangement.

The conclusion is that the plaintiff has a valid copyright under our law, and is entitled to an injunction to restrain the defendants from infringing it[10]..

Far from being flushed with the success of this result, Carte and his partners had more immediate worries. The pirate producers in New York, Philadelphia, and Chicago, decided to pay no heed to the Boston judge, produce and see what would happen. A New York producer,

John Duff of the Standard Theatre, had failed in a bid to purchase the American rights of *The Mikado;* however he announced that he would put on the show regardless. Carte's answer was a unique and brilliant military-style operation that secretly transported the whole company to New York, and to a Fifth Avenue premiere five days before Duff. Carte naturally followed his opening with an action to stop the Duff production, however to his surprise and consternation appearances before two judges resulted in failure.

In the first, an application before Judge Wallace of the New York Circuit Court, Carte sent Causten Browne again, but this time also sent Choate; Duff also had top attorneys, ex-Judge Dittenhoefer and Aaron Vanderpoel. The judge was openly sympathetic for Carte's position, but having delivered the facts, his judgement continues:

> Both upon reason and authority it must be held that by the publication of the whole opera, except the instrumental parts, the authors abandoned the entire dramatic property in their work to the public. The right to represent it as a dramatic composition thereby becomes public property, although they still retain the sole right of multiplying copies of their orchestral score. If the orchestration of an opera is not a dramatic composition, certainly the piano-forte arrangement cannot be... While it is much to be regretted that our statutes do not, like the English statutes, protect the author or proprietor in all the uses to which literary property may be legitimately applied, it is not the judicial function to supply the defect.
>
> In view of these conclusions it is not necessary to consider whether a valid statutory copyright for the pianoforte arrangement of Tracy had been obtained. ...Of course the defendant could not be permitted to produce the opera as though it were containing the orchestration of Gilbert and Sullivan. He would not be permitted, by deceptive advertisements or representations calculated to mislead the public, to enter upon an unfair competition with the complainant. He does not profess to employ their orchestration, and the case is free from any element of actual fraud. The motion for an injunction is denied[11].

The more forthright statement made by Judge Divver of New York City caught the imagination of the pirates: though not officially reported, or even positively associated with a Savoy case, this Irish expatriate is thought to have said:

Copyright or no copyright; commercial honesty or commercial buccaneering, no Englishman possesses any rights which a true-born American is bound to respect.

Later, Alexander Browne wrote to the *North American Review* in disgust:

> A Union of classes, the worthy and the worthless, showed well the lamentable state of public opinion then existing as to the propriety of appropriating other people's ideas without paying for them. In those days even the newspapers laughed at our efforts to protect such property in the courts, and in this way did much to salve the consciences of those managers who appeared to possess any[12].

The legal battles over *The Mikado* failed: only the superior quality of the legitimate productions organised by Carte had a saving effect. The opera became commercially exploited on a vast scale, and it was not until 1891 that any protection could be afforded it or the other Savoy operas in its wake. Sullivan, in a surprisingly bitter attack for his quiet and selfless nature, made a speech from the conductor's podium after the Gala Performance at the Fifth Avenue Theatre, which he had conducted, on 24th September 1885:

> We should have been grieved indeed if you received first impressions of our work from a spurious imitation - an imitation in which the author's intentions are ignored, for the very good reason that the performers do not know what our intentions are, and in which the music, though having been patched up from a pianoforte arrangement, must necessarily be mutilated, and a misrepresentation of the meaning of the composer.
>   It may be that some day the Legislation of this magnificent country may see fit to accord the same protection to a man who employs his brains in Literature and Arts as they do to one who invents a new bear-trap, or who accidentally gives an extra turn to a screw, thus doing away with the necessity of boring a hole first. On that day these unfortunate managers and publishers who, having no brains of their own, and content to live by annexing the brain properties of others, will be in an embarassing and piteous position. Like Hamlet, their occupation will be gone...

That day, which had come to the rest of the civilised world, but was so long in coming to the United States, arrived at a time when the house of Savoy was in disarray. However despite their piratical antics, both author and composer knew that whilst they had lost a small fortune over the years, in commercial terms, they had also seen popularity and publicity on a scale so vast that through the American reaction to *Pinafore* alone, their place amongst the immortals was secured.

The Lord Chancellor

Henry Lytton

De Wolf Hopper

John Reed

Iolanthe Act II with John Ayldon as Earl Mountararat, John Reed as the Lord Chancellor, and Geoffrey Shovelton as Earl Tolloller. *(photo: Courtesy D'Oyly Carte Opera Trust)*

Iolanthe Act II finale with Patricia Leonard as the Fairy Queen, Lorraine Daniels as Leila, Suzanne O'Keeffe as Celia, John Reed as the Lord Chancellor, Patricia Ann Bennett as Fleta, Barbara Lilley as Phyllis, and Geoffrey Shovelton as Earl Tolloller. *(photo: Courtesy of D'Oyly Carte Opera Trust)*

Act II finale of *Patience* with Kenneth Sandford as Archibald Gros-venor. *(photo: Courtesy of D'Oyly Carte Opera Trust)*

Patience curtain call with John Reed as Reginald Bunthorne. *(photo: Courtesy of D'Oyly Carte Opera Trust)*

Appendix

Arias cited in text

H.M.S. Pinafore: Act I
Sir Joseph Porter, K.C.B.

When I was a lad I served a term
As office boy to an Attorney's firm,
I cleaned the windows and I swept the floor,
And I polished up the handle of the big front door.
 I polished up that handle so carefullee
 That now I am the Ruler of the Queen's Navee!

As office boy I made such a mark
That they gave me the post of junior clerk.
I served the writs with a smile so bland,
And I copied all the letters in a big round hand -
 I copied all the letters in a hand so free,
 That now I am the Ruler of the Queen's Navee!

In serving writs I made such a name,
That an articled clerk I soon became;
I wore clean collars and a bran-new suit
For the pass examination at the Institute.
 That pass examination did so well for me,
 That now I am the Ruler of the Queen's Navee!

Of legal knowledge I acquired such a grip
That they took me into the partnership.
And that junior partnership, I ween,
Was the only ship that I ever had seen.
But that kind of ship so suited me,
That now I am the Ruler of the Queen's Navee!

I gew so rich that I was sent
By a pocket borough into Parliament.
I always voted at my party's call,
And I never thought of thinking for myself at all.
I thought so little, they rewarded me
By making me the Ruler of the Queen's Navee!

Now landsmen all, whoever you may be,
If you want to rise to the top of the tree,
If your soul isn't fettered to an office stool,
Be careful to be guided by this golden rule -
Stick close to your desks and never go to sea,
And you all may be Rulers of the Queen's Navee!

Trial by Jury
The Learned Judge

When I, good friends, was called to the bar,
I'd an appetite fresh and hearty,
But I was, as many young barristers are,
An impecunious party.
I'd a swallow-tail coat of a beautiful blue -
A brief which I bought of a booby -
A couple of shirts and a collar or two,
And a ring that looked like a ruby!

In Westminster Hall I danced a dance,
Like a semi-despondent fury;
For I thought I should never hit on a chance
Of addressing a British Jury -
But I soon got tired of third-class journeys,
And dinners of bread and water;
So I fell in love with a rich attorney's
Elderly, ugly daughter.

The rich attorney, he jumped with joy,
    And replied to my fond professions:
'You shall reap the reward of your pluck, my boy,
    At the Bailey and Middlesex Sessions.
You'll soon get used to her looks,' said he,
    'And a very nice girl you'll find her!
She may very well pass for forty-three
    In the dusk, with a light behind her!'

The rich attorney was good as his word;
    The briefs came trooping gaily,
And every day my voice was heard
    At the Sessions or Ancient Bailey.
All thieves who could my fees afford
    Relied on my orations,
And many a burglar I've restored
    To his friends and his relations.

At length I became as rich as the Gurneys -
    An incubus then I thought her,
So I threw over that rich attorney's
    Elderly, ugly daughter.
The rich attorney my character high
    Tried vainly to disparage -
And now, if you please, I'm ready to try
    This Breach of Promise of Marriage!

Iolanthe: Act I
The Lord Chancellor

When I went to the Bar as a very young man,
    (Said I to myself - said I)
I'll work on a new and original plan
    (Said I to myself - said I),
I'll never assume that a rogue or a thief
Is a gentleman worthy implicit belief,
Because his attorney has sent me a brief
    (Said I to myself - said I!).

Ere I go into court I will read my brief through
And I'll never take work I'm unable to do
My learned profession I'll never disgrace,
By taking a fee with a grin on my face,
When I haven't been there to attend to the case.

I'll never throw dust in a juryman's eyes
Or hoodwink a judge who is not over-wise
Or assume that the witnesses summoned in force
In Exchequer, Queen's Bench, Common Pleas, or Divorce,
Have perjured themselves as a matter of course.

In other professions in which men engage,
The Army, the Navy, the Church, and the Stage,
Professional licence, if carried too far,
Your chance of promotion will certainly mar -
And I fancy the rule might apply to the Bar.

The Gondoliers: Act II;
The Duke and Duchess of Plaza-Toro

Small titles and orders
For Mayors and Recorders
    I get - and they're highly delighted!
M.P.s baronetted
Sham Colonels gazetted,
    And second-rate Aldermen knighted.

Foundation-stone laying
I find very paying:
    It adds a large sum to my makings -
At charity dinners
The best of speech-spinners,
    I get ten per cent of the takings.

I present any lady
Whose conduct is shady
    Or smacking of doubtful propriety -
When Virtue would quash her,
I take and whitewash her,
    And launch her in first-rate society.

I recommend acres
Of clumsy dressmakers -
    Their fit and their finishing touches.
A sum in addition
They pay for permission
    To say that they make for the Duchess.

Those pressing prevailers,
The ready-made tailors,
    Quote me as their great double-barrel -
I allow them to do so,
Though Robinson Crusoe
    Would jib at their wearing apparel.

I sit, by selection,
Upon the direction,
    Of several Companies bubble.
As soon as they're floated
I'm freely bank-noted -
    I'm pretty well paid for my trouble.

At middle-class party
I play at écarté
    And I'm by no means a beginner.
To one of my station
The remuneration -
    Five guineas a night and my dinner.

I write letters blatant
On medicines patent -
    And use any other you musn't -
And vow my complexion
Derives its perfection
    From somebody's soap - which it doesn't!

We're ready as witness
To anyone's fitness
    To fill any place or preferment.
We're often in waiting
At junket or feting,
    And sometimes attend an interment.

In short if you'd kindle
The spark of a swindle,
    Lure simpletons into your clutches -
Or hoodwink a debtor,
You cannot do better
    Than trot out a Duke or a Duchess!

Notes

Chapter 1

1. Hesketh Pearson: *Gilbert - His Life and Strife*, p.19
2. *Scribner's Monthly* (1879), vol.XVIII,p.754.
3. Following Isaac Goldberg's *The Story of Gilbert and Sullivan*, p.23.
4. Gilbert's name first appeared in *Foster's* in the 1864 edition, being the first after his call. His details remained in subsequent editions until his death.
5. Edith Browne: 'W. S. Gilbert' Ch.II.
6. MS. Northern Circuit Records, 1866.
7. Hesketh Pearson: '*Gilbert and Sullivan*', pp.23-7.
8. 'An Autobiography', *Theatre* 2nd April 1883, p.217.

Chapter 2

1. This 'piece of absurdity' in two acts was from Meilhac and Halevy's *Le Reveillon*, produced at the Globe from 24th January 1874; it was revived as *On Bail* at the Criterion on 12th February 1877.
2. All extracts taken from the 6th edition, 1908
3. Dark and Grey; *W. S. Gilbert - His Life and Letters*.

Chapter 3

1. Related in Adair-Fitzgerald's *The Story of the Savoy Opera*, p.41.
2. Hesketh Pearson: *Gilbert - His Life and Strife*, p. 40.
3. Ibid., p.59
4. She also produced Gilbert's *Fortune Hunter* in both Birmingham and Edinburgh, 1896-7. On the day of his death, she was the last person Gilbert visited, after which he returned home and was drowned in his lake at a bathing party.
5. *c.* 9th July 1892.

Chapter 4

1. Monday, 6th January 1873, p.10.
2. This remark is sometimes attributed to the 4th January edition of the *Gazette* though it certainly does not appear there.
3. Peyton Wrey: *Notes on popular dramatists: No.III, W. S. Gilbert, London Society,* January 1875.
4. Hollingshead: *The Gaiety Chronicles,* p.72; 'J.B. Buckstone beside being a versatile player and a manager of the Adelphi and the Haymarket, wrote over seventy plays and burlesques'. Southern: *The Victorian Theatre; a Pictorial Survey.*
5. Edward Righton: *A Suppressed Burlesque - The Happy Land. The Theatre,* 1st August 1896.

Chapter 5

1. 'An actress of individuality and high technical accomplishment, Henrietta Hodson was seen at her best in characters where she could mingle demureness with an underlying sense of fun and mischief. When pathos or sentimentality was demanded she was found wanting. Her act was somewhat too delicate and refined for burlesque, in which she showed a lack of animal spirits.' *Dictionary of National Biography, 1901-1911,* supp., p.275.
2. *Theatre,* 1st, 8th, 15th, 22nd May; 5th June 1877.
3. *Op. cit.*

Chapter 6

1. *The Times,* Monday 29th March 1875.
2. Abolished by the Marriage Act, 1970.
3. Lawrence: *Arthur Sullivan, Life Story, Letters and Reminiscences,* p.106.
4. It depicted Lord Coleridge; p.9
5. Edward Vaughan Kenealy (1819-1880) LL.D. Trinity College Dublin; friend of Thackeray, called at Gray's Inn. Q.C. 1868. Retained in the Tichborne case in 1873. 'A barrister who ceases to be merely the advocate of his client's cause puts himself into a very false position through departing from that sound policy of impersonal advocacy which is the tradition and glory of the English Bar. That Dr. Kenealy's conduct at the trial was most unfortunate, and unprofessional, is to say the least. He made uncalled-for strictures on many witnesses of great position and undoubted rectitude, and flouted, and even insulted the Bench. In its verdict of guilty against the Claimant at the Old Bailey, the jury added a rider of censure on the demeanor of his leading counsel, and in the course of the same year, 1874, Dr. Kenealy was disbarred. He became the editor of a vigorous, if not violent, newspaper *The Englishman* and became M.P. for Stoke.' B.W. Kelly: *Famous Advocates and Their Speeches.* London: Sweet & Maxwell, 1921.
6. See Appendix, p.216

Chapter 7

1. Hollingshead: *Good Old Gaiety*, p. 26.
2. Gilbert wrote to Sullivan on 6th August 1879 that 'a gang of fifty roughs' had been involved.
3. This letter is undated but appears in Hollingshead's *The Gaiety Chronicles*, pp. 275-6.

Chapter 8

1. Around mid-February, 1876.
2. *The Times*, Friday 28th August 1903.
3. Saturday 30th August 1903.

Chapter 10

1. Gilbert's courtroom battles took on the trait of employing the greatest advocates of his day, either for his cause or to oppose him. His legal escapades involved twenty silks, fourteen additional juniors, and came before fifteen judges.
2. Sir Charles Frederick Sigismund Day (1826-1908). 'While a sound and capable lawyer, he showed little interest in the problems of law which came before him sitting in Banc, and his apparent inattention, continued with his habit of never taking notes, made him very unpopular with civil litigants.' *Dictionary of National Biography, 1909-11*, supp.ii.
3. 'When the jury retired the affections of the twelve good men and true were divided between the wonderful rhymester and the brilliant advocate, and they came back to state to the judge that there was no prospect of being able to decide between the two favourites.' Marjoribanks: *Life of Lord Carson*, vol. 1. The jury were in fact out for two and a half hours.
4. Caryl Brahms, in her book *Lost Chords and Discords*, attributes this letter to Gilbert's concern over an American copyright case. No references or authority are offered, however, nor did she disclose a source in correspondence; this idea is extremely unlikely.
5. Sent from Sorrento, 12th April 1898.

Chapter 11

1. Percy M. Young: *Sir Arthur Sullivan*, p 247.
2. 7th June 1909
3. 22nd June 1910.

Chapter 12

1. Hesketh Pearson: *Gilbert - His Life and Strife*, p 219
2. Marked by a plaque set in the wall on the sixtieth anniversay of the accident.

Chapter 13

1. Repealed by Theatres Act 1968 in consequence of removing from the Lord Chamberlain's Office the function of censorship.
2. Hollingshead: *Good Old Gaiety*, p.26.
3. Gladstone was approaching the conclusion of his great ministry, 1868-74, the first of four prime-ministerships.
4. Various authorities indicate that Gilbert wrote to Whistler to ask permission that 'Bunthorne' should be made up as the famous artist.
5. Minutes of Evidence: Joint Committee Paper 1909 (333), pp. 190-91, paras 3418-430, etc.

Chapter 14

1. Mr. Justice Talfourd edited Charles Lamb's letters and writings; he was the author of the first modern Copyright Act; Dickens dedicated *Pickwick* to him.
2. Extracts from *Bleak House* (1852-3) from Everyman Edition 1907; introduction and ch.1, pp1-3.
3. John Singleton Copley, Lord Lyndhurst (1792-1863). b. Boston, Massachusetts. Came to UK 1775. Trinity College Cambridge, Lincoln's Inn. Called 1804; Serjeant by 1813. Became Canning's Chancellor in 1827; also under Peel, 1834, 1840.
4. Dickens' Mr. Justice Stareleigh was based on Stephen Gaselee, (1762-1839), Judge of the Common Pleas, 1824-1837; Serjeant Buzfuz was based on the greatest of Serjeants of the day, Bompas.
5. All extracts from the Savoy Operas taken from the two-volume 1962 OUP edition, World Classics Series. All extracts from the *Pickwick Papers* taken from the 1964 Macmillan edition. Cf. pp.443-8, 462.
6. *Pickwick* was still a best-seller with 100,000 one-shilling copies sold by 1878: a vast number considering the national standards of literacy even in the late 1870s.
7. *Great Expectations*, Library Edition (London: Chapman and Hall, *c.* 1890) Vol XXIV, ch. XX.
8. *A Tale of Two Cities*, Vol XXIII, book II, ch ii.
9. Although in the particular plot the set being Cornwall, pirates that were apprehended would be sent to local assizes at Bodmin, Truro, or further east to Exeter; if local feeling made it impossible for a trial to be without prejudice they could be sent further away.

10. 35 and 36 Vict. c38.
11. Although Peel first introduced it out of wartime, Gladstone was the first Prime Minister to make income-tax a feature of an annual budget.
12. Goldberg, *op. cit.*, p.280.

Chapter 15

1. Sir William Henry Smith (1825-91); First Lord of the Admiralty 1871-7; First Lord of the Treasury and Leader of the Commons 1886. M.P. for Westminster from 1868.
2. Sir Garnet Joseph, First Viscount Wolseley (1833-1913); massacred the Ashanti in his greatest triumph on a punitive expedition.
3. Frederick Sleigh, First Earl Roberts of Kandahar. Campaigned in Afghanistan 1879 and relieved Kandahar. Commander-in-Chief in the (1899-1902) Boer War in South Africa.
4. Heard in the Court of Exchequer before Baron Huddlestone: Ruskin had written: 'I have seen and heard much of Cockney impudence before now but I never expected to hear a coxcomb ask two hundred guineas for flinging a pot of paint in the public's face.' Libel was proven, but damages were assessed at merely one half-penny.
5. See commentary on the Wilde article; *Palace Peeper* (publication of the New York Gilbert and Sullivan Society), March 1979.

Chapter 16

1. A Royal Commission on the Interpretation of Statutes had been set up at that time, but did not report until three years later, when its recommendations formed the basis of the Act of 1889.
2. The Albert Borowitz article in the *American Bar Association Journal*, 1973 at p.1276 is most informative in this area.
3. 19 & 20 Vict. c.47
4. 25 & 26 Vict. c.89
5. See Appendix.
6. This reference shows Gilbert's cautious attitude - it refers to the early repeal of the South Sea Bubble Act, 1820.
7. A large number of late nineteenth-century bank failures occurred during Gilbert's period of writing; however this is probably an allusion to the October 1878 City of Glasgow Bank fraud: see Arthur Griffiths: *Mysteries of Police and Crime*, (London: Chapman and Hall, 1899.)
8. This could be an allusion back to the 'Diddlesex Junction' song, or merely the railway boom of the 1840s.
9. Eight months before this production, in February 1893, Ferdinand de Lessops was convicted of fraud in an attempt to raise money by bond for the Panama Canal project. Corruption in all tiers of the French

government was subsequently discovered and a man closely involved with the scandal escaped to the Tankerville Hotel, Bournemouth, where he obtained political asylum.
10. Eventually abolished as a crime by S.I. Suicide Act 1961. (9 & 10 Eliz.2) c.60

Chapter 17

1. 5 & 6 Vict. c.45 'to afford greater encouragement to the production of literary works of lasting benefit to the world' (preamble).
2. Protection had developed through the Common Law from 1474. This was the first time government intervened, except for the medieval Crown grants of monopolies.
3. *Law Times*, LXVIII, N.S. 263.
4. 2nd August 1879: Gilbert and Sullivan were both in Europe. Carte was in America.
5. *Entr'Acte*, 3rd October 1885.

Chapter 18

1. Short on Copyright, p.12; International Copyright Act 1838.
2. (1839) 10 Sim. 329; 59 E.R. 641
3. Nowell-Smith: *International Law and the Publisher in the Reign of Queen Victoria*, (O.U.P., 1968)
4. 2nd May, 1783.
5. Act of July 1870, s.4952: 'any citizen of the U.S.'.
6. Article 2, 9th Sept. 1886.
7. 7th-14th Sept. 1886.
8. Lawrence, *op.cit.*, p.130.
9. *Ibid.*
10. 1886 *Federal Reporter*, 861; Goldberg intimates in *The Story of Gilbert and Sullivan*, p.330 that Nelson restored the deadlock; this is clearly an error.
11. *Ibid.*
12. *Sir Arthur Sullivan and Piracy: North American Review*, June 1889.

Glossary of legal terms as used in the Savoy Operas

ACT (Tr. Sor. Utop. G.D.), of Parliament   End product of Legislature; until Gilbert's death literally made by the sovereign with the advice and consent of the Lords Spiritual and Temporal and the Commons in Parliament assembled. After 1911 the concurrence of the Lords became practically unnecessary.

AFFIDAVIT (Iol. Rud.)   Statement in writing made on oath, sworn before someone who has the authority to administer it.

ARREST OF JUDGMENT (Iol.)   A staying or withholding of a given judgment in an action on the grounds that an error has appeared which precludes the plaintiff's right to recover, or prevents the sentence of a prisoner.

ATTORNEY (Tr. Pin.) -AT-LAW   Formerly officers of the Superior Courts of Law sitting at Westminster Hall; they appeared to prosecute or defend actions where partners to the suit were absent. In 1873 the Judicature Act restyled their title as Solicitors of the Supreme Court.

ATTORNEY-GENERAL (Mik.)   The principal law officer of the Crown, and the head of the Bar of England, prosecutor for the Crown.

BAILEY (OLD), (ANCIENT) (Tr.)   The Central Criminal Court situated on the corner of Newgate Street and Old Bailey, principal court of

227

criminal jurisdiction at first instance in England and Wales. In Gilbert's day the building he was acquainted with stood until 1906 attached to the famous Newgate Prison where executions and flogging were carried out.

BANC, IN (Tr.)   Banco sittings of the superior Westminster courts formerly to determine matters other than the trial of actions. After 1873 jurisdiction transferred to the divisional courts of the High Court of Justice. In Banc was the opposite to sittings at Nisi Prius where a judge sitting with or without a jury tried an action.

BANDS (Iol.)   The weepers of linen worn like a cravat by all British judicial officers with robes as a remnant of the links between the law and the Church.

BAR (Iol. Tr.)
(1) the place where prisoners stand to be tried: 'prisoner at the bar';
(2) the place where barristers stand 'within the bar' (Q.C.s) or 'out of the bar' (outer or 'utter' barristers);
(3) of the profession of a barrister, 'the Bar' being members of and the profession itself; hence, being 'called to the Bar', i.e. within the profession;
(4) the place in the House of Commons or Lords beyond which strangers may not pass.

BARRISTER (Tr.)   The advocating branch of the British legal profession. Regarded as the senior branch, from which the Judges are almost exclusively appointed.

BENCH (Iol.)   Word used with reference to judges and magistrates collectively.

BOMBAZINE (Iol.)   The 'stuff' gown material for robes worn by 'junior' barristers, and also used in ushers and solicitors gowns.

BREACH OF PROMISE OF MARRIAGE (Tr.)   Popular suit in Gilbert's time until its abolition as late as 1970 by the Marriage Act.

BRIEF (Iol. Utop.)   Written instructions sent by the solicitor to the barrister for the conduct of civil or criminal proceedings.

CAPITAL PUNISHMENT (Mik.)   As far as Gilbert was concerned, death by hanging. Abolished as a punishment for murder in Britain only as late as 1965.

CENTRAL CRIMINAL COURT (Pir.)   see BAILEY, OLD. Court established in 1834 for trial of major offences committed in London, Middlesex and certain parts of Kent, Essex and Surrey.

CHANCELLOR OF THE EXCHEQUER (Mik.)   Formerly (and in Gilbert's day until 1873) judicial officer that presided over the Barons of the Court of Exchequer. His former secondary function remains, being now the minister of the Crown having control over the national revenue and expenditure.

CHANCERY, (COURT OF) (Pir. Iol.)   Until 1873 had two jurisdictions: (a) 'ordinary' being a common law court; (b) 'extraordinary' being a court of equity. After 1873 only equitable jurisdiction remained. Dealt with trusts, mortgages, complicated contracts, wardship, in Gilbert's time.

CHANCERY LANE (Pat. Iol.)   Thoroughfare running from Fleet Street to Holborn, in Gilbert's time bordered by Lincoln's Inn, Rolls Gardens, Barnard's Inn, Clifford's Inn. Then the site of the Chancery Court and Master of the Rolls Court out of term. Present day site of the Public Record Office and Law Society, professional headquarters of the solicitors.

COMMITTAL (Iol.)
    (a) for trial: from magistrates courts to higher court before judge and jury;
    (b) to prison: after sentence, or for contempt of court.

COMMON PLEAS, COURT OF (Iol.)   Also called Court of Common Bench. Superior court of common law; exclusive jurisdiction over actions concerning real property; jurisdiction over all actions between subject and subject. Merged with Queen's Bench Division of High Court 1880.

CONTEMPT (OF COURT) (Iol.)   Anything tending clearly to disregard courts' authority; open insult or resistance to presiding judges, or

disobedience of their orders. Punishable by immediate imprisonment for unlimited period at judge's discretion until contempt is
'purged'.

COUNSEL (Tr.)   Word used to denote Barrister-at-law.

DAMAGES (Tr.)   Monetary sum awarded by a judge or jury in a civil
action in satisfaction for the wrong suffered by the plaintiff.

DEED (Sor.)   A written instrument, signed, sealed and delivered.

DEFENDANT (Tr.)   A person sued in a civil action or charged in a
criminal action with a lesser offence. Persons charged with
criminal offences were in Gilbert's day, and until recently,
referred to as 'prisoner'.

DIVORCE (Iol.)   Gilbert is here referring to the 'Divorce Division' of the
High Court, more properly known as the Probate, Divorce and
Admiralty Division, 1873-1970, now known as the Family Division. It was first set up by a statute of 1857 as the Court of Divorce
and Matrimonial Causes.

EQUITY (Iol.)   A body of rules and procedure based on the concepts of
conscience and justice which grew up separately from the common
law and were administered by different courts. Could give a
remedy in equity where a plaintiff had no legal remedy. Jurisdiction almost wholly contained within the Court of Chancery until
1925 when all divisions of the High Court enabled to use equity.
Where equity and law conflict, equity prevails.

EVIDENCE (Iol.) rules of.   System for controlling anything which can
be introduced into a court of justice to help determine the truth or
otherwise of the point in issue.

EXCHEQUER, COURT OF (Iol. Tr.)   One of the superior courts of Common Law sitting in Westminster Hall, it had its equitable jurisdiction poached by the Chancery Court in 1841. Prime function to
bring in the revenues of the Crown and to recover the King's debts
and duties. Named after the chequered cloth, scaccarium, cover-
ing the table where in medieval times the King's accounts were

made up and marked with tally-stick counters. Apart from working out property rights of the Crown it dealt with subjects'
disputes. Was merged with Queen's Bench in 1873.

FIRST LORD OF THE TREASURY (Mik.)   Titular office held by the Prime
Minister.

'GOOD CONDITION OF SUBSTANTIAL AND DECORATIVE REPAIR'
(Utop.)   Common exclusion in covenants to maintain premises
due to fair wear and tear having effect on their condition.

INTERIM ORDER (Gon.)   An order made to take effect provisionally
until a further order or other directions are given.

INSTITUTE (Pin.)   Popularly thought to be intended as the Law
Society in Chancery Lane.

JUDGE ORDINARY (Mik.)   Judge of the former Court of Probate, then
President of the Probate, Divorce and Admiralty Division; now
the President of the Family Division.

LAWYER (Utop.)   Colloquial or literary term that has no technical
application in British law whatsoever. More often used to
describe the functions of a solicitor; used in a technical sense in
America.

LEGAL FICTION (Gon.G.D.)   Application of law for practical convenience which creates a situation of unreality.

LORD (HIGH) CHANCELLOR (Gon. Iol. Mik.)   Highest judicial officer in
the kingdom. Head of the judicial system and minister of the
administrative department concerned with its running. Cabinet
Minister, Speaker of the House of Lords, Privy Councillor,
judge.

LORD (GREAT) CHAMBERLAIN (OF THE QUEEN'S HOUSE) (Gon.
Mik.) Crown appointee, administrative head of Queen's
Household and Palace of Westminster when in session. Until
1968 empowered to license theatres in London, its environs, and
any place resided in by the sovereign.

LORD CHIEF JUSTICE (Mik.)   Title given to heads of the Courts of King's Bench and Common Pleas. Now given to the President of the Queen's Bench Division of the High Court.

MASTER OF THE ROLLS (Mik.)   Formerly one of the judges of the Court of Chancery, and keeper of the rolls of all patents and grants that pass the Great Seal and all Chancery Records. A master in Chancery, he attended as an assessor to the Chancellor. Before their destruction in 1834 in the fire that destroyed the Houses of Parliament he kept the tally rolls of the Court of Exchequer. Granted an independent court by George II. Presently ex-officio judge of and head of the Court of Appeal, but not when Gilbert was writing. Then sitting as a Chancery judge determining questions of disputes as to records.

NOTARY (PUBLIC) (Sor.)   No application in British law, the function being to attest deeds, now performed by solicitors acting as Commissioners for Oaths. Term widely used in other countries.

NISI PRIUS (Mik.)   In Gilbert's sense, a judge sitting with a jury to try an action, in a civil court sitting then at Westminster Hall. To be distinguished from a trial at bar, a criminal trial, or a trial in an inferior court.

PLAINTIFF (Tr.)   Any person who askes the court for a remedy against another person by way of proceedings.

PLEADINGS (Tr.)   The formal written arguments between the parties in a suit or action which develop and determine the exact points to be decided.

PRIVY PURSE (Mik.)   Used by Gilbert as the official of the Royal Household that deals with the sum of public money voted to the Sovereign for her own purposes. The term refers to the sum itself.

Q.C. (QUEEN'S COUNSEL) (Sor. Utop.)   Barristers appointed by letters patent as Her Majesty's counsel learned in the law. They wear a silk gown instead of a stuff one and are nicknamed 'silks'. They give up writing pleadings and can only appear in court if they are supported by a junior barrister.

QUEEN'S BENCH (DIVISION) (Iol.) Formerly Court of Queen's Bench. Now the principal division of the High Court of Justice, since 1873, in terms of business.

REVISING BARRISTER (G.D.) Junior barristers of not less than seven years call appointed annually to revise the register of the parliamentary electorate in each district. The appointments ceased in 1918.

SECRETARY OF STATE FOR THE HOME DEPARTMENT (Mik.) Minister of the Home Office responsible amongst other things for the role of the police at a national level.

SESSIONS (Tr.) The sitting of justices in a commissioned court. Reformed in 1971, formerly Petty Sessions were held by lay magistrates and Quarter Sessions before visiting judges.

SOLICITOR (Pat.) Formerly officers of the Court of Chancery until 1873. Some rights of audience as an advocate but chiefly concerned with preparation of litigation, drafting documents, conveyancing and probate. See ATTORNEY.

SOMERSET HOUSE (Pat.) In Gilbert's day headquarters of the Board of Inland Revenue. More famous as the registry for births, marriages, and deaths.

STAKEHOLDER (Utop.) A person with whom a stake is deposited depending the outcome of a wager.

SUBMISSION (Tr.) Presentation of legal argument.

SUBPOENA (Tr.) A writ sent to a person ordering him to appear at court to give evidence, on penalty for failure.

UNDERTAKING (Gon.) A promise given in the course of legal proceedings which may be enforced.

USHER (Tr. Iol.) The court door-keeper.

WARD (Pir. Iol.) A minor under the protection of the Chancery Division, called a ward of court.

WESTMINSTER HALL (Tr.)   St Stephen's Hall, Westminster, formerly home of the superior courts until the opening of the Royal Courts of Justice in the Strand in 1884.

WOOLSACK (Iol.)   The seat of the Lord Chancellor in the House of Lords, reflecting the importance of the wool trade to England in the Middle Ages.

Select Bibliography

Books

Adair, St. J. Fitzgerald. *The Story of the Savoy Opera*. London: Stanley Paul, 1926.

Allen, Reginald. *The First Night Gilbert and Sullivan*. New York: Heritage, 1958 (for the Limited Editions Club.)

Anonymous. *Charles Dickens, The Story of His Life*. London: J.C. Hotton, 1870.

Aye, John. *Humour in the Theatre*. London: Universal, 1934.

Ayre, Leslie. *The Gilbert and Sullivan Companion*. London: Pan, 1972.

Bailey, Leslie. *The Gilbert and Sullivan Book*. 2nd Edn. Cassell, London 1952.

Bailey, Leslie. *Gilbert and Sullivan and Their World*. London: Thames and Hudson, 1973 (for Book Club Associates Edition.)

Ball, H. G. *Law of Copyright and Literary Property*. New York: Albany, 1944.

Browne, Edith A. *W.S. Gilbert*. London: John Lane, 1907.

Burnand, Sir Francis. *Records and Reminiscences*. Vol II 2nd Edn. London: Methuen, 1904.

Copinger and Skone James. *Law of Copyright* 12th Edn. London: Sweet & Maxwell, 1980.

Dark, S. and Grey, R. *W.S. Gilbert - His Life and Letters*. London: Methuen, 1923.

The Dictionary of National Biography, 1909-11, supp ii, 1912-21 supp. London: Oxford University Press, 1917.

Dickens, Charles. *Bleak House* London: Everyman Edition, 1907.

Dickens, Charles. *The Posthumous Papers of the Pickwick Club*. London: Macmillan, 1964.

Dickens, Charles. *Sketches by 'Boz'*. London: Macmillan, 1892.

Eddy on Copyright. London: Sweet and Maxwell, 1957.

Foster's Hand-List of Men-At-The Bar. London: Reeves and Turner, 1883.

Gilbert, W.S. *The Bab Ballads*. 6th Edn. London: Macmillan, 1908.

Gilbert, W.S. *Original Plays*. (3rd Series) London: Chatto and Windus, 1919.

Gilbert, W.S. *The Savoy Operas* (2 vols). London: Oxford University Press, 1962 (The World's Classics Series 592/3.)

Glover, James. *Jimmy Glover His Book*. 4th Edn. London: Methuen, 1911.

Goldberg, Isaac. *The Story of Gilbert and Sullivan*. New York: Crown, 1935.

Griffiths. *Mysteries of Police and Crime* (2 vols) London: Cassell, 1899.

Harmsworth. *A History of English Law* (16 vols). London: Methuen, 1972.

Holdsworth. *Charles Dickens as a Legal Historian*. New Haven: Yale University Press, 1929.

Hollingshead, John. *The Gaiety Chronicles*. London: Constable, 1898.

Hollingshead, John. *Good Old Gaiety* London: Constable, 1903.

Hyman, Alan. *The Gaiety Years*. London: Cassell, 1975.

Jacobs, M.C. *An Outline of Theatre Law*. New York, 1949.

Lawrence. *Sir Arthur Sullivan - Life Story, Letters and Reminiscences*, London: James Bowden, 1899.

Lockwood, Frank, Q.C. *Law and Lawyers of Pickwick*. London: Roxborough Press, 1893.

Lytton, Henry A. *Secrets of a Savoyard*. London: Jarrolds, 1921.

Mander and Michenson. *The Lost Theatres of London*. London: Hart-Davis, 1968.

Mander and Michenson. *The Theatres of London*. London: New English Library, 1975.

Marjoribanks, Edward. *Life of Sir Edward Marshall Hall*. London: Gollancz, 1929.

Marjoribanks, Edward. *Life of Lord Carson*. (Vol 1.) London: Gollancz, 1932.

Mathew, Theobald. *For Lawyers and Others*. London: Hodge, 1937.

Maugham. *The Tichborne Case*. London: Hodder and Stoughton, 1906.

Nowell-Smith and Barnes. *International Law and the Publisher in the Reign of Queen Victoria*. London: Oxford University Press, 1968.

Pearson, Hesketh. *Gilbert and Sullivan*. London: Hamilton, 1935.

Pearson, Hesketh. *W.S. Gilbert - His Life and Strife*. London: Methuen, 1957.

Putnam, G. H. *The Question of Copyright*. New York and London: G.P. Putnam & Sons, 1891.

Rees, Terence. *'Thespis' - An Enigma Reconsidered* London: Dillon's University Bookshop, 1964.

Settle and Baber. *Law of Public Entertainment*. London: Sweet and Maxwell, 1915.

Sherson. *London's Lost Theatres of the Nineteenth Century*. London: Bodley Head, 1925.

Southern. *The Victorian Theatre, A Pictorial Survey*. London: David and Charles, 1970.

Steadman, Jane W. *Gilbert Before Sullivan*. Chicago: University of Chicago Press, 1967.

Wilson, A.E. *The Lyceum*, London: Yates, 1952 (Theatre Book Club Edition.)

Young, Percy M. *Sir Arthur Sullivan* London: Dent, 1971.

Periodicals and Miscellaneous

American Bar Association Journal (1960) Vol 46, 386; (1973) Vol 59, 1276;

The (London) Athenaeum 3rd April 1875, p. 466;

Blackwood's Magazine July 1875, vol. CXCIX p. 121;

Cornhill Magazine December 1863, vol. VIII pp. 11-16; 1882 Annual p. 159;

Daily Mail (London) 30th May 1911, pp. 6, 8;

Daily Sketch (London) 25th November 1932, p. 10;

Daily Telegraph (London) 19th November 1877, p. 3;

D'Oyly Carte Centenary Programme, 1975 (in toto)

D'Oyly Carte North American Tour Programmes, 1976 p. 2; 1978;

D'Oyly Carte Provincial Tour Programme, 1881;

Edinburgh Evening Dispatch 5th October 1897, p. 2, 4th October 1897, p. 4;

Entr' Acte (London) 21st March 1885, p. 8; 22nd August 1885, p. 9; 3rd October 1885, pp. 6, 11;

The *Era* 3rd August 1879, pp. 4, 5, 8; 17th August 1879, p. 3; 5th July 1890, p. 10; 23rd August 1890, p. 9; 30th August 1890, p. 8; 6th September 1890, p. 8;

Evening Standard (London) 17th November 1936, p. 17; 17th June 1942, p. 4;

Figaro (London) 1st June 1878, pp. 3, 6;

Fun 11th April 1868, p. 54;

Gasbag (Michigan, U.S.A.) 7th March 1977, vol. VIII p. 7.; 7th August 1977, vol. VIII p. 10;

Gilbert and Sullivan Journal vol X pt. 10; vol X pt. 14 p. 289;

Graphic (London) 23rd December 1882, pp. 689, 691;

Hansard 2nd May 1907, col. 1062; 6th May 1907, col. 1323;

Hornet 25th May 1878;

Illustrated London News 24th November 1877, p. 510; 23rd February 1878, p. 173; 2nd August 1879, p. 110; 17th January 1880; 1st May 1880, pp. 427-8; 8th January 1881;

Illustrated Sporting and Dramatic News 8th January 1876, pp. 354-5, 359; 11th March 1876, pp. 574, 576; 6th May 1876, p. 126; 12th March 1881, p. 635; 7th May 1881, p. 189; Minutes of the Joint Select Committee on Stage Plays (Censorship) 1909, Joint Committee Paper (1909) 333 pp. 190-1 paras 3418-3430;

Justice of the Peace 16th August 1975, p. 474;

Letters to the Dramatic Profession, W.S. Gilbert; Henrietta Hodson; (1877) London: printed for private circulation.

Law Society Gazette 24th May 1978, (vol. 75 no. 19,) p. 528;

London Society January 1875, p. 13;

News Chronicle 10th October 1933, pp. 1, 16; 11th October 1933, p. 6;

An Operatic Glossary from 'Abudah Chest' to 'Zoffany' - Gilbert and Sullivan Society 1975 (toto).

Palace Peeper March 1979.

Pall Mall Gazette 4th January 1873, p. 13; 6th January 1873, p. 10; 1st April 1907, p. 5; 1st May 1907, p. 2;

Punch or the London Charivari 12th March 1881 p. 118; 9th December 1882, p. 268; 28th October 1893, p. 204;

The Referee 4th June 1911, p. 4;

The (London) Star 3rd September 1890, p. 3; 23rd October 1894, p. 1-2; 24th October 1894, p. 1-2;

Solicitor's Journal 8th June 1976, p. 426;

Solicitor's Monthly vol. XVIII (1879) p. 754;

The *Theatre* 1st, 8th, 15th, 22nd May, 5th June 1877; 1st August 1879; 2nd April 1883 p. 217; 1st August 1896, p. 63;

The Times (London) 29th March 1875, p. 10; 17th November 1877, p. 9; 25th May 1878, p. 9; 27th p. 11, 28th p. 6, August 1903; 19th January 1910, p. 3; 9th August 1955, p. 5;

Legal Authority

REPORTS

Federal Reporter (1886) 860
Law Reports (1881) 16 Ch D 594
Law Times Reports   (1881) XLIII NS 665
                      (1894) LXXII NS 4,263
Time Law Reports 27th August 1903.

STATUTES.

Copyright Acts 1842 5 & 6. Vict. c.100; 1911 1 & 2, Geo.5 c.46.
International Copyright Act 1886 38 Vict. c.12 (21 LJ 432)
Theatre Acts 1843 6 & 7 Vict. c.68; 1968 16 & 17 Eliz. II c.54
Act of Congress on International Copyright July 1870. S.4952

Index